# Ryokan

# Ryokan

## Mobilizing Hospitality in Rural Japan

*Chris McMorran*

University of Hawai'i Press
Honolulu

Printed in the United States of America

**Library of Congress Cataloging-in-Publication Data**

Names: McMorran, Chris, author.
Title: Ryokan : mobilizing hospitality in rural Japan / Chris McMorran.
Description: Honolulu : University of Hawai'i Press, 2022. | Includes
    bibliographical references and index.
Identifiers: LCCN 2022010485 | ISBN 9780824888978 (hardback) | ISBN
    9780824892289 (pdf) | ISBN 9780824892296 (epub) | ISBN
    9780824892265 (kindle edition)
Subjects: LCSH: Health resorts—Japan—Kumamoto-ken—Employees. |
    Women in the hospitality industry—Japan—Kumamoto-ken. | Family-
    owned business enterprises—Japan—Kumamoto-ken.
Classification: LCC RA922.K9 .M36 2022 | DDC
    613/.1220952/25—dc23/eng/20220314

ISBN 9780824892272 (paperback)

*Cover art:* (front) "Japanese Hospitality" and (back)
"A Taste of the Four Seasons" by Sakaguchi Yoshie

*To Hisako*

# Contents

Acknowledgments / ix

Prologue: Work to Do / 1

Chapter 1. Retreat / 6

Chapter 2. Landscaping the Countryside / 25

Chapter 3. Pariah in Paradise / 44

Chapter 4. Inside Job / 56

Chapter 5. How to Succeed in Business / 78

Chapter 6. A Day in the Life / 95

Chapter 7. Women without Homes / 123

Chapter 8. Professional Care? / 142

Chapter 9. Policing Ryokan Space / 164

Epilogue / 170

Notes / 173

Bibliography / 189

Index / 199

# Acknowledgments

THIS BOOK took many years to complete and accumulated many debts along the way. My first and greatest debt is to my coworkers, supervisors, acquaintances, and friends in and around Kurokawa Onsen who supported my research and made life a constantly engrossing experience. I was fortunate to be buffeted by the shifting responsibilities, obligations, and desires at the heart of ryokan work, and my deepest gratitude goes to everyone who not only tolerated my presence, but trusted me enough to share your stories. I wish I could thank you all individually.

At the University of Colorado, I could not have asked for a more supporting and inspiring PhD committee than Timothy Oakes, Elizabeth Dunn, Rachel Silvey, Linda White, and Marcia Yonemoto. Special thanks to Tim for taking a chance on me as an advisee. In so many ways, this book was only possible because of you. I was also fortunate to be surrounded by a supportive group of fellow grad students, especially Alicia Davis, Jamie Gillen, Aimee Kelly, Aloe Yu Luo Rioux, Monica Ogra, Dan Trudeau, and Kiyoshi Yamashita, as well as our Boulder friends and my colleagues at the Center for Asian Studies. In Japan my research was supported by Tsutsumi Kenji and the Human Geography Department at Osaka University, Yamazaki Takashi and Kumagai Mika in the Department of Geography at Osaka City University, and Yokoyama Satoshi at Kumamoto University (now at Nagoya University). Steven Ybarrola at Central College first inspired me to study anthropology, a decision that eventually led me to Japan. I owe him so much.

I have been fortunate to call the National University of Singapore (NUS) my professional home since 2010. In the past decade colleagues across the University have supported me, but the Department of Japanese Studies and the Social and Cultural Geography Research Group have provided constant engagement and encouragement. In particular, I wish to thank Timothy Amos, Simon Avenell,

Tim Bunnell, T. C. Chang, Jamie Gillen, Scot Hislop, Elaine Ho, Lee Bee Ling, Lim Beng Choo, Hendrik Meyer-Ohle, Michelle Miller, Emi Morita, Ryoko Nakano, Kamalini Ramdas, Jonathan Rigg, Deborah Shamoon, Tracey Skelton, and Thang Leng Leng.

Research in Kurokawa Onsen was funded by the Japanese Ministry of Education, Culture, Sports, Science and Technology (MEXT), the Japan Foundation, and the US National Science Foundation (DDRI #0602711). Since 2011, I have been fortunate to return to Kurokawa nearly every year with a group of NUS students, thanks in part to funding from the University and the Japanese Chamber of Commerce & Industry Singapore Foundation. In particular, I wish to thank my Field Studies in Japan students. Seeing Kurokawa and Tsuetate through your eyes continually rekindled my fascination with the area and reminded me why this research was important. Thank you also to the thousands of students I have had the pleasure to teach over the years at NUS. I have been blessed.

Special gratitude goes to Michiel Baas, Eli Elinoff, Abirami Ashok Kumar, Jason Morris-Jung, and Shiori Shakuto for reading chapters early in the process and providing valuable feedback. Thanks also to Jyoti Vasnani for proofreading assistance when I needed it most. I am grateful to have finally met Sakaguchi Yoshie, whose beautiful original artwork graces the cover. I have long admired the playful way you see Kurokawa, and I am so happy you agreed to share your talents to bring the cover to life. Thanks also to Mrs. Lee Li Kheng for designing the map of Kurokawa and to Tokunaga-san at ST Planning for allowing me to use two photos. Finally, thank you to Pamela Kelley and Stephanie Chun at the University of Hawai'i Press: Pamela for seeing promise in my proposal, and Stephanie for ushering the project to the end.

On a more personal note, thank you to my family, who are all so distant in space but close to my heart: my parents, Jan and the late Jack McMorran, and everyone else who means so much: Ayao, Chris, Claire, Colby, Dillon, Emily, Jennifer, Karen, Megan, Randy, Riley, Rod, Sarah, Sue, Takashi, and Xavier. Thank you also to my friends in Singapore who fill my life with so much joy and provide happy distractions from work. Your names would fill too many pages. I am lucky to have you.

Finally, I can never put in words the depth of my appreciation for Hisako, who has been by my side throughout this long journey. I look forward to enjoying ryokan with you for the rest of our lives.

# Ryokan

# Prologue

## *Work to Do*

Iawoke smelling of mildew and *tatami* (rush mat). My afternoon nap on the floor of the empty dining hall left my dark blue uniform littered with bits of *tatami*. I brushed them away and stepped out into the blinding mid-September sun. I needed to prepare mentally and physically for the afternoon check-in and the busy evening to come.

It would be another full house at Yamazakura. Yamazakura was one of two dozen ryokan, or traditional Japanese inns, in the hot springs resort of Kurokawa, located deep in the mountainous interior of Kyushu.[1] On this night in late 2006, fifteen coworkers and I would welcome forty-four guests: couples, small groups of friends, and families with young children, all coming to enjoy the food, hot springs, natural surroundings, nostalgic atmosphere, and hospitality (*omotenashi*) designed to make guests feel "at home."

We returned to work at 3:00 p.m. following our afternoon break, with a long list of tasks to complete over the next few hours. While our guests arrived at unpredictable times, we had to fold towels, fill carafes with hot water, wipe serving trays, sweep the lobby, pick up guests from the bus stop, check the temperature of the baths, help guests park in the narrow lot, and prepare for the evening meal. I would spend the first hour spraying a fine mist on the paths, trees, and bushes. Amid the late summer heat, the glistening grounds would offer a cool welcome after the two-hour drive or bus ride from Fukuoka, Oita, and Kumamoto, Kyushu's urban centers and points of entry from the rest of Japan. The afternoon sunlight shimmered through the thick canopy of trees, before dropping behind the mountain and abandoning our narrow river valley in the long, dark night.

On my way to the tool shed, I passed the lobby just as Tanaka emerged.[2] I did not have time to engage in small talk or translate an email from an overseas guest. However, something seemed different today, as she called me and Sakamoto, the driver and handyman sweeping a path near the entrance. "Excuse me. Can you please help?" Despite her professional air, Tanaka's wide eyes and shaky voice betrayed a genuine emergency. "Please hurry." We followed her into the building, stepping out of our shoes and onto the lobby's dark wooden floor. When Tanaka neglected to change into slippers, I sensed the situation was serious. We raced to catch up as she explained in a hushed voice, "*Shachō-san* was pale and weak all morning, and now he collapsed." Her voice broke, before adding, "I think he stopped breathing." We reached the room behind the lobby just as our boss, Yamazakura's owner, burst through the door. "Carry him outside. I'll get the car."

The man Tanaka still calls *Shachō-san* (*shachō*: company president, owner) lay motionless on the floor of the one-bedroom apartment. Since arriving at the inn six weeks earlier, this was the only room I hadn't entered: a private living space adjacent to the inn's most public space, the lobby. A quick glance revealed decades of middle-class clutter mingled with signs of the man's failing health: unopened seasonal gifts, tourist trinkets from family and friends, furniture pushed into corners to accommodate a hospital bed, bags of adult diapers. Now fully retired, the former owner and his wife founded Yamazakura in this remote, mountainous corner of Kumamoto Prefecture in the 1970s and still live on site. From this room they nurtured the family business and helped transform Kurokawa from sleepy hamlet into one of the country's best-known tourist destinations.

Japan's economy famously boomed in the decades following World War II. Japan boasted the second-largest economy in the world by the late 1960s, and most citizens enjoyed a prosperous middle-class life. However, while cities grew due to state and corporate investment, aided by inexpensive labor from the countryside, rural villages like Kurokawa suffered. Farmers enjoyed generous government agricultural subsidies, but the exodus of young people for education and work left many rural communities in crisis. Since then, state and local actors have tried to stem the decline of rural life through infrastructure, tourism, and community-building efforts. Such programs were designed to do double duty—reducing urban congestion and reviving rural areas. They hoped to draw industries and people to the countryside, which has long held a powerful place in the nation's geographical imagination as the landscape of Japanese identity.[3]

While most efforts to revive the countryside failed, Kurokawa Onsen succeeded. In the 1970s, when the Sakai family opened a six-room inn, Kurokawa was suffering the same problems as most rural villages: a shrinking population and a lack of economic diversity. However, local residents like the Sakais claim that a combination of cooperation, hard work, and creativity has helped Kurokawa avoid the fate of other rural communities. Instead of lamenting their remote location, they used it to their advantage. They created a nostalgic village atmosphere modeled after the *furusato* (hometown), an aesthetic that appeals to both Japanese and non-Japanese visitors searching for the "real" Japan.[4] According to local business owners, they worked collectively in ways that mirror cherished cultural ideals often tied to the countryside and brought the village back from near collapse. Even in 2020, more than a decade after I conducted the core research for this book, Kurokawa boasts a steady resident population, dozens of successful businesses, regular community events, and a strong sense of local pride. Remarkably, this tiny hamlet with an official population of around two hundred people attracts around one million visitors per year.[5] Consequently, Kurokawa has become the envy of other rural villages throughout Japan that hope tourism can save them, too.

As the resort rose in popularity from the 1980s, the ryokan I call Yamazakura experienced slow, steady growth, occasionally expanding and renovating. By the time I arrived in 2006, it had fifteen rooms and twenty full- and part-time employees, and it was fully booked nearly every night of the year. Guests arrived from around the country and over time from places as diverse as Australia, South Korea, Hong Kong, Switzerland, Canada, and Thailand. Along the way, the Sakai family realized a dream shared by many small business owners in Japan: passing a successful business to the next generation. In the late 1990s they began handing responsibility to their eldest son and his wife. They even built a house next to the inn to lure the young couple and their children home, while the founders continued to reside in this dark cramped space behind the lobby. Now retired, the former owners seldom leave the room due to *Shachō*'s poor health and dementia. At mealtimes his wife collects a tray of food from the kitchen, and she helps him to the bath on weekday afternoons, when they are least likely to encounter guests. Even staff like me rarely see the couple. They live like ghosts in their own home.

Now, our founder lay at our feet. We carefully scooped him up—Sakamoto and I holding his head and torso, Tanaka his legs—and maneuvered him through the door and across the lobby. As I felt in vain for a pulse, I wondered why no one called an ambulance. The nearest hospital was twenty minutes away, and he needed assistance as soon as possible. Were they afraid sirens would disturb guests about to arrive?

We reached the entrance, stepped into our sandals, and continued out the door. We struggled to keep his limbs off the ground as we waited for the car. Our boss backed his black sedan to the entrance, just as I had done with guests' cars to load their luggage. This time there were no smiles and well wishes for a safe journey from a line of uniformed staff. The younger Sakai whispered instructions as we wedged his father's body into the back seat. I held his head as his wife slid into the back seat, ready to cradle his head in her lap. I gently closed the door, and the car pulled out the long driveway.

I looked back at Tanaka and Sakamoto, who breathed heavily, their faces full of concern. We had all been through a shock, but no one said a word. Then Tanaka looked past me and beamed. Confused, I followed her gaze and understood. "*Irasshaimase!*" she enthusiastically welcomed a middle-aged man walking toward us. We all smiled and bowed as he passed through the space just vacated by our ailing founder. The tourist, a short white towel around his neck, smiled. "Wow, this place really takes me back. It's so beautiful, isn't it!" We all humbly agreed. "Can I take a bath?" he asked. Tanaka led him to the lobby, and the moment was gone. We had no time to worry about our founder. Guests would arrive soon, and we all had work to do.

This book is about work. It is about the physical and emotional work required to produce one of Japan's most relaxing and rejuvenating places: the ryokan. I show how ryokan create a nostalgic, comforting atmosphere that helps guests—both domestic and foreign—feel "at home" in the Japanese countryside. Ryokan use both landscapes and hospitality considered uniquely Japanese to take advantage of powerful cultural beliefs about where national identity and women's work belong: in the countryside and in the home, respectively. *Ryokan* is based on twelve months of intensive fieldwork in Kurokawa Onsen, where I welcomed guests, cleaned rooms, washed dishes, and scrubbed baths in a handful of family-run inns. Like all places, Kurokawa is unique. Its rise from obscurity to the top tier of hot springs resorts merely one generation ago means it is still suffering from growing pains as it struggles to find its identity. Therefore, while this book highlights the behind-the-scenes work that can be found in all ryokan, I also explain the geographical and historical context that makes Kurokawa's ryokan unique, including the collective exterior work of men to design and maintain this rural idyll and existential threats to that idyll in the form of outside capital and a national controversy in 2003 involving former victims of Hansen's disease (leprosy).

*Ryokan* also features the individualized interior work of women to produce hospitality and reproduce the next generation of owners. *Ryokan* features the people who keep these family businesses running, with the first half concentrating on the family business owners and the second half zeroing in on the maids, cleaners, drivers, chefs, and front desk clerks who shoulder much of the everyday burden of hospitality. In particular, I highlight the women who are most responsible for mobilizing hospitality in this remote corner of Japan: the female co-owners known as *okami,* and the maids/cleaners known as *nakai.* By revealing these women's personal paths to the ryokan, their physical and emotional labor, and their reflections on their work, I explore the contradictions and opportunities wrapped up in ryokan hospitality. *Ryokan* tells the story of one hot springs resort's remarkable rise from obscurity and the messy realities of the work—celebrated, invisible, exploited, liberating—that maintains it.

# Chapter 1

# Retreat

Like a house from a folktale brought to life.
Like something you saw as a child.
Like returning to your hometown.
A nostalgic landscape; a nostalgic smell.
> (Okyakuya, "Yado Okyakuya" brochure)

**I** first stepped into a ryokan in 1996. I had graduated from university and moved to Japan to teach English as a second language in mid-1995, just months after the devastating Kobe Earthquake and the Aum Shinrikyō sarin gas attack in Tokyo.[1] While growing up in the United States, I had been taught to admire Japan for its rise from the ashes of World War II to the status of economic superpower. Japan promised to be a place of endless discovery, where high-tech postmodern urban life supposedly coexisted with rural traditions. But six months into my new job in the peripheral prefectural capital of Kumamoto City, I had experienced neither.

Kumamoto City was comfortable, but it lacked the excitement of Tokyo or the charm of the countryside. Instead of innovative architectural design, neon lights, and cutting-edge fashion, or idyllic villages surrounded by rice fields and forests, my everyday landscape consisted of forgettable grey concrete blocks. When some fellow expat English teachers suggested we escape the city and experience the "real Japan" at a hot springs village I jumped at the chance.

Nine of us squeezed into two cars for the long drive. We passed through the vast caldera of Mt. Aso and along the winding mountain roads of the Yamanami Highway before arriving at Kurokawa Onsen. Nestled among steep forested hills, we found no train station, factory, shopping center, or tall buildings. There were no bright lights, karaoke boxes, or convenience stores. There were only a few dozen inns, shops, and homes clustered along the Tanohara River. Steam rose behind squat wooden buildings, and each inn beckoned visitors with a warm glow in the cold winter dusk. This was a side of Japan I had heard about but not yet experienced. It was a landscape of nostalgia that I later heard Japanese visitors call a "time slip."

Outside the entrance of our inn was a sign listing the night's guests, with one friend's name appearing awkwardly in vertical English letters next to a dozen Japanese names. We entered the lobby, and a young woman behind the counter bowed slightly and welcomed us. While our friend who made the booking registered for the group, the rest of us explored the lobby. We admired the flower arrangement and leafed through tourist brochures and the village map. Soon a pair of older maids (*nakai*) arrived. They bowed deeply and welcomed us in Japanese, scanning the group for the most competent speaker and explaining the layout of the inn. They led us to our rooms—men in one, women the other—and showed us where to step out of our shoes at the entrance. We settled around the low table at the center of the room, the only furniture besides floor cushions, while the *nakai* prepared a pot of green tea. She made small talk in basic Japanese and select English words, asking about our jobs and our home countries, "*Okuni wa?...*Country?...*Amerika?*" She explained where to find the baths and other facilities and demonstrated how to properly wear a *yukata*, the light cotton robe provided to each ryokan guest. With gestures and simple Japanese, she asked what time we wanted dinner and breakfast and did her best to make us feel welcome. Finally, she encouraged us to explore the village and try the baths at other inns, before leaving us in privacy.

We spent the early evening strolling along Kurokawa's lanes, shopping, taking photos in the picturesque scenery, and greeting other visitors, as if we were reproducing some ideal sense of community that seemed to only exist in the distant past and this magical place. Then we returned to our rooms and enjoyed an extravagant dinner served by the *nakai*. For nearly two hours we feasted on Japanese favorites and local specialties, each presented with seasonal garnishes in a unique bowl or plate. The *nakai* served each dish at its ideal temperature, bringing wave upon wave of colorful new items and clearing empty dishes that threatened to crowd the table. When we could eat no more, she set before each of us a delicate glass plate with two immense grapes and a slice of melon. Somehow we found space for dessert. Too full to move, we relaxed for a while, before enjoying a final soak in the hot springs. We returned to the room to find our bedding where the dinner table had been. As a light snow fell outside, I drifted to sleep beneath the thick comforter into one of the most restful nights of my life. The next morning we had a huge breakfast and a final bath before checkout, when a line of uniformed staff bowed and waved goodbye.

### Japanese Retreat

This was my first exposure to ryokan, or Japanese inns. In Japan's massive and competitive tourism industry, ryokan stand alongside hotels as accommodation options for travelers. However, hotels are by definition Western-style (yōfū), while ryokan are Japanese-style (wafū) in both design and hospitality.[2] This distinction was etched into Japanese law in the middle of the twentieth century, as Japan welcomed a growing number of Western tourists who expected a certain standard of amenities and service. At the time, ryokan ranged greatly in quality, with too many falling below international standards. In response, authorities instituted separate legal categories for hotel and ryokan, to assure foreign visitors they would receive a certain standard when booking a "hotel." Even today, ryokan range in quality from basic to five-star and beyond, and they can range from small wooden buildings with a handful of rooms, to massive concrete "ryokan hotels" that accommodate hundreds of guests per night. However, style matters more than size, and the distinction in design and hospitality from hotels remains. By design, ryokan offer a uniquely Japanese retreat.

Ryokan are found throughout Japan, from major cities to tiny villages, including hot springs resorts like Kurokawa and other tourist destinations like central Kyoto. However, ryokan numbers have been declining for decades. A 2019 report by the Ministry of Tourism noted a substantial drop in the number of ryokan, from approximately 75,000 inns in 1994, to 42,000 in 2014.[3] By 2017, the number of ryokan had sunk further to 38,622, while the number of hotels grew from around 7000 in 1994 to over 10,000 in 2017.[4] Despite these downward trends, ryokan continue to be the preferred accommodation for many Japanese guests and a "must try" for many non-Japanese visitors, despite the fact that ryokan often cost two to three times more per night than most hotels.

Government agencies, trade associations, and travel agencies often translate ryokan as "traditional Japanese inn," a definition that emphasizes the ryokan's Japanese characteristics and links it with a time and place unsullied by contact with the West. The Japan National Tourism Organization proclaims, "There's no better way to experience Japan's traditions and culture than a stay at a traditional Japanese inn (ryokan) experienced in the art of hospitality."[5] Similarly, the Japan Ryokan & Hotel Association trade group asserts ryokan are "imbued with the traditional culture of Japan."[6] In countless brochures and webpages, individual ryokan attempt to evoke sights, feelings, and even smells that make domestic tourists glad to be Japanese, while attracting foreign visitors hoping to experience traditional Japanese life. Even the English-language Lonely Planet guidebook associates the ryokan with traditional Japan: "For a taste of traditional Japanese life, a stay at a ryokan is mandatory."[7] Regardless of the guest, the aim is to produce an explicitly Japanese retreat.

One key element of Japaneseness found in all ryokan is the bath. Since the 1960s, most Japanese homes, and even the smallest apartments, have been able to include a bath. However, this privatization of bathing has reduced the number of opportunities for what Scott Clark calls "bathing together," which can strengthen existing relationships and create unique social connections with strangers.[8] Most ryokan feature a shared bath for men and for women, which can make for awkward encounters with strangers, but which might also provide a chance encounter with someone without interference from the usual markers of social status like clothing. These shared baths also make it possible for family members who would normally never bathe together, such as sisters-in-law, or an elderly father and his son, to share time doing nothing but relaxing. Plus, ryokan baths are larger than most home baths and often feature a constant trickle of water, which increases the feeling of decadence and luxury, and further reminds guests they have escaped from everyday concerns like the cost of the water bill.

The bath becomes even more important in ryokan located in hot springs resorts (*onsen*). These inns proudly display the temperature and minerals found in their waters, along with the ailments they supposedly treat, and their online and print advertising always highlights the size and atmosphere of their baths, particularly when they have one or more outdoor baths (*rotenburo*). Visitors can choose their ryokan based on the purported health benefits of the hot springs (treating arthritis, infertility, or stress), the unique attributes of the water (milky white, rusty red, salty, or carbonated), or the view from the bath (the Pacific Ocean, Mt. Fuji, or a remote river gorge). In highlighting their baths, ryokan are portrayed as a uniquely Japanese retreat.

Media are instrumental in producing this image. Bookstores overflow with guides and glossy travel magazines devoted to entire regions or specific resorts with information on the price, scenery, water quality, and meals of ryokan.[9] Travel agents display colorful brochures advertising the cuisine, scenery, and baths found at inns around the country. Travelers, travel agents, business owners, and industry groups host countless ryokan-centered blogs and websites.[10] Travel programs that pepper the television schedule often feature minor celebrities visiting historic sites and staying in inns around the country, with the programs often devoting more time to the ryokan than the sites. They describe each inn's nostalgic (*natsukashii*) and traditional (*dentōteki*) qualities, the delicious local cuisine, the beauty of the landscape, and the quality of the baths. Ryokan are even a popular setting for television dramas, films, and novels.[11] Not surprisingly, the focus is nearly always on the tourist experience: the food, the scenery, the service, and the bath, especially if the ryokan is located in a hot spring resort. In all these media, ryokan provide an escape from the everyday.

If all of this sounds exceedingly wholesome, it is worth noting that ryokan have long been associated with sex, too. Ryokan remain a favorite destination for extramarital affairs, providing yet another kind of escape for guests from their daily lives. Moreover, many ryokan are found in hot springs resorts (*onsen*), some of which have a reputation for attracting businesses related to the sex industry, including snack bars and cabaret clubs.[12] Indeed, just steps beyond the ryokan lobby, guests in some resorts can satisfy many sexual desires. However, this association between ryokan and sex, or even *onsen* and sex, seems to be waning. According to ryokan owners and workers with decades of experience, there has been a significant shift in clientele over the past few decades, from large groups of men (often colleagues) staying together, to smaller groups and more families. This change has led to a decline in the demand for the sex industry around ryokan. Increased numbers of young couples, young families with children, multigenerational families celebrating birthdays, and small groups of female friends have helped ryokan largely shed their association with sex and the sex industry.[13]

### Ryokan Work

In the years since that first visit in 1996, I stayed at ryokan in Kurokawa and elsewhere around Japan. As I did, I grew curious about what the ryokan was like for those who worked and lived there. I learned that many small family-run inns hire outside help to create their Japanese retreat. In some cases, this labor is only required on busy weekends or high-volume travel seasons like the month of August, New Year's, and the cluster of public holidays in late April and early May called Golden Week. However, the intensely personal interaction at the core of ryokan hospitality, so-called Japanese-style hospitality, means that even a small inn with a dozen rooms needs a staff of ten or more, while larger ryokan require dozens of employees at the front desk, back office, gardens, parking lot, rooms, corridors, and kitchen. Indeed, ryokan with a steady stream of guests like the two dozen inns around Kurokawa have far more happening behind the scenes than one might expect from a so-called family business. They require a small army working year-round. Who are all these people who welcome guests, cook and serve the meals, tend the grounds, and clean the rooms? Where do they come from? Why do they choose this line of work, and what are the working conditions, especially in family-run inns like Yamazakura?

In mid-2006 I returned to Kurokawa, hoping to answer these questions and study the ryokan workplace. To do so, I put on a uniform and worked. For a year I worked over one thousand hours at Yamazakura and six other inns. Cleaning rooms, scrubbing baths, washing dishes, and carrying trays was the only way to access the backstage areas and experience the daily routines, routine conversations, bodily aches and pains, and emotional highs and lows of making guests feel at home.

In a way, the time and space of the workplace determined the method. I realized early that it would be nearly impossible to understand the working conditions and social relations in a ryokan without being on the job. Guests arrive in mid-afternoon, eat a large meal between 6:00 and 9:00 p.m., sleep, wake, eat breakfast from 8:00 to 9:00 a.m., and check out by 10:00 a.m. Meanwhile, employees work around the guests. They arrive at 7:30 a.m. or earlier to serve breakfast. They clean rooms after the 10:00 a.m. check-out. They eat lunch around 12:30, then take a short break. They return at 3:00 p.m. to help guests check in. Then they serve dinner and prepare the dining room for tomorrow's breakfast. The workday finally ends at 9:00 p.m. or later. When could I talk to employees except at work? Interviewing at 6:00 a.m. or 10:00 p.m., or interrupting their short afternoon break, would be impractical and rude. Plus, if I really wanted to learn about the ryokan as a workplace, I wanted to do the work.

Like many workplaces, ryokan contain spaces exclusively for employees and nonemployees. Anyone not falling into these two categories presents a dilemma. I could shadow employees, but an early attempt in 2004 failed. Workers were always tripping over me, since they were constantly on the move, cleaning rooms or delivering food in the inn's narrow spaces. More than a decade later, Eguchi still recalls with amusement the first time I followed her around Yamazakura. "I wondered, who is this strange foreigner, and why is he following me asking these questions?" Eguchi and her coworkers did not seem bothered by our differences—a non-Japanese man in his thirties closely watching Japanese women in their fifties and sixties at work. They seemed more bothered that I was not a tourist or an employee. I was an object out of place. Between the long hours and most ryokan work occurring behind closed doors, my best option was to put on a uniform and get to work. Only then could I understand the emotional and physical stresses and joys of ryokan work, as well as the realities of flexible labor in contemporary Japan.

So I approached the owner of Yamazakura and promised to both pull my weight and protect the anonymity of the inn and its staff as an unpaid worker. He agreed, and in 2006 I returned to Kurokawa. His wife, whom everyone simply called "*Okami*-san," met me in the lobby the day I arrived and asked with a mischievous smile, "Are you sure you want to work here? You might regret it, since we are so busy."

During the next twelve months, I washed dishes, carried luggage, scrubbed baths, laid out bedding, parked cars, vacuumed *tatami*, prepared dinner trays, and cleaned toilets. I worked alongside those who produce and embody this intentionally Japanese retreat. I learned how to move through space, how to interact with guests, coworkers, and management, and most importantly, how to translate each owner's nostalgic, gendered conception of home and hospitality into what my *okami* called "service from the heart" (*kokoro kara no sābisu*). I found myself shortening and quieting my steps in hallways and guestrooms, working with quick, polite humility in the presence of guests, and conjuring a sincere smile when necessary in order to fool both guests and coworkers.[14] I also learned how to deflect requests by coworkers who took advantage of my position as the newest staff member, and over time, how to bargain in the complicated marketplace of favors, expectations, and refusals that are common to all workplaces, but which must be delicately negotiated in the presence of guests.

By embedding myself in a ryokan, I joined a long line of researchers since the 1970s who have worked blue-, white-, and pink-collar jobs in order to understand Japanese society. These workplaces have included factories, banks, hostess bars, tea houses, educational institutions, grocery stores, tanneries, non-profit organizations, convenience stores, and more.[15] Despite this diversity of workplaces under the microscope, however, the popular imagination about work in Japan has tended to focus on secure white-collar employees in large corporations protected by the so-called lifetime employment system. This system, which guarantees employment for its core workers from graduation to retirement and includes regular pay raises and generous bonuses and benefits, expanded during the 1960s and inspired many popular reports on the stability of the system and its impact on both its core male employee, the so-called salaryman (*sararīman*), and his partner, the professional housewife (*sengyō shufu*).[16] In the system, which is often portrayed as uniquely Japanese, the full-time permanent employee's life revolves around his (usually "his") company, with all other social relationships—family, neighbors, friends—taking a backseat. The salaryman has been portrayed as a corporate warrior expected to devote his life to the company, while his spouse is expected to devote herself to both helping him be the best company man possible and raising successful children who will take their place. Popular reporting has long emphasized these two figures, which in turn has perpetuated myths about Japanese homogeneity, specifically the security of work in Japan and the centrality of work and home to men and women, respectively.

Scholars of Japan have long complicated this picture, in part by accessing a broad range of workplaces and employees beyond white-collar bankers. Scholars have revealed considerable diversity in working conditions, job security, and the centrality of work to one's identity, for both men and women, by spending time in small family enterprises.[17] They have shown the challenges faced by women navigating full-time and part-time employment during their life course and alongside their responsibilities at home.[18] And they have shown the systematic growth in more precarious forms of employment, including contract-based dispatch work (*haken*) and positions in the service economy.[19] In some ways, this has accompanied both the stagnation of the lifetime employment system since the 1980s and the increase of both women's participation in the workforce and the number of non-permanent jobs during that period.[20] However, a focus on the salaryman and housewife always overlooked the underlying precarity that always existed throughout the Japanese postwar economy.[21]

Since at least the 1980s, workplace studies have undermined the lingering belief still held by so many casual observers of Japan that the country remains a homogeneous, overwhelmingly middle-class society with a shared set of experiences and values, particularly when it comes to work. Instead, studies focused on Japanese work in particular have highlighted the fact that there seem to be two Japans: one populated by permanent employees and their families secure in the bubble of the lifetime employment system, and another Japan populated by everyone else, including farmers, fisherfolk, dispatched workers (*haken*), seasonal domestic migrant workers (*dekasegi*), day laborers, and perpetual part-timers.[22]

I follow this trend by featuring small family businesses in Japan's economically and demographically troubled countryside that rely on highly flexible, vulnerable employees. In the pages that follow I introduce the people whose lives and labor converge in the ryokan, from the family business owners, to the chefs, cleaners, drivers, gardeners, and front desk clerks employed to make tourists feel at home. These diverse characters reveal not only the physical and emotional work that produces a ryokan, but also the divergent expectations of family, career, and self that is found among ryokan employees and owners. As I show, the ryokan provides a last resort for many individuals to reach divergent goals, including regional socioeconomic revival, household continuity, skill development, economic freedom, and even escape from domestic violence. Throughout the book, I explain what draws people to ryokan work, the work they do, and the sacrifices and joys they experience in the workplace. In doing so I highlight the precarity of not only employees whose personal circumstances make them particularly vulnerable to exploitation by employers, but also small business owners trapped in the countryside and struggling to compete in the cutthroat tourism industry.

### Workers' Retreat

Owners, guests, and the media frequently depict the ryokan as a retreat and a home away from home. However, it surprised me that some employees do, too, especially given the physically and emotionally demanding nature of the work. One of the first people to bring this to my attention was Suzuki, a coworker at Yamazakura. Her entry into ryokan work and her situation sharply contrasts with that of her employer, and provides valuable insights into the ryokan workplace and Japanese society.

Suzuki is a *nakai,* whose job is to care for guests throughout their stay.[23] Frequently translated as "hostess" or "maid," *nakai* is written with the characters for "relationship" (仲) and "to exist, to be" (居). Appropriately, she occupies a space in between. She embodies the relationship between the inn owners and their guests. Plus, she shuttles food and beverages between the kitchen and the guestroom. Importantly, *nakai* only refers to women. I encountered very few inns that even considered hiring men to do the feminized work of the *nakai.* Ryokan owners, employees, and guests usually dismissed the notion, sometimes with laughter, suggesting it would be strange for a man to do what they considered women's work (*onna no shigoto*). In inns where dinner is served in the guestroom, *okami* and *nakai* thought it inappropriate for a man to come and go freely. On the other hand, it was perfectly normal for a woman to enter guestrooms, even of male guests. While men commonly serve food in restaurants and bars, they seldom serve food in a ryokan. Rare exceptions when male staff enter guestrooms are when a window or a heater needs to be fixed, or when male staff help move the dining table and lay out *futon* after dinner. The latter typically only occurs when guests are not in the room.

*Nakai* are often called the "face of the inn" (*ryokan no kao*), since theirs is the one seen most by guests. In most inns, one *nakai* cares for the guests of one to three rooms, thus creating an intimate relationship with guests that lasts from check-in to check-out. The *nakai* welcomes her charges in the lobby and shows them the facilities and to their room, before serving tea and wishing them a pleasant stay. Later, she serves dinner in their room, returning time and again over the course of an hour, with a new dish and lively conversation. Eventually she clears the dishes, pushes aside the dining table, and lays out the bedding. The next morning she serves breakfast and cleans the rooms after her guests check out. For the *nakai* in Yamazakura, this is a cycle of hospitality that lasts ten to twelve hours a day, five to six days a week, all year long.

Suzuki was one of the employees at Yamazakura who gave me a crash course in how to create a nostalgic, harmonious, and purposefully Japanese atmosphere for guests. Everyone knew the purpose of my research and seemed eager to help, but since I arrived in August just days before the Obon holiday season, one of the busiest travel periods of the year, few of my new coworkers had the time or energy to do more than correct my constant errors.

The hot days of August and September were grueling. We shuttled food, laundry, and a heavy vacuum cleaner around the inn, always ready with a smile and a bow when we encountered guests. Although we chatted in spare moments during the long days, my coworkers were too exhausted to sit down with me for an extended conversation. And our afternoon break between lunch and the 3:00 p.m. check-in was sacrosanct. Everyone watched television or napped to conserve energy for the unpredictable evening to come.

When the pace of work slowed slightly in mid-October, Suzuki asked about my research as we cleaned a guestroom. When I indicated that things were progressing slowly and that I hoped to have a longer conversation with everyone at some point, she replied "You can talk with me if you like. Come to my room during break."

So after eating lunch and jotting some notes, I took the narrow path to Suzuki's room. I gently tapped on the door. A faint voice came from deep within the room. "Come in." I slowly slid open the door, expecting to see her walking toward me, welcoming me. Instead, she sat in the center of the dimly lit room, her legs stretched under the low table, eyes glued to the television. She took a long drag from her cigarette. I stepped out of my shoes and onto the *tatami* floor, and closed the door behind me.

Suzuki stayed in a small, dank, windowless room below the guestrooms. It lacked any visible sign of her normally cheerful personality. Breaking the awkward silence, I offered, "It's cool in here, isn't it?" It was such a pleasant contrast to the heat outside. As my eyes adjusted to the dim light, however, I felt the dampness and noticed that the wall behind the television was black with mold. Suzuki had covered it with pages from a travel agency calendar. Mold crept around the edges of images of Mt. Fuji, the Sapporo Snow Festival, and an Okinawan beach.

On one side of the room lay her unmade *futon*. With no storage closet or visitors, she had no reason to tidy up each morning. Plus, there was nowhere to hang the *futon* in the sunshine and out of the sight of guests. A few shirts hung on a moveable rack. She shared the ten-mat room, along with a toilet and sink, with another employee who had the day off.[24] Like the others living on-site, she lacked a shower and bath. She had to use one of the inn's baths after 10 p.m., when most guests were finished. Suzuki had lived in this makeshift space for six years. For her, it was not home; but it was the best she could expect.

She invited me to sit, and we half-heartedly watched television for a few minutes. Then, sensing her lack of interest in the program, I asked how she came to work in a ryokan.

"I grew up in a small town," she began, "so after high school, I moved to Osaka. I soon found a job as a hostess in a snack bar." Now in her late-fifties, Suzuki's graying hair and fine wrinkles accentuate her beauty, which brought her so much attention in her youth. At the snack bar her job was to pour drinks, talk with male customers, and look attractive. "A lot of people didn't like the job, but I really enjoyed it!" Her eyes lit up as she recalled those days of glamour and attention, filled with fashionable clothes and gifts from customers. "Every night I met people who paid attention to me. I was young and beautiful." She was popular and earned a good living for several years. In addition to her looks, she developed a quick wit and an ability to make small talk with strangers, crucial yet undervalued skills in the service industry. She continues to be adept at teasing, often with sexual innuendo, a skill she uses with guests and coworkers, including me. Her gift of gab served her well in the snack bar.

"That was where I met my husband." Some of the excitement left her voice as she mentioned him, but she recalled the romance of the courtship with a hesitant smile. "He was kind and persistent. He came to see me nearly every day. Eventually, I gave in." She agreed to return to his home in Kyushu, where they married. He was the eldest son, so they moved into the ancestral home with his parents, a practice common at the time. And like many of her peers, Suzuki "retired" from paid employment in her mid-twenties and dedicated herself to homemaking and raising a family. To this day, she regrets sacrificing her independence and leaving behind her exciting life in Osaka.

Suzuki paused to light another cigarette, before resuming in a quieter voice. Years passed and two sons were born. But things began to fall apart. "My husband often came home drunk. He started chasing other women." Looking away, she continued, "He also began to hit me."

Feeling unsafe, Suzuki decided to leave. But where would she go? Her parents lived in the same prefecture, but she wanted to put some distance between herself and her husband. A job ad in a magazine drew her attention: "Don't worry about clothing, food, and shelter (*ishokujū shinpai nai*). Childcare available (*kodomo takujisho ari*)." The job was at a large ryokan hotel, which offered a decent salary, a uniform, a dormitory room, three meals a day, and childcare for her younger son (5). More importantly, Suzuki could escape her husband's violence and gain financial independence. It helped that she needed no prior experience. As she explained, "I only needed to be a woman."

She called to arrange an interview, and she left home in the middle of the night. She dropped her older son (8) at her parents' house, where he could continue school, then boarded a bus with her second son, bound for the Izu Peninsula. She soon began work at a ryokan hotel with hundreds of rooms. "I had no experience," she recalled. "Before that I had been only a housewife." But for Suzuki the job was simple. She served food and cleaned rooms, or as she put it, "Exactly what I'd done as a housewife."

She worked with over fifty women, many in similar situations. "There were almost no locals, like you find in Kurokawa. They were from Hokkaido, northern Honshu, and many other places; so many women running from something (*nigete kiteiru hito*), including husbands and other terrible things. The ryokan attracts that kind of person. It is a refuge for women (*kakekomidera*[25]). That's why ryokan advertise far and wide, telling women from elsewhere, 'Don't worry. Come, work here and you'll have food and a place to live.'"

For the next twenty years, Suzuki worked in ryokan around the country, eventually arriving in Kurokawa in the late 1990s, around the time I first visited. "It was not as well-known as it is today," she recalled. "And the roads were terribly narrow and winding. I couldn't believe there was a resort in such an inconvenient place." After working in another inn for several years, she came to Yamazakura and has been here for six years. She is a part-timer (*pāto*) who works five or six days a week. She has complaints—insufficient staff, long hours, no bonus despite the inn's success, plus a few annoying coworkers—but she also praises the ryokan industry for providing an avenue for women to escape their husbands and survive on their own. In fact, even after complaining that *Okami* fails to even occasionally thank everyone for their hard work, Suzuki calls her "a god" (*kamisama*) for employing her.

After nearly an hour of revealing her work history and her litany of complaints and praise for the industry and her boss, Suzuki paused. An awkward silence hung in the room. When scheduling the meeting I had not expected her to reveal so much. After a pause, I remarked that her life had been difficult. But she quickly corrected me, saying her life was not unusual, nor so difficult. In her few decades working in ryokan around the country she had met many women who had been through worse. Then she glanced at the clock and reminded me that we needed to be upstairs soon for check-in. As she lit another cigarette, I thanked her and let myself out.

### Between Escape and Exploitation

I walked away feeling the weight of privilege and responsibility familiar to ethnographers entrusted with the intimate details of another's life. Anthropologist Nancy Scheper-Hughes calls the ethnographer an empathetic keeper of records: "one who listens, observes, records, and tries to interpret human lives."[26] The burden lies in interpreting. In this case, I needed to make sense of Suzuki's precarious circumstances, alongside her enthusiastic praise of Yamazakura and the ryokan industry.

The ryokan's role as an escape for divorced, abused, and otherwise destitute women is a widely known fact in Japan. When I point out the prevalence of such women in ryokan to Japanese acquaintances, they often remark something to the effect of, "Yeah, I guess so." Some even mention a divorced aunt or widowed grandmother who worked in a ryokan. Yet few seem bothered by the potentially exploitative nature of these women's relationship with the ryokan. There is a cold logic to the connection: ryokan need the labor and women need the job and benefits. Suzuki receives a room, meals, a uniform, and a decent daily wage of 8000 yen (approximately US$80, or $8 an hour for a normal 10-hour day). For a woman fleeing an abusive husband, or simply dissatisfied in marriage, the ryokan is preferable to imposing on relatives or becoming homeless. Suzuki even equates a ryokan with *kakekomidera*, an Edo period (1600–1863) Buddhist temple that offered women refuge and helped them initiate divorce, which they were legally unable to do themselves. In Suzuki's eyes the ryokan serves a similar function in contemporary Japan by providing refuge from her abusive husband. And Suzuki is not alone. During the twelve months I worked in and around Kurokawa Onsen, and in the years since, I met dozens of women who used the ryokan to escape dangerous or unbearable conditions at home.

Plus, thanks to ryokan work many *nakai*, particularly those in their forties and older, feel a freedom rare among women of this age in Japan. After decades of being "retired" from full-time employment and dependent on their husband's income, these women can live independently. The ryokan offers a liberating last resort when they have, as several put it, "no place to go" (*iku tokoro ga nai, ibasho ga nai*).

At the same time, Suzuki and the dozens of *nakai* I worked with around Kurokawa frequently pointed out the economic disparity around them. They had no job security, had received no pay raise or bonus in over ten years, and were still officially part-timers, despite working up to sixty hours a week. While inn owners built spacious new homes or remodeled existing ones, most employees were transplants from elsewhere and lived in tiny rooms in aging dormitories, often with shared toilets and always under surveillance of their employers. There was no union, and they could be fired for no reason, simply by being told, "Don't come in tomorrow" (*ashita konakute ii*).

Of course, working women in Japan have long faced such issues, and recently Japan has seen growth in the number of nonregular employees among both women and men.[27] These realities contrast with the job security of the model salaryman. Such changes in the labor force have shone light on these precarious lives. Some have even characterized Japan as a "disparity society" or "gap society" (*kakusa shakai*).[28] Amid such disparity, however, the vulnerability of my *nakai* coworkers stood out: their usefulness to the ryokan comes in part from their precarious personal circumstances. Many are divorced or separated from their husbands. This not only frees them to work the long hours required by the ryokan, but it also compels them to work due to a lack of economic security provided by a spouse or family. Indeed, for *nakai* who stay in the company dormitory, losing a job could mean homelessness. Unable to use a computer and often having spent years or decades outside the formal workforce, they have little work experience and few recognized job skills. Moreover, while the remoteness of Kurokawa draws tourists nostalgic for a rural landscape, that same location isolates workers from other job opportunities. They lack opportunities to meet potential employers and cannot easily reach a job interview because of

Kurokawa's location. Matters are worse for women who cannot drive and who must rely on the slow and irregular public transportation system or a ride from friends. They can easily get stuck.

More importantly, however, my colleagues knew that their long workdays helped perpetuate not only their employers' relatively wealthy lifestyles, but also each household (*ie*) into the distant future. For me, this connection was made painfully clear just a week after my chat with Suzuki, as I helped carry our founder's body through the lobby (prologue). It reinforced whose home we were reproducing with our warm smiles and tireless bodies. Outsiders frequently praised Kurokawa's ryokan owners for revitalizing the region and protecting a slice of traditional Japan for others to enjoy. In contrast, we were unskilled, replaceable workers doing the chores that made the inn feel like home, and which reproduced the home of our bosses. We embodied the owners' hospitality to guests, as well as the long-cherished rural values associated with rural landscapes like those found in Kurokawa. However, we enjoyed none of the long-term economic and social safety net that our labor wove for these families.

For Suzuki, Yamazakura meant both escape and exploitation, leaving her balanced between respect and contempt for the inn and its owners. I dwell on Suzuki's tale in order to highlight the gulf between the precariousness of her life and the permanence of her workplace. Work provides the tenuous yet meaningful ties binding these realms together.

### A Last Resort

*Ryokan* tells the story of how Kurokawa Onsen became one of Japan's best-known tourist destinations, despite its remote location and lack of historical or geographical significance. The first half introduces the families who own the ryokan and do the long-term work to keep the resort and their businesses running. The latter half focuses on employees like Suzuki, whose everyday embodied labor makes each ryokan feel like a home away from home and thus perpetuates the family business. The book is based largely on research conducted in 2006–2007, when I worked at Yamazakura, with short stints at six other inns around Kurokawa Onsen. In the years since, I have returned to Kurokawa nearly every year, spending several days each time following up with former coworkers and inn owners, making new acquaintances, and hearing about coworkers and friends who moved on, and in some cases, passed away. I also draw upon a number of primary and secondary sources related to

Kurokawa, including journalistic accounts published in books, magazines, and newspapers; tourist ephemera like brochures, maps, and pamphlets; ryokan websites; landscape-planning documents; travel guides; and documents related to a long-vacant lot in the heart of the village, which is the subject of chapter 3.

For owners, a ryokan like Yamazakura is a family business, that if successful, can lure an adult child back to the countryside and help fulfill a common dream among small business owners: to pass a successful business to the next generation.[29] Ryokan owners and their families around Kurokawa feel tremendous stress, not only to keep enough fickle tourists coming through the door, but also to keep their households and communities intact. They are not corporations lured to the area by tax incentives, inexpensive land, and cheap labor. Most grew up in the hamlet. They struggled in hard times and are now reaping rewards in an unpredictable tourist market. They embody the region's successes and failures and cannot move away to escape difficulties, unlike much of their workforce. Ryokan provide a last resort for these families to counter the demise of rural Japan and ensure the continuity of their households and communities.

Chapter 2 begins by exploring why Kurokawa looks the way it does. More than most workplaces, the ryokan is a bulwark of tradition in the face of globalization, through its use of Japanese space and Japanese hospitality. In particular, ryokan owners in and around Kurokawa have capitalized on widespread belief in the countryside as a powerful source of national identity. To take advantage of the ideological power of Japan's rural landscapes, Kurokawa's leaders have manipulated the built and natural environment to recreate their version of the *furusato,* or hometown. As chapter 2 demonstrates, the result is a village that appears to have been untouched for centuries; a hidden gem lost in space and time. Men have done most of the work of shaping the landscape, labor that has given them the power to claim who belongs in Kurokawa and who does not. This is clearly seen in one of the darkest chapters in Kurokawa's history and the subject of chapter 3. In the wake of a national scandal involving former sufferers of Hansen's disease (leprosy), Kurokawa's local leaders expelled one hotel from their business community, arguing that it was always an outsider that did not think like a local. This chapter shows how local leaders have used the landscape itself as a disciplinary tool to determine who is local, pressure the departure of one hotel, and successfully delay the construction of a new hotel for more than a decade.

In chapter 4 I step inside the ryokan, to shift attention from men's exterior work on the landscape to women's interior work. Both are essential to the ryokan. The former impacts how the ryokan *looks,* the latter how it *feels.* In a country where "the customer is god" (*okyaku wa kamisama*), satisfying the "gods" is emotionally and physically demanding work, and the person most responsible is the wife and co-owner, the *okami.* Beyond caring for the emotional and physical needs of guests, she must also care for the *family* of this family business: as wife, daughter-in-law, and ideally, mother of a successor to the family business. In fact, biological reproduction is every *okami*'s most literal and vital "interior work." *Okami* know that a willing successor, along with a steady stream of satisfied guests, can produce a social and economic safety net that honors one's ancestors, provides for today's family members, supports the neighbors, and extends the family *and* business far into the future. Chapter 4 explores the pasts, obligations, and dreams of the women who embody the ryokan and give each one its distinctive *aji* (flavor, taste).

Chapter 5 examines the challenge of succession. How does a family choose and train a successor willing to move back to Kurokawa and take over the family business? Chapter 5 shares the journeys of several successors, from their relative freedom through education and work far from Kurokawa, to their eventual return to this remote hamlet, where they too will one day be obligated to find their replacement. For some families the choice is simple and based on a long-standing preference for the eldest son. But what happens when a family lacks a son? And what challenges do these young people face back home in this isolated village? Chapter 5 examines multiple paths to succession and the ways that marriage and the inconveniences of rural Japan complicate the transfer of a successful business from one generation to the next.

The second part of the book shifts attention from ryokan owners to the small army of employees who keep a busy inn buzzing. In contrast to the long-term, even generational timeframe in which ryokan owners operate, their employees follow a basic daily routine that may be interrupted at any moment by the need of a guest. Chapter 6 introduces this daily routine through timestamps across twelve months of fieldwork, in order to provide a sense of the regular and irregular rhythms of the ryokan workday, the joys and frustrations of hospitality, the spaces and technologies of the work, and the people that keep a ryokan running through their physical and emotional labor.

Chapter 7 introduces the figure on the front lines of providing hospitality in a busy ryokan: the *nakai*. When the *okami* can no longer care for all of her guests, she hires women who reproduce her flavor of hospitality for her. However, because of the demanding schedule of the ryokan, the only women able to do this work are those without homes and families of their own. Through interviews and conversations in the spaces between work, I reveal how *nakai* fall into ryokan work, due to a lack of options available. At the same time I show that some women find new freedom in ryokan work. Chapter 7 demonstrates the role of the ryokan in providing a livelihood for strong, independent Japanese women, while acknowledging the limitations of this celebratory stance for women without a home. Women like Suzuki trade one form of exploitation for another—a husband for a ryokan owner—both of whom rely on her physical and emotional labor. The expectations tied to her sex—to be polite, subservient, hospitable, attentive—and the spaces of that labor—the home and the ryokan— are similar. Chapter 7 examines this highly vulnerable, mobile, flexible workforce and its ambivalent relationship with the workplace.

Chapter 8 reveals long-standing tensions among *okami* and *nakai* surrounding the professionalization of hospitality, between those who valued professional development and those who thought it undermined the very soul of the ryokan. These tensions came to the fore at Yamazakura as we prepared for a VIP visitor in the fall of 2006. In chapter 8 I show that these tensions were about more than the professionalization of hospitality. They struck at the heart of what it means to be a working woman in Japan today, as well as the potential evolution of ryokan. Chapter 9 focuses on a single, transformative moment in my relationship with the ryokan and ryokan work. It is the story of policing ryokan space, through the assertion of who belongs and who does not. As I learned in a painful encounter with my own coworkers, ryokan are spaces for hosts and guests. Anyone else is geographically out of place.

*Ryokan* examines the work entailed in producing the nostalgic, welcoming destination that is the ryokan. I share the histories and conflicting desires of individuals who use the inn for vastly different purposes—regional socioeconomic revival, household continuity, job skill development, financial independence and prosperity, self-fulfillment, and even escape from physical and emotional violence— in order to highlight the rich complexity of this space and the people who produce it.

## Chapter 2

# Landscaping the Countryside

"**W**hy all the smoke?" I asked Sakai as I stepped from the cool air outside into his thatched-roof hut. Yamazakura's owner stood in the middle of his latest project and replied, "I'm giving it some age." It was April 2004, and local builders had just finished the structure. They had stained the walls black and placed benches around an open hearth (*irori*) that would provide a place to rest in all seasons. Guests could escape the hot summer sun or warm themselves by the fire in winter. It would be especially useful for day visitors waiting for family or friends of the opposite sex to finish their baths. Sakai was eager for guests to use it, but first he needed to make it look old. So he was burning bundles of *susuki* (Japanese plume grass, *Miscanthus sinensis*) cut from a nearby hillside. A layer of soot would soon hide the shiny black walls and add a veneer and odor of age that better suited Kurokawa's landscape.

As I waved the smoke from my eyes and admired his ingenuity, Sakai told me a story to emphasize his point. An Italian restaurant had recently opened in the village center. The owner had wanted to build a concrete café decorated in the colors of Italy's flag. When word reached Sakai, he and several other inn owners dropped by the restaurateur's home and asked them to reconsider. Italian food was fine, but the building should not look out of place. Any structure that failed to match Kurokawa's nostalgic atmosphere might undermine decades of hard work.

"Fortunately," Sakai concluded with a satisfied smile, "they saw our point." The restaurateur erected a small wooden building in a grove of trees that blended into the surrounding landscape. From the exterior, one would never guess it served Italian cuisine.

Kurokawa's landscape is serious business for ryokan owners like Sakai. It is credited with much of the resort's growth since the 1980s, and it is the star of each ryokan's website and the multilingual travel guides found on the dashboards and dining tables of Yamaza-kura's guests. Outdoor baths and wooden inns framed by autumn foliage or cherry blossoms beckon potential visitors to this remote destination, while the accompanying text contrasts the traveler's long and arduous journey with the "healing" (*iyaseru*) scenery and expe-rience that awaits. The Lonely Planet description of the landscape echoes that found in Japanese guidebooks: "This low-key resort still seems like it's a tiny, forgotten village that you've been lucky to stumble upon."[1] For many visitors, Kurokawa's landscape triggers a "time slip" to a destination removed from the present; a distant, yet familiar place on the verge of vanishing.

Of course, Kurokawa has not been "forgotten," nor is it "stum-bled upon" by roughly one million annual visitors. And while the landscape may look like a remnant of preindustrial Japan, it is largely a recent product of luck and hard work by business owners like Sakai and their employees. As Gotō Tetsuya, Kurokawa's best-known ryokan owner, admits, "This landscape is not just left over from long ago. We made all of this over many years. We planted the trees and built the baths with our own hands. It's all man-made." Importantly, he adds, "We built it so that it doesn't look like a lot of different people built it, but like it appeared long ago."[2] In fact, since the 1980s ryokan owners like Sakai and Gotō have been shaping Kurokawa's landscape to fit a nostalgic ideal that serves two intertwined—yet sometimes contradictory—needs: a nation longing for the past and a local community looking to secure its future.

What does Kurokawa look like today, why does it look that way, and who is the "we" (*bokutachi*) credited with its transformation? The answers to these questions reveal not only the enduring role of the countryside as a touchstone of national identity, but also the role of the rural landscape in producing Kurokawa's "locals" (*jimoto no hito*).

These two scales of identity—the national and the local—intersect in Kurokawa, revealing the dynamic politics of rural space in contemporary Japan. Kurokawa's creation and success attests to the resilience of the aesthetic and cultural values associated with the countryside. While many rural communities suffer from economic and social collapse, Kurokawa satisfies an enduring national desire for a rural "anyplace" that is imagined to be removed and protected from the economic, cultural, and political uncertainties associated with globalization. Kurokawa's ongoing production of an idyllic rural landscape shows that the value of rural space serves both the national and local scales in mutually reinforcing ways.

But Kurokawa is not just anyplace. By appealing to a national aesthetic, its residents and business owners have been singled out for keeping alive the spirit of rural Japan in general, as well as for strengthening the local economy and local sense of identity. As a result, local and national senses of identity sometimes clash, such as when Kurokawa's residents challenge dominant flows of political and economic power from Japan's urban centers to its peripheral regions. Kurokawa's leaders claim that their success has, in fact, come despite a postwar political economy that systematically prioritized urban growth over rural towns and villages. Interestingly, Kurokawa's narrative thus questions the legitimacy and decision-making of the state, while at the same time embodying the state's image of where Japanese identity and cultural values come from. Kurokawa's leaders refuse to simply reproduce a rural theme park for the urban political and economic elite, and instead show how the countryside can be a tool for political action against outside forces perceived to threaten local interests and local identity.

### The Death and Rebirth of the Countryside

Less than a generation after its defeat in World War II, Japan boasted the world's second-largest economy. By 1973, it had experienced more than a decade of double-digit annual growth and most of the population enjoyed unprecedented affluence. However, the country's so-called economic miracle had been geographically uneven. Beginning in the 1950s, the state prioritized infrastructure and industrial projects in urban areas, which were supported by a steady influx of surplus labor from the countryside.[3] The resulting loss of population and economic vitality in the countryside led to both problems and opportunities.

Japan's long rural decline affected residents of every town and village in locally specific ways. In extreme cases, formerly thriving villages gave way to abandoned homes, schools, fields, and forests. However, the slow depopulation of the countryside had a deeper impact on the nation as a whole, due to the long-held belief in the importance of the countryside in defining what it means to be

Japanese. Many believe that the country's long agricultural history developed a set of values and beliefs that remain deeply ingrained in the population, even generations after most people left the family farm. Rice-growing practices, in particular, are believed to have made the Japanese naturally cooperative and willing to put the needs of others before themselves.[4] For over a century, such beliefs have served the interests of Japan's political, business, and cultural elites, who benefit from the idea that the country's agricultural past developed a unique, homogenous, group-centered, cooperative national identity.[5] The simplicity and historical inaccuracy of these beliefs are irrelevant. For many, the countryside remains an idyll whose always-imminent loss stimulates longing for its aesthetic and affective qualities.[6]

The threat of a vanishing countryside, in turn, offers opportunities to capitalize on urban Japan's desire to experience the aesthetic and affective rewards unique to this space before it is lost. Kurokawa's business leaders recognized this starting in the early 1980s, when Gotō and others decided to produce just such an idyllic rural landscape. As Gotō puts it, "Kurokawa was just a backwards hot springs village deep in the mountains (*inaka no yama no naka no onsenchi*). There was nothing to do but sell itself to guests interested in such a place."[7] The key to turning Kurokawa's backwardness into its charm (*miryoku*) was to create "Japan's hometown" (*Nihon no furusato*), a landscape that would envelop tourists in a time and space removed from their stressful everyday urban lives.

Literally "old village," *furusato* indicates a point of origin and a place of deep emotional connection shaped by time, space, and gender. *Furusato* often refers to one's birthplace, whether a fishing village in Kyūshū or a neighborhood in Tokyo. However, your *furusato* might also be the village of your ancestors, where your grandparents live(d) and the family grave is located. In either case, your *furusato* is often distant in both time and space from the present: a place you or your family moved away from decades ago and only visit once or twice a year. *Furusato* is also commonly associated with a maternal figure who is always waiting, ready to care for you when you return home. In this way, the gendered division of labor commonly associated with the family home in Japan is mapped onto the rural village to which one can ultimately return for existential comfort.

Like the idea of home, *furusato* identifies an emotionally charged place where your roots lie. It is a place that should be remembered and protected. However, just as the questions "Where are you from?" or "Where is your home?" lead to different responses depending on the context, the geographical scale of the *furusato*—neighborhood, municipality, prefecture, or nation—often differs depending on who is asking and where. A university student in Osaka who grew up hundreds of kilometers away in Kumamoto might consider the entire prefecture, a particular municipality, a neighborhood, and a residence all her *furusato*, depending on who is asking. Similarly, a citizen living overseas might consider the entire archipelago of Japan his *furusato*.

The *furusato* is a place that figures powerfully in one's sense of identity and to which one longs to return, like the distant homeland of an exile. But first, one must feel separated from it. As Jennifer Robertson explains, "The recognition of a place as *furusato* is possible only once that place is, or is imagined as, distant, inaccessible, lost, forsaken, or disappearing."[8] Given the scalar flexibility of *furusato* and its association with a distant or disappearing home, it also refers to the countryside in general in contemporary Japan. Politicians, marketers, and citizens use *furusato* to refer to a rural "anyplace" where Japanese culture and society is thought to have emerged but is currently vanishing. Robertson notes that *furusato* is used "in an affective capacity to signify not a particular place—such as a real 'old village,' for example—but rather the generalized nature of such a place and the warm, nostalgic feelings aroused by its mention."[9] The warm, nostalgic feelings associated with *furusato* are evoked through music, literature, and images of "forested mountains, fields cut by a meandering river, and a cluster of thatch-roof farmhouses."[10] This landscape evokes a simpler time and place and provides contemporary Japanese, even those lacking a connection to a specific rural village, roots in the country's rural origins.

### Consuming the Countryside to Preserve It

For decades, politicians, artists, corporations, and others have tapped into the tension underlying *furusato*: the demise of the countryside alongside the warm and fuzzy feelings this landscape evokes. Local governments and entrepreneurs initiated projects like the One Village, One Product (*isson ippin*) movement and the renovations in Kurokawa.[11] However, most efforts have been spearheaded by the state, which has tried to protect Japan's rural origins by curbing depopulation and encouraging economic development in the countryside by commodifying the *furusato*.[12] This has meant encouraging urban residents to travel to the countryside or purchase products directly from rural villages.

An early example was Japan Railways' (JR) use of *furusato* as an emotional trigger to stimulate travel not to specific locations, but to the countryside in general. In posters and television spots in its highly successful *Discover Japan* (1970s) campaign, the national railway featured trendy young (urban) women visiting shrines, pulling radishes from fields, and mingling with elderly (rural) residents, thus demonstrating that tourists could find their Japanese selves in any *furusato*.[13]

A decade later, the state again called on the power the *furusato* to support rural villages through the Furusato Parcel Post, started by Japan Post in 1985. Customers waiting in line to send a letter or sort out their banking could leaf through brochures and select food and other products for direct purchase from towns and villages throughout the country. The Furusato Parcel Post provided a direct connection between the consumer and a distant village, whose inhabitants not only shipped their apples or cabbages, but also treated the purchaser as an honorary resident, sending handwritten thank you notes and newsletters about local life and upcoming events. Unlike ethical consumption practices found today, which are often designed to bridge massive economic and social gaps at the global scale, the Furusato Parcel Post had a decidedly national and regional agenda, as Japanese citizens were asked to use their purchasing power to help undo decades of economic and social decline, and thus protect Japan's precious rural communities.[14]

The *furusato* was again invoked in the Furusato Creation Plan of 1988. Recognizing the continued plight of many towns and villages, but wanting to encourage bottom-up solutions, the state offered a one-time grant of one hundred million yen (approx. US$800,000 at the time) to each of Japan's 3,268 municipalities. The aim was to fund projects developed by local residents that would improve their lives and potentially attract tourists, such as hot springs facilities, museums, or centers to celebrate local crafts.

Unfortunately, such projects failed to change the fate of most rural towns and villages. By the early 1990s, Japan's economic bubble had burst, leaving the countryside more vulnerable than ever to depopulation and economic stagnation. The state attempted to build its way out of economic trouble, in part by adding roads, rail-

roads, bridges, and tunnels to further link urban areas to the countryside. However, the state also recognized that more drastic measures were needed to solve rural problems.

One fiscal belt-tightening strategy devised in the 1990s aimed
to reduce the number of cities, towns, and villages in half, to around
1,500 by the year 2005. This process of amalgamation involved the
absorption of smaller municipalities by neighboring cities or the
joining of multiple villages and towns into single units. Reducing the
number of municipalities would reduce the number of boards of education, mayors, and so on throughout the country. The state nearly
met its goal, with the number of municipalities reaching 1,730 by the
year 2010.[15] However, the effort unleashed a backlash, with many
complaining that this would speed the disappearance of rural towns
and villages. Titles like *Vanished Village: What Was the Great Heisei
Amalgamation?* and *Vanishing Village, Surviving Village: Mountain
Villages Buffeted by City/Town/Village Amalgamation* exemplify both
the continued fear of the potential loss, and by extension, the continued importance of the countryside in the Japanese imagination.[16]

Even today, the Japanese government uses the appeal of the
*furusato* to revitalize the countryside, again through its commodifi-
cation and consumption. A recent example rekindles memories of
the 1980s Furusato Parcel Post, by again directly connecting struggling rural communities with the generosity of concerned city dwell-
ers. This is the Furusato Tax (*furusato nōzei*), established in 2008.[17]
In this scheme, individuals reduce their taxable income by donating
to one or more *furusato* of their choice. In return, the community
thanks them with attractive local products (typically food, which increases in value depending on the size of the donation) and news in
an effort to strengthen the donor's bond to the place.[18] As was the
case in the earlier scheme, the *furusato* is not limited to one's birthplace. It can be anywhere, or multiple locations.[19]

With most of Japan's major educational, entertainment, commercial, and political centers, along with a majority of its population,
located in a narrow belt between Tokyo and Osaka, rural villages like
Kurokawa seem more peripheral than ever. However, the continued
popularity of the countryside and concern about its disappearance
demonstrates that as the countryside becomes more economically,
politically, and socially marginal, it also becomes more celebrated
as a touchstone of national identity. Similar shifts in political
economy around the world, including Europe and elsewhere in Asia,

have brought similar cultural outcomes.[20] Rural villages have been abandoned or transformed, leading to both the loss of, and nostalgia for, their aesthetics, values, and ways of life.

Through initiatives like those outlined above, *furusato* remains locked in productive tension between a spatially diffuse symbol of national identity and a precise, mappable location peopled by folks who embody those celebrated social values and relations. Indeed, the nostalgic appeal of the countryside persists amid continued depopulation and aging, desperate attempts at rural revival, and municipal amalgamations. The tension between the *furusato* as specific location and generic rural village becomes productive when tourists seek actual destinations to satisfy their longing for vanishing rural landscapes. It is into this gap that Kurokawa comfortably rests.

### Kurokawa Rising

Kurokawa sits in the northern part of Kumamoto Prefecture, sandwiched between Oguni to the north, Aso to the south, and Oita Prefecture on the east and west. This is the mountainous central portion of Kyushu where narrow river valleys are filled with rice fields and hillsides are blanketed with plantation forests of Japanese cedar, locally referred to as Oguni *sugi*. Kurokawa is part of the hamlet of Manganji, one of three hamlets in the municipality of Minami-Oguni. The village has long experienced the same economic and population pressures felt by rural areas elsewhere in Japan. Farming and forestry have long been vital to the economy, not only providing jobs and income, but also helping keep households intact for generations. However, the widespread mechanization of farming and sudden drop of lumber prices in the late 1960s led many to abandon the region for good. After a peak of 7,761 in 1955, Minami-Oguni's population dropped to 3,957 in 2020.[21] These days, most families cannot survive on farming and forestry alone. Landowners typically have a full-time job and tend their fields and forests in their free time.

Tourism has become essential to Minami-Oguni's survival in the past few decades, and many locals credit it with stabilizing the village population compared with similar rural communities. Local residents credit Kurokawa in particular with boosting the economy, not just of the hamlet of Kurokawa, but the village of Minami-Oguni and the wider Oguni region. Kurokawa's two hundred-plus permanent residents and thirty ryokan host around three hundred thousand overnight stays per year and purchase goods and services from

FIGURE 1. Location of Kurokawa, in the center of Kyushu. Courtesy Lee Li Kheng.

dozens of regional businesses, including producers of rice, vegetables, meat and dairy products, and soy sauce, as well as flower shops, laundromats, and woodworkers. Moreover, while its young people leave home to pursue educational and work opportunities in distant cities, just like young adults in other rural communities, many eventually move back to the region to take over family businesses, protect old traditions, and create new ones.

The key to Kurokawa's revitalization has been the production of a *furusato* landscape. Landscape is a silent but powerful tool. For many, landscape is merely what one sees out the window; it is only scenery. But Kurokawa shows that landscape is much more than scenery. Landscape reflects hegemonic ideals about what our surroundings should look like, not only through the protection of natural and built elements we cherish (scenic vistas at national parks, particular buildings and architectural styles), but also through the exclusion of elements, activities, and even people we consider out of place.[22] In this way, landscapes become powerful tools that assert and reinforce who and what belongs in a particular space. As Patricia Price puts it, landscapes "allow us to tell stories about ourselves to ourselves" and "construct collective identities," by making visible the values we hold dear and covering over that which we do not cherish. The result is a palimpsest, an ever-changing visual (and verbal) narrative built up over time about who we were, who we are, and who we want to be.[23]

Kurokawa's landscape epitomizes this ability of a landscape to construct identities through the stories it tells. The collective identity constructed in Kurokawa's landscape links to the idea of *furusato*. However, far from being just a theme adopted to attract weary urban residents seeking healing in the countryside, Kurokawa appears to embody the *furusato* ideal. The way Kurokawa looks and who receives credit for creating its appearance comprise important elements of its landscape narrative: equal parts historical remnant, modern invention, and success story steeped in social values that have long been praised in mainstream Japan and associated with the idyllic rural *furusato*.

The story of how Kurokawa came to appear as it does today relies heavily on a truncated history that begins in the late-1970s, when a new generation of owners returned home to take over their family businesses. Since the 1980s, the tale that is often repeated about these men (sic) and their vision for a new, but nostalgic, Kurokawa has drowned out counternarratives, and as I emphasize in the second half of the book, has largely ignored the army of workers behind the scenes whose labor is essential to creating the hospitable space of each ryokan and the hamlet as a whole. However, it is instructive to understand the story that Kurokawa's residents tell themselves and the world, not only because of the way it emerges from and is reiterated in the landscape, but also because of how it helps construct collective identities of both locals and the Japanese population in general.

### A Place Left Behind

Kurokawa claims a history as a therapeutic resort (tōjiba) since the early Edo period. The oldest ryokan, Okyakuya, for instance, was established by order of the Hosokawa clan of Higo (current-day Kumamoto Prefecture) in 1722.[24] However, travel restrictions during the Edo period and poor accessibility due to its remote, mountainous location limited Kurokawa's growth. In fact, the most common tale of the resort's history begins well into the postwar era in 1961, when the Kurokawa Onsen Ryokan Association (ryokan kyōdō kumiai) was founded by six inns. Tourism had begun to rebound throughout the country and onsen were gaining popularity.[25] This travel boom was enabled by improved transportation networks, epitomized by completion of the Shinkansen high-speed railway in time for the 1964 Olympic Games in Tokyo, as well as the completion of more highways around the country to suit a growing middle class of car owners.

Even Kurokawa, never connected by rail, benefitted from an expansion in the country's transportation networks. Most notably, the completion of the Yamanami Highway in 1964, which linked Oita Prefecture to the Aso region of Kumamoto Prefecture, brought more visitors and eventually more inns. Between 1961 and 1968, seven new inns opened. Unfortunately, this boom was short-lived. As nearby onsen like Tsuetate (Kumamoto), Yufuin (Oita), and Beppu (Oita) welcomed busloads of guests and constructed ever-larger hotels, snack bars, and other amenities to suit their needs, Kurokawa's distance from major urban centers, comparably poor road access, and lack of space to host such large groups of guests slowed its growth.

Today's ryokan owners consider the 1970s and early 80s Kurokawa's dark, "anonymous period" (mumei jidai). As Gotō notes, at that time nothing distinguished Kurokawa from the hundreds of remote hot springs resorts scattered throughout the archipelago. Residents continued to abandon the village and guests stopped coming, leading owners to engage in side businesses. Endō Keigo, for instance, ryokan owner and former head of the Ryokan Association, recalls that during long stretches with no guests he had no choice but to use the inn's shuttle bus to drive groups of the elderly around Kyushu. "I wasn't sure if my real job was ryokan owner or bus driver."[26] Other owners struggled to afford building repairs and often went weeks without a guest.[27] Most inns only operated around holidays or busy months, or they hosted long-term guests who cooked their own meals and used the hot springs for medicinal purposes. When they were busy during holidays, these family businesses relied on siblings, aunts, cousins, and grandmothers for part-time help, but otherwise business was slow enough to allow the owners to care for their guests by themselves. One owner still recalls those days fondly as a time when he could indulge in long softball games. By the mid-1980s, his softball days were over.

Those anonymous days can now be seen as a stroke of luck, since they left the resort underdeveloped compared to their more accessible competitors. Continued urbanization, a massive increase in consumers with disposable income, widespread car ownership, and most importantly, growing nostalgia for the aesthetics and values of rural life, laid the groundwork for Kurokawa to suddenly become attractive. Owners still recall tourists accidentally driving through Kurokawa in the early 1980s and asking, "What is this place" (*koko wa doko ka?*).[28] It was not on any tourist maps or in the major guidebooks. It was like a village lost in time and space.

### Building Japan's *Furusato*

Kurokawa's subsequent rise to prominence is featured in books, magazines, web pages, and video specials. They depict a village teetering on extinction in the late 1970s and suffering the same problems as other rural areas in the postwar era: depopulation, a weakening economic base, a lack of infrastructure, an aging population, and a bleak future.[29] Critically, instead of succumbing to petty rivalries, closing businesses, or abandoning the area, Kurokawa's ryokan owners worked together to create what they called "Japan's *furusato*" (*Nihon no furusato*). In doing so, they not only made the hamlet look like a *furusato*, they also embodied its cherished cultural values of group harmony and cooperation.

One hero of this tale is Gotō Tetsuya, second-generation owner of Shinmeikan. Media and other inn owners like Sakai often credit Gotō with first understanding the shift in visitor tastes toward smaller, quieter ryokan and destinations that evoked the *furusato*. Other owners thought they needed to compete with resorts like Beppu by offering more snack bars and entertainment. Gotō countered that Kurokawa's future lay not in attracting busloads of tourists, but accommodating emerging segments of the tourist population, namely small groups of friends and families arriving by car. He felt that Kurokawa's charm was precisely its lack of imposing concrete hotels and glowing neon lights. He put his ideas to the test by building an outdoor bath (*rotenburo*), intended to satisfy guests' desire to be close to nature.[30]

While bookings at Gotō's inn increased, he worried that Kurokawa's other dilapidated inns would detract from the *furusato* atmosphere he was trying to create. At regular meetings of the Ryokan Association, he implored others to follow his lead.[31] He later recalled, "It was no good for just one inn to have a rustic atmosphere (*inaka no fun'iki*) and attract guests. We all had to do it, . . . to create Japan's hometown."[32] He urged others to emulate the *furusato*, even as the negative aspects of life in places like Kurokawa—depopulation, aging population, stagnant economy, and inconvenience bound up in his term *inaka* ("the sticks")—became more pronounced.

The early-1980s also saw a handful of eldest sons of ryokan families return home. Most had been away from Kurokawa for around a decade, attending university and working in cities like Tokyo and Osaka. Many were reluctant to return, due to Kurokawa's poor prospects. However, many felt they had little choice, since their freedom to leave for school and work had always been contingent on returning when summoned. As their parents neared retirement and this next generation of inn owners settled into their struggling businesses, Gotō's ryokan boomed. Despite their parents' resistance to change, the young returnees witnessed Gotō's success and soon followed his lead.

The first two steps in creating the *furusato* involved planting trees and building baths. Like many mountain villages in Japan, Kurokawa was surrounded by neat rows of a single species of tree, the Japanese cedar (*sugi*).[33] In order to diversify species and soften the hamlet's landscape, ryokan owners began transplanting saplings from nearby mixed forests to the front of inns and along roadsides.[34]

FIGURE 2. Aerial view of Kurokawa. ST Planning, used with permission.

FIGURE 3. Mixed species of trees planted along streets (called *michi no ryokka*, lit. "street greening") softens the landscape. Photo by author.

They chose trees and shrubs that would make an immediate impact, including dogwood, beech, maple, birch, magnolia, camellia, verbena, azalea, elm, and honeysuckle.

Next, nearly all inns built an outdoor bath like Gotō's, where guests could sit under the stars or falling snow. They planted trees around the baths to both surround guests with nature and protect their bodies from unwanted eyes. Unfortunately, two inns lacked the space to build an outdoor bath, and as more tourists arrived hoping to experience Kurokawa's outdoor baths, these inns suffered. The solution to this problem proposed by the Ryokan Association neatly fit the social ideal associated with the *furusato*. It developed a small wooden bath pass, called *nyūtō tegata*, which allowed the purchaser to enter any three outdoor baths in the village. Thus, even guests staying at an inn without an outdoor bath could enjoy soaking outside at the other inns.

Introduced in 1986, the bath pass not only served as a tangible reminder of the cooperation among all inns, but also generated income for each ryokan and the Association.[35] Sales were slow at first (around six thousand in the first year); however, the bath pass soon attracted media attention. Within months of its launch, two television programs devoted to hot springs aired episodes on Kurokawa, followed by stories in dozens of newspapers and magazines.[36] The timing was ideal, with the country experiencing both an *onsen* boom and a *furusato* boom.

The bath pass put Kurokawa on the map, attracting both overnight guests and day trippers.[37] Like a pub crawl, the bath pass popularized a "bath crawl" (*onsen meguri*) and encouraged repeat visits by tourists eager to try new baths each time. The Ryokan Association aided this effort by printing and distributing colorful maps that indicated the location, view, and special properties of each bath.

More importantly, the cooperation among businesses inspired a new vision for the resort: Kurokawa as "one ryokan," with "each inn a guest room and the street the hallway" (*yado ga heya de, rōka ga michi*).[38] The Ryokan Association hired full-time staff, ran publicity campaigns, and continually expanded efforts to develop a "Kurokawa-like" (*Kurokawa-rashii*) atmosphere, while ryokan that participated in the scheme (i.e., all of them), underwent renovations and tree-planting in order to fit the nostalgic, natural model. Again, the landscape was more than a scene to observe or walk through. It was also a model for cooperative social relations.

FIGURE 4. Outdoor bath, surrounded by trees and shrubs. Photo by author.

FIGURE 5. Used *nyūtō tegata* hung by tourists at the Kurokawa Jizō Temple. Photo by author.

In the decades that followed, Kurokawa continued to attract visitors and shape the landscape to fit the *furusato* ideal. It established uniform signs (color, shape, size) for all businesses (1987), standardized outdoor light fixtures (1988), built and staffed a tourist information center that distributes maps, *nyūtō tegata,* and accommodations info (called Kaze no ya, 1993), painted all roadside guardrails dark brown (1996), constructed a community events and meeting center (called Betchin-kan, 2003), installed large tourist maps and information signs throughout the resort (2003), and added greenery throughout the village (1999–present).

In the early 2000s, the Ryokan Association also worked with residents and other non-ryokan businesses to identify and codify the previously informal aesthetic choices that attracted tourists. The result was a set of guidelines for all new construction and renovations by both businesses and homes, which would maintain the landscape and hopefully avoid potentially thorny situations like the one with the owner of the Italian restaurant featured earlier in this chapter. The guidelines, called the "Kurokawa Area Town-Making Pact," appeared in a colorful pamphlet that was sent to each household and business. It indicated preferred 1) building height and color, 2) roof color and pitch, 3) appropriate greenery, 4) height and materials of garden walls, 5) billboards (only "designs that suit Kurokawa"), and even 6) vending machines (painted brown or placed under a structure "built with wood or highly wood-like materials").[39] These guidelines have helped solidify the Kurokawa-like theme beyond ryokan and held everyone responsible for maintaining the landscape.

Over the decades, Kurokawa's efforts to produce a nostalgic landscape have attracted more than guests. They have also attracted the attention of planners, scholars, politicians, and residents of other small communities. Everyone wishes to learn from the success of this remote village that revitalized itself by satisfying nostalgia for the countryside held by both Japanese and non-Japanese visitors.

Of the resort's many accolades, one stands out for highlighting not only how timeless and effortless Kurokawa's landscape appears, but also the work necessary to create and maintain it. This is the "Good Design Award" from the Japan Institute of Design Promotion, which praises Kurokawa's carefully designed landscape for appearing "undesigned."[40] The notion of "undesigned design" (*dezain shinai dezain*) suggests that Kurokawa looks this way not because of decades of planning, negotiation, and the establishment of guidelines,

FIGURE 6. Tourists crossing the Tanohara River and admiring the *furusato* land-scape. Notice that all shops and inns use the prescribed colors and materials. Incidentally, when the state rebuilt this bridge in 2003, they painted it red. For six months, Gotō and others pleaded with the state to repaint it dark brown in order to suit the *furusato* landscape. The state eventually complied. Photo by author.

but because of an innate aesthetic sense among locals. This supports a state-driven narrative that locates long-admired cultural values in rural space, where they are thought to exist naturally. At the same time, the award acknowledges that any design that seems effortless, in fact, requires a lot of work. And while some of this must be completed by outside contractors with special skills and tools, the daily, monthly, and annual practices done by locals are emphasized in the narrative and most visible to the public: sweeping roads, planting and tending trees and shrubs, cleaning the river, repairing stone walls, conducting fire prevention drills, and hosting concerts and festivals.

Participation in such mundane activities, which are all publicly visible and often photographed and shared online and in print, demonstrates how "local" (*jimoto*) one is and justifies one's right to belong in Kurokawa.[41] Gotō always claimed that it was not enough for one ryokan to look old in order to attract guests: "We all had to do it, . . . to create Japan's *furusato*." For Gotō, the most important thing was the collective effort and resulting scenery, and only those who participated in landscaping activities and upheld the landscaping guidelines constituted Kurokawa's "we." Those who did not risked being cast out of the *furusato*'s protective shell, as the next chapter shows.

## Chapter 3

# Pariah in Paradise

In May 2013, I stood before a vacant lot near the center of Kurokawa, my heart racing. Until May 2004, the Ai Ladies Hotel (officially the Ai Redīzu Kyūden Hoteru) occupied this prominent spot, near the intersection where visitors exit highway 442 to enter the heart of Kurokawa. Standing five stories tall, it had ample parking, bold red carpeting in the lobby, and a beautiful garden behind it. In a chain of unpredictable events that began in late 2003, this prominent business went from successful hotel to demolition. Since mid-2004, the lot has stood virtually untouched, its future in limbo.[1]

The "no trespassing" sign on the gate was clearly visible, but I considered it a polite request. There was no visible danger and nothing to steal on the flat sea of white gravel. Eventually, I ventured inside. I winced as the rocks loudly crunched beneath my feet, causing me to stop every few steps to scan my surroundings and listen for something that might compel me back outside. As I pressed forward, my thoughts wandered back to the incident that produced this rare piece of empty space in an otherwise congested resort. What began with a botched hotel reservation soon brought Kurokawa unwanted international attention, as well as an opportunity for business leaders to reiterate who belongs in Kurokawa—who is local and who is not—in their effort to embody "Japan's *furusato*."

I first visited the property in 1997 as a guest of the hotel. As I crossed what used to be the parking lot, I recalled the white concrete tower that always seemed out of place in Kurokawa. The hotel always proudly advertised its outdoor bath and garden, but with space for ninety guests, twice that of most other ryokan in town, it always stuck out like a sore thumb. In 2002 the Japanese landscape garden pictorial magazine "Niwa" devoted an entire issue to "The Gardens of Kurokawa Hot Spring Resort." Following dozens of pages of rich color

FIGURE 7. The empty lot owned by Kyōritsu Mentenansu, where the Ai Ladies
Hotel stood before closing its doors in April 2004. Photo by author.

photos of small traditional-looking family-run inns that epitomized
the *furusato* aesthetic, the magazine briefly described Ai Ladies: "This
is a rare 'hotel' (*hoteru*) in Kurokawa."[2] Although the magazine
praised its bath, the author implied that the modern (*kindaiteki*)
"hotel" exterior clashed with Kurokawa's *furusato* landscape.

In the early 2000s Kurokawa was regularly featured in travel
magazines, television programs, newspapers, and books. In October
2003 it was honored as the subject of the second issue in a new magazine series devoted to hot springs, *Shūkan Nihon no meiyu* (Japan's
famous hot springs weekly).[3] Among Japan's thousands of hot
springs, only thirty were eventually featured, and Kurokawa's place
as the second issue after Kusatsu Onsen signified its prominent
status. However, weeks before the magazine's publication, a series
of events began unfolding that would bring new, unwanted attention
to Kurokawa.

In September of 2003, an employee of the Kumamoto prefectural office telephoned Ai Ladies to make a reservation for twenty-
two guests. The guests would stay in mid-November as part of the
prefecture's "Furusato Return Project" (Furusato hōmon satogaeri

jigyō). About a week before check-in, the hotel received a faxed guest list, along with information showing that the guests were not government employees, but residents of Kikuchi Keifuen, a state-run Hansen's disease (*hansenbyō*) sanitorium. *Hansenbyō*, more commonly known as leprosy, has a long, tragic history in Japan.[4] Those infected have been ostracized and forced to live on the edges of society since at least the twelfth century. In its race to become a "civilized country" (*bunmeikoku*) at the turn of the nineteenth century, Japan followed a Western model of complete isolation by constructing institutions like Kikuchi Keifuen.[5] In 1907, the state passed the Leprosy Prevention Law, which provided accommodation and treatment for sufferers, but also controlled their movements. Historian Ryūichi Kitano notes that over the course of the twentieth century such state-run leprosaria "increasingly came to serve as places for quarantine rather than treatment."[6]

Hansen's disease attacks nerve endings, causing loss of feeling, particularly in the hands, feet, and face. Simple cuts and burns can cause permanent scarring, skin discoloration, and even loss of skin and extremities. Given its reputation as both contagious and disfiguring, the disease has long been feared around the world. Effective treatment discovered in the 1940s means that someone infected may always carry the scars of the disease, but poses no danger to others after treatment. However, instead of seeing this as an opportunity to allow *hansenbyō* patients to return to society following treatment, Japan maintained its policy of forced isolation until 1996, when the Leprosy Prevention Law was finally repealed.[7] Unfortunately, this long history of separation from Japanese society meant that fear and confusion about *hansenbyō* did not end with the repeal of the law.

Ai Ladies canceled the reservation in question a few days before check-in out of concern for its other guests. The response from the government, business interests, and citizens was swift, and the incident soon made headlines throughout Japan and around the world.[8] Kumamoto Prefecture, along with the Ministry of Justice in Tokyo, charged the hotel with violating both the would-be guests' human rights and hotel industry laws. Japan Travel Bureau, the country's largest travel agency, and a handful of other agencies broke ties with Ai Ladies. *Hansenbyō* patients, their doctors, family members, and advocacy groups denounced the hotel for adding insult to centuries of injury so soon after repeal of the Leprosy Prevention Law.

At first, the hotel's general manager blamed Japanese society for its decision: "Under the current circumstances, in which general social recognition and acceptance (of the disease) is insufficient, we, as a member of the hospitality industry, cannot accept (the former patients) as guests."[9] However, Ai Ladies and its parent company, Tokyo-based cosmetics manufacturer Aistar, Co, Ltd., soon realized that it was on the wrong side of the issue. The hotel was overwhelmed by angry faxes and telephone calls, and the Aistar president resigned.[10] In the weeks and months that followed, the hotel's general manager and Aistar's new president made frequent (unscheduled and uninvited) visits to leprosaria around the country, where they read formal letters of apology and offered free hotel accommodations to patients. However, *hansenbyō* patients and their supporters were unmoved, accusing the company of "social grandstanding."[11]

### Patrolling Kurokawa's Boundaries

The "accommodation denial incident" (*shukuhaku kyohi jiken*), as it came to be known, quickly reverberated throughout the nation. Justice Minister Nozawa Daizō even noted that the government hoped to use the incident to address national problems: "We'd like to learn from this case as we strengthen efforts to eliminate misunderstanding and prejudice toward leprosy sufferers."[12] The incident provided an opportunity for the nation to reconsider the historically marginalized status of *hansenbyō* sufferers and address continued injustices against them. However, the incident also had a profound and lasting effect at the local scale, with Kurokawa's landscape at the heart of the matter.

The Ryokan Association met soon after the news broke. Since every story about the incident named both the hotel and the resort, every ryokan in and around Kurokawa was implicated by association. As Association members received questions and cancellations from guests in those early weeks, they worried about the future. How would this impact the vital New Year's holiday? Would Kurokawa's reputation be permanently damaged? Two weeks later, on December 2, 2003, the members decided to distance themselves from the incident and from Ai Ladies by ousting the hotel from the Ryokan Association. They hastily reprinted tourist maps without the Ai Ladies building and removed its brochures from the info center. The hotel stayed in business, but it was no longer part of Kurokawa's symbolic "single ryokan with many rooms."

The legal repercussions for the hotel were minimal. It paid a small fine of 20,000 yen ($180) and was punished with a mandatory three-day closure in March 2004. Former employees I spoke with claim that business was largely back to normal by that time. So they were shocked when Ai Ladies announced in April that the hotel would permanently close its doors on May 6. Weeks later, the entire compound was razed, leaving nothing but the gravel lot visible today.

### The Art of Becoming Local

In May 2004, just after the hotel closed, I ran into Kondo, a ryokan owner in Kurokawa. I asked what he thought about Aistar's decision to close the Ai Ladies Hotel and vacate Kurokawa. Usually a talkative man, he simply shrugged. Since the previous December, when the Ryokan Association officially removed Ai Ladies, I had wondered what had become of the community that produced this landscape. Could the collective spirit of the *furusato* so easily exclude Ai Ladies? I pressed him, asking, "Do you think the Association would have removed another ryokan in the same situation?"

Kondo took a long drag on his cigarette before answering. "They never drank with us. And their kids didn't go to school with ours."

He did not directly answer my question, but his message seemed clear. The community embodied in the idea of the *furusato* was alive and well in Kurokawa, at least among those who follow local principles.[13] Kondo implied that if the company's president or general manager had been a regular drinking buddy with the other *kumiai* members, or if the manager's children had attended a local school—in other words, if the hotel had made the effort to act local—the incident might have turned out differently.

From Kondo's perspective, locals understand the value of cultivating social bonds over a long period and in multiple spheres. They know that enrolling one's children in local schools means investing in the future social life of the village, and that socializing together is how social ties are built and how collective decisions get made. In other words, if Ai Ladies management had drunk with other business owners on a regular basis, they might have sought their advice from the beginning. Locals might have convinced the management to allow *hansenbyō* patients to stay or helped the hotel better manage the fallout of its decision. Kondo suggested that Aistar was motivated by a set of values that did not match those of Kurokawa locals.

Instead of the Aistar president living in or near Kurokawa, as is the case with nearly all other businesses, the company sent a new manager from Tokyo every few years. Each new Ai Ladies manager lived in company housing, but his or her family did not join, thus limiting the possibility of becoming local. It is normal for employees of large corporations to circulate around the country, and in some cases around the world, to branch offices and factories.[14] However, this practice contradicts the principle of a small family business like a ryokan, where trust is built between households over generations and "company presidents" are owner-managers who live on site, scrub the baths each night, organize and participate in festivals, and plant trees together. In other words, company presidents embody the *furusato* by creating it day by day, generation by generation.

When the Aistar president visited, he often arrived by helicopter, creating a scene and punctuating the economic disparity between himself and locals. A former neighbor of the hotel shuddered when recalling the commotion caused by those whirring helicopter blades, which often blew her laundry from the clothesline.

According to some, Ai Ladies cemented its outsider status by shirking its landscaping duties. It ignored the design guidelines of the Town-Making Pact, refusing to paint its exterior brown or mustard. And while ryokan owners are often the most visible and active participants in regular landscaping activities like tree-planting, garbage collection, and river cleanup, the Aistar president was permanently absent. Instead, the hotel sent an employee as representative. Most inns in Kurokawa are enterprises passed through the generations, thus embodying the integration of family and business. Ai Ladies, on the other hand, was just another business in Aistar's expansive corporate portfolio. While locals had cooperated with Ai Ladies for years, it operated by a different set of principles that kept it a permanent outsider.

As several people told me years later, the "accommodation denial incident" showed the incompatibility of local and non-local values. One friend explained, "The real problem is that Ai Ladies was not local. It was from Tokyo." Another resident and former Ai Ladies employee agreed, "No one talks about it, but Ai Ladies is gone because it was from Tokyo, not because of the *hansenbyō* problem." Indeed, the *hansenbyō* incident simply verified what most people already knew: Ai Ladies did not come from Kurokawa, and it made no serious effort to become local over the decades.

### Fearing Outside Capital

Today's visitor to Kurokawa can easily miss the vacant lot where the Ai Ladies Hotel once stood. In fact, the longer the property stands empty, the more it may seem that the 2003 episode has faded into the background. However, the space has not been benign. For over a decade Kurokawa's leaders and residents have reflected on the memory of the Ai Ladies episode and worried about what will replace it. The result has been heightened emphasis on the *furusato* landscape as a model of both aesthetic design and social behavior in negotiations with the property's new owners.

Immediately after the Ai Ladies Hotel was demolished, people worried what would replace it. Would Aistar rebuild? Would it sell? And what would a new owner build? Such questions weighed heavily on ryokan owners like Gotō Tetsuya, who pinpointed his concern: what if a non-local, or "outside capital" (*gaibu shihon*), purchases the land? It may not respect Kurokawa's past or maintain its *furusato* landscape for the sake of future generations. Gotō fears that all "outside capital" is necessarily driven by motivations, values, and interests that lie elsewhere, making the purchase or rental of property to a non-local a constant threat to Kurokawa's future. While other outsiders have purchased land in recent memory, the size of the Aistar lot, which is several times larger than most other properties in Kurokawa, and its prominent location, mean that any refusal to follow the established design rules would be broadcast on a massive scale. The Town-Making Pact only provides design suggestions, with no teeth for enforcement. Therefore, leaders like Gotō and Kondo had to visit new businesses and explain the logic behind Kurokawa's success, stressing the uniformity of its landscape, and in turn, suggesting that their new neighbors follow suit. This strategy worked in the past, but each property sale or rental required Gotō and others to begin the process anew.[15] The Aistar property would be no different.

Locals hoped to avoid this uncertainty by keeping the land local. At one point the Association even attempted to pool its resources and purchase the property collectively. However, it was too expensive. In desperation, Gotō even petitioned the national and prefectural governments to purchase the land for public use like a park. Both refused.

In October 2006, two and a half years after closing the Ai Ladies

Hotel, Aistar sold the property to Kyōritsu Mentenansu (hereafter KM), a Tokyo-based firm with over 3800 employees and interests in multiple industries, including construction, food services, and senior citizen housing. However, it is best known for managing student and company employee dormitories and for operating the "Dormy Inn" chain of hotels throughout Japan.

### Thinking Like a Local

The sale of the property has triggered years of negotiations between KM and Kurokawa's business owners and residents.[16] Association members first met KM management in 2008. Like Gotō and Kondo had done with other non-locals, the Association explained the history of Kurokawa's emergence from obscurity and provided KM with the design guidelines outlined in its Town-Making Pact. KM assured the Association that it wanted to be a good neighbor. Therefore, it would follow the rules and build something that suited the Kurokawa aesthetic.

Relations soured when the Association learned that KM proposed to build a hotel with approximately ninety rooms. Kurokawa's largest accommodations, Yusai, has only sixty-five rooms, while most businesses are small inns like Yamazakura, with fifteen to twenty rooms.[17] Its predecessor, Ai Ladies, had only had forty rooms on the same property. In other words, KM's proposed hotel might technically follow the design guidelines of the Town-Making Pact, but it would contradict its spirit. The Association countered that in order to fit the "Kurokawa-like" (*Kurokawa-rashii*) landscape, the hotel should have no more than fifty rooms. According to a letter from the Ryokan Association to the mayor of Minami-Oguni dated February 2015, leaders from both sides met an additional nine times between October 2006 and February 2015, trying to reach agreement on this thorny issue. However, the company still intends to break ground on an eighty-nine-room hotel.

I first learned about these consultations in May 2013. After walking around the empty lot in the afternoon, I brought up the subject over a late-night drink with Kondo and a friend who owns a souvenir shop. They had just come from a meeting of the residents' association (*jichikai*), which consists of farmers, professionals, business owners, and other people residing in Kurokawa. The Ryokan Association (*kumiai*) had just shared with the group a strongly worded letter to KM, expressing the Association's opposition to the hotel construction plans. After much discussion the *jichikai* supported the Association and its letter.

Given the dire straits of most remote communities around Japan today, it may have been unthinkable to KM that Kurokawa would stand in the way of its plans. Over drinks the shop owner explained that the *jichikai* members did not come to this decision easily. After all, there were numerous potential benefits to welcoming a large new business like the one KM proposed: local jobs, increased tax revenues, and more tourists purchasing souvenirs at her own store. However, *jichikai* members agreed with the Association about the problems of "outside capital," which would follow instructions from Tokyo and thus likely have a "different way of thinking" (*kangaekata ga chigau*) that would not lead it to act in the best interests of the community.

The shop owner suggested that given its size, KM might offer deep discounts that would threaten some of the smaller inns and potentially lead to the loss of long-standing family businesses. Kondo also mentioned the potential environmental impact of welcoming such a large new neighbor. With more than double the number of rooms, the proposed hotel would likely use twice as much of the hot springs as Ai Ladies had, which might negatively affect the hot springs source of other inns. Given all these concerns, the *jichikai* members agreed with the Association's continued resistance to the planned hotel and the Association's request that KM build something smaller and more "Kurokawa-like."

Halfway through our conversation, Kondo passed me a copy of the Association's letter, dated May 20, 2013, and stamped "confidential" (*maruhi*). Clearly, these negotiations were a delicate matter. KM was a powerful outside force whose impending arrival might unravel generations of work and destroy the very fabric of society in Kurokawa. How could the residents of this tiny remote village resist the allure of "outside capital"?

In these negotiations, Kurokawa's leaders use the resort's name brand, as well as the moral authority of the *furusato*, to assert both what KM should build and how it should behave. In documents to KM they reiterate the landscape narrative that has become central to local identity, emphasizing the collective effort that led to the development of the "regional brand" (*chiiki burando*) of Kurokawa that KM hopes to profit from.[18] Interestingly, they acknowledge KM's business prowess, praise its status as a top-tier corporation (*ichiryū kigyō*), and speak respectfully of its business "culture" (*kigyō no* '*bunka*'). However, they claim Kurokawa has its own "culture" (*Kurokawa bunka*), which is less concerned with profits than the legacy left for the next generation. According to its leaders, these two cultures cannot coexist in Kurokawa.

Kurokawa's explicit appeal to culture in its negotiations with KM disrupts the typical urban-rural power relations found in contemporary Japan. By using the language of culture Kurokawa's leaders emphasize their unusual position at both the periphery and center of Japanese power and identity. Theirs is a small village in a remote mountainous area distant from Tokyo and the nation's major economic, cultural, and political institutions. However, this distance also seems to protect Kurokawa from the negative impacts of modernization, Westernization, globalization, and other changes that have been imagined to threaten the sources of a unique national identity. Indeed, as praise for the *furusato* by those same urban-based economic, cultural, and political institutions over the years has shown, villages like Kurokawa provide a desperately needed core of Japanese identity in turbulent times. In its negotiations with the Tokyo-based KM, Kurokawa complicates the typical flow of power from the urban center to rural periphery by telling the Tokyo-based business how it should look, think, and behave in order to be welcomed into the rural community. Kurokawa asserts its authority to make such suggestions by referencing its unique position at both the core (as *furusato*) and periphery (in the countryside) of Japanese society.

For decades, the state has insisted that rural Japan, idealized in the form of the *furusato*, comprises a time and space that should be preserved as a touchstone of Japanese culture. By claiming that Kurokawa and KM have two different "cultures," local residents suggest that theirs, which is tied up in the mythos of the *furusato*, is the authentic Japanese culture. KM, on the other hand, is the culture of "outside capital." Put another way, KM has a business culture, while Kurokawa has a *family* business culture. In the former, KM is motivated by profit, which it seeks through a geographically dispersed network of enterprises with a minimal stake in each community. From the perspective of Gotō, in particular, this makes it morally suspect as a new neighbor.[19] In the latter, Kurokawa's family businesses may aim for a profit, but each family's primary motivation is to perpetuate the family through a single enterprise. This ties the livelihood to a single location that, in Gotō's logic, makes it more trustworthy and willing to cooperate to benefit its neighbors. The assertion that KM has a different culture does not blame KM for its way of thinking or behaving. However, it chastises KM for failing to understand and follow Kurokawa's more admirable, Japanese principles.

While these negotiations have been the source of stress, they have also provided an opportunity for the community to articulate its values and goals, as well as to make explicit the unspoken connection between the landscape and who belongs in it. In documents related to the negotiation, Kurokawa's residents have drawn on the moral authority of the *furusato* to stake a claim to the legitimacy of their way of life.

### Realizing Their Inner *Furusato*

Producing a *furusato* landscape in Kurokawa has meant more than enhancing the village scenery to match some national vision of an ideal time and place in the countryside. It has also meant embodying the *furusato:* becoming a cooperative group of villagers working toward a common goal. The cooperation extends beyond the Ryokan Association (*kumiai*) to other stakeholders like the local residents' association (*jichikai*), the tourism association (*kankō kyōkai*), and the young adults' organization (*seinenbu*), each of which aims to enhance the local quality of life and the tourist experience by continually improving the glue that holds them together: the *furusato* landscape. KM claims it is a willing participant in Kurokawa's vision for the future. However, its unwillingness to bend to the will of local commercial and civic groups by following their *furusato* principles, threatens to paint KM as a permanent outsider before it even pours any concrete foundations.

Kurokawa's business owners and other residents do more than create a tourist façade through their *furusato* landscape. The visibility of their landscape work strengthens the village's status as an exemplar of the idealized aesthetics and social relations of the past, as well as a rare rural community adapting to the present. Indeed, Kurokawa's very success seems to support the claims that the so-called unique Japanese culture associated with the countryside can adapt and survive in an increasingly globalized world. Through community-wide efforts like planting trees and agreeing on a common design aesthetic, Kurokawa's residents have both shaped a *furusato* and embodied one. Themed tourist landscapes may seem benign or superficial, but Kurokawa's "undesigned design" demonstrates the relevance of the *furusato* theme and its associated cultural values in contemporary Japanese society. The similarity of the built landscape to a culturally shared nostalgic aesthetic makes it feel "undesigned" and therefore, exactly what a rural village should look like.

As Kurokawa's success story gets repeated, its repercussions ripple through contemporary Japan's political economy. In fact, the narrative's connection to the landscape—which can be seen and walked through—reinforces the cultural ideals tied up with the *furusato*. Japanese virtues of communal effort and interdependence seemingly come to life in the landscape itself. Indeed, Kurokawa's success reaffirms and perpetuates the Japanese cultural ideal that only by sacrificing the interests of the self (or inn) can the group (Kurokawa) prosper. Here, Kurokawa perpetuates the myth of the *furusato*, precisely as the political economic realities of present-day Japan continue to hollow out the countryside.

Moreover, Kurokawa's narrative of emergence from obscurity and its physical appearance as a timeless ideal not only lionizes Kurokawa's business leaders and family businesses, but also implicitly blames other rural villages for their economic and social woes. When Gotō complains, "Everywhere you go in Japan, landscapes have come to look the same," he implicitly blames residents of other towns and villages for failing to learn from their surroundings, nurture a sense of local identity, and resist incursions by "outside capital" (*gaibu shihon*)—businesses owned by non-local Japanese corporations whose presence (and landscape choices) threatens to destroy any coherent local identity.[20]

Therefore, Kurokawa's landscape does important ideological work for the nation. It answers a national longing for the perceived simplicity of the past and concern that Japan has lost its roots in its push for modernization, while its residents epitomize the cherished cultural values associated with the countryside feared to be vanishing elsewhere: group harmony and cooperation. Finally, the landscape implies that Japan's twentieth century story of rural depopulation and decline was not the result of the systematic prioritization of urban development at the expense of the countryside. Indeed, walking through Kurokawa one might think that any rural village could be revitalized if only its residents were sufficiently cooperative, interdependent, hardworking, and innovative. In this way, the *furusato* becomes more than an aesthetic and affective set of associations evoking nostalgia for a simpler rural past. It becomes a normative force admonishing other rural villages for not realizing their inner *furusato*.

# Chapter 4

# Inside Job

In late 2012 my wife and I treated her parents to an overnight stay in Tsuetate Onsen, a small resort twenty minutes from Kurokawa. It was a last-minute trip to celebrate birthdays and relax in the countryside. After a quick online search we called and booked two rooms for the following night.

We arrived in mid-afternoon after a two-hour drive into Kyushu's mountainous interior. Steam punctured the December air from pipes scattered about the village. We found our destination, a squat three-story ryokan facing the river, and stepped into the lobby. It was made cozy by a kerosene stove and seasonal decorations. A Christmas tree and a large poinsettia sat next to a decorative wooden staircase with drawers (*hakokaidan*), covered in one-of-a-kind wooden and bamboo objects that displayed the creative personalities of the owners of this six-room inn. As we closed the door, a gentleman in his sixties emerged from a back room, his smile as warm as the kerosene stove. He crossed the lobby and joined us at the front desk. He opened a paper ledger and confirmed our last name, before announcing that we were tonight's only guests. He led us up a narrow staircase to two adjacent rooms, where he briefed us on the location and times of the baths and dinner. Then he departed, adding, "Please enjoy your stay. Call the front desk if you need anything."

At 6:30 p.m. a young woman in her late twenties tapped on our doors and announced it was time for dinner. Arakawa wore a chic apron of colorful, intricate patchwork over a loose-fitting black uniform designed for ease of movement. Her makeup and hair were simple yet flawless: shoulder-length dark-brown hair swept into a ponytail. Light foundation, with a hint of pink on her cheeks and little more. She had an understated, wholesome beauty. She was the picture of rural femininity.

She escorted us into an adjacent room, where a low table

exploded with the shapes and colors of our first course (fig. 8). Raw tuna shared a small square plate with raw horse, a regional specialty served with grated ginger and sesame-infused soy sauce. Boiled and steamed vegetables rested on a large green leaf: pumpkin, carrot, fiddlehead fern, and a taro root delicately carved into the shape of a mushroom.

We oohed and aahed at the feast as Arakawa knelt beside the table and asked about our drive. Noticing my wife's phone, she offered to take our picture. She seemed to sense that this family trip might one day be a cherished memory. During the next hour, she did her best to help make it so.

As we ate, she made ten trips to the kitchen, each time removing empty plates and returning with drinks or a new dish: salted grilled sweetfish (*ayu*), savory egg custard, locally raised beef grilled on individual braziers set before us. She announced each item, then lingered, watching us savor each morsel and humbly accepting each compliment. She appeared to be in no hurry and seemed to enjoy our company. Between trips to the kitchen, she inquired about our lives and answered questions about hers.

FIGURE 8. The first course of dinner. Photo by author.

Two years previously Arakawa married the eldest son of the gentleman we met in the lobby, the inn's third-generation owner. A year later she gave birth to a son, and the young couple moved from Fukuoka in order to begin the process of taking over the family business. Arakawa's husband is the fourth-generation owner of this family business, and their son promises to be the fifth. Her husband is the handyman and chef, while she serves meals and cleans rooms. The in-laws assist when necessary: he at the front desk, she behind the scenes babysitting, cleaning, and endlessly giving advice.

Arakawa has struggled to adjust to life in the countryside. "I guess I'm still getting used to it. Tsuetate is so inconvenient. There is no grocery store, and it is far from any shopping. Plus, business is slow."

A generation ago Tsuetate swarmed with tourists. Its glory days are briefly visible in the 1978 installment of Japan's long-running film series *Otoko wa tsurai yo* (It's Tough Being a Man). In an early scene of the twenty-first film in the series, "*Torajirō wagamichi wo yuku*," the lead character Tora-san steps off the bus in a bustling Tsuetate, before quickly transferring to the less hectic Tanohara Onsen. In the film Tsuetate is the congested tourist enclave that Tora-san escapes in an attempt to escape his troubles. However, during the 1980s Tsuetate began a slow downward spiral, just as Kurokawa began capitalizing on its own version of the unhurried rural escape.

Today Tsuetate is an empty husk of its past self. Tall abandoned ryokan lurk along the river, their rusted window frames and crumbling staircases giving the village a sense of abandonment. However, the Arakawas have not given up hope. In part, this is because they feel a duty to maintain the family business. By doing so can they honor past generations, support the community, and provide a stable future for their son. Arakawa sounded optimistic, "At least Tsuetate is quiet and the people are friendly. It should be a good place to raise a child. Hopefully, business will pick up." We echoed her wish and complimented her hospitality, before turning our attention back to the meal.

Sensing a lapse in the conversation, Arakawa excused herself and returned with the final course: rice, miso soup, pickled daikon, and fresh fruit for dessert. "Breakfast will be served at 8:00. If you need anything else, please call the front desk." At the doorway, she kneeled, bowed one last time, and wished us good night. Then she stepped out of the room and gently closed the door.

In Tsuetate we experienced the essence of the ryokan: a small family business caring for guests like visitors to their own home. With only six rooms and rarely a full house, Arakawa does not employ any outside staff, nor can she afford to. Instead, her family, which lives on-site, does whatever necessary to make guests feel comfortable. This makes Arakawa's hospitality direct, intimate, and vital to her survival. Dissatisfied guests threaten the future of not only the business, but the family itself. Too few guests can shutter a ryokan, even one that has operated for centuries, while too many guests may alienate them, making them feel they are not receiving the personal attention they deserve. Getting the balance right is the Arakawa family's last resort to honor their ancestors, remain in Tsuetate, and pass the family business to the next generation.

Twenty minutes down the road, Kurokawa's ryokan seem to operate in another world. While Arakawa struggles to stay afloat, Yamazakura's fifteen rooms were at or near capacity nearly every night of the year I worked there, and the inn has remained as popular in the years since. Beginning in the 1980s, Kurokawa's dozen ryokan (gradually increasing to over two dozen when I worked there) filled and expanded, eventually becoming too large for owners to personally care for guests the way Arakawa does. Kurokawa's ryokan owners came to rely on full- and part-time employees in increasingly specialized positions, creating layers of professionalized care between themselves and their guests. However, the owners I met in Kurokawa still see their inns as essentially the same as Arakawa's: small family businesses welcoming strangers into their home and providing the best hospitality they can until they pass the baton to their heirs.

### Stepping into the Ryokan

Kurokawa Onsen's *furusato* landscape reassures visitors that the Japanese countryside endures in an ever-changing world. This landscape is considered foundational to Japan's *national* identity, and it has solidified the *local* identity of Kurokawa's business owners. They have been credited with reenergizing the region and avoiding the economic and demographic crises facing other rural communities. Most acclaim has gone to the male owners of its ryokan, in part because they are its visible landscapers. They are on the streets and in the press making Kurokawa look the way it does. Less attention has gone to their wives, the *okami*, whose emotional and physical labor maintains both the *family* and the *business* of this quintessential family business.

In this chapter I step inside the ryokan, shifting from the exterior work of men like Sakai to the interior work of women like Arakawa. Both are essential to the ryokan. The former impacts how the ryokan *looks*, the latter how it *feels*. The person ultimately responsible for a ryokan's interior work is the *okami*. The way she talks to guests, moves through the inn, serves a dish, decorates to match the seasons or to express her personality, even the way she smiles, all reflects the unique flavor (*aji*) of her hospitality. In a country where "the customer is god" (*okyaku wa kamisama*), satisfying the "gods" is emotionally and physically demanding work that a skilled *okami* makes look effortless.

The *okami*'s interior work also involves caring for the *family* of this family business: as wife, daughter or daughter-in-law, and ideally, mother of a successor. In fact, biological reproduction is every *okami*'s most literal and vital "inside job." She must also identify and train her replacement. *Okami* like Arakawa know that excellent service may bring profits, but success without a successor is meaningless. Only the combination of a willing successor, a competent *okami,* and a steady stream of satisfied guests will produce a social and economic safety net that honors one's ancestors, cares for today's family members, and supports the neighbors, thus reproducing the family *and* business, in this specific location, far into the future. Indeed, the *okami* is stuck in place, immobilized by her obligations to the family business, while also reaping the long-term benefits that come with being tethered to it.

### The Business of Family

Owning a family business has long been a respected way of life in Japan. Today artisans, shopkeepers, and innkeepers around the country run businesses that have been passed through families for decades or even centuries. Each generation aims to maintain or improve the reputation of the business. As the Arakawas know, the future of the family, the business, and the community depends on it. Small family businesses like ryokan provide the backbone of social and economic life in urban neighborhoods and small villages alike, providing jobs, keeping profits local, and contributing the funds and labor for festivals and other activities vital to the celebration and reproduction of local identity.

For instance, Kurokawa may only have two hundred permanent

residents, but it holds eight annual festivals, all organized by groups like the Kurokawa Onsen Ryokan Association (Kurokawa Onsen Kankō Ryokan Kyōdō Kumiai), the Kurokawa Onsen Tourist Association (Kurokawa Onsen Kankō Kumiai), and the Minami-Oguni Town Chamber of Commerce and Industry Youth Branch (Minami-Oguni Machi Shōkōkai Seinenbu), whose members are mostly local family business owners. In other words, ryokan owners in Kurokawa do more than just perform the community through the group landscaping projects mentioned earlier. They also strengthen local identity and demonstrate their long-term stake in the community by representing their family businesses in such local organizations.

Japanese employees, especially those with lifetime positions, are notorious for working long hours and being "married to the company." But these tendencies intensify for owners of any family business. It is a full-time, year-round commitment intimately tied to the reputation of one's family—past, present and future. A Toyota engineer may feel connected to the company, but the Arakawas *are* the company. Plus, they live where they work, which leaves no meaningful separation between the family and the business.

Take the village of Oguni, where I lived during a year of fieldwork in Kurokawa. Within a ten-minute walk of the town hall were nearly a dozen restaurants and cafes, a pharmacy, a butcher shop, a fishing tackle store, a clothing shop, a furniture store, several hair salons, a dentist, and even a soy sauce manufacturer. All these family businesses were located inside or attached to the owner's residence. Even the official post offices in Kurokawa and nearby Nakabaru are located in the front room of the postmaster's home. And while each of these has separate spaces for business and family purposes, the boundaries are often fuzzy.

These fuzzy boundaries between home and work are common in ryokan, where the family typically lives on-site.[1] In Kurokawa I met several families who live in a few rooms just behind the lobby. Others are lucky enough to have a separate entrance for the family. Another family lives at the back of the inn, along a hallway of guestrooms. They always lock their door to avoid embarrassment for curious or confused guests who might accidentally enter, thinking it is their room. Elsewhere, a three-generation family shares a windowless basement apartment only accessible through the ryokan kitchen. The luckiest families live in free-standing homes, but even these are just steps from the inn. There is simply no escaping the business.

These ryokan owners lack the domestic privacy most Japanese take for granted.[2] They must look presentable whenever they step outside their cramped living quarters, and they must always be prepared to answer questions from staff or guests. But this is the bargain ryokan owners make. Many enjoy the convenience of living where they work, and they willingly put the needs of customers above family in the short term, in order to meet the needs of the family in the long term.

For ryokan owners, superior hospitality means providing delicious food, comfortable bedding, a relaxing space, and a warm smile. But it also means avoiding loud domestic quarrels, having family gatherings at a restaurant (or skipping them altogether), and meeting friends for a drink only in a bar. It means family members avoid arriving home during check-in or check-out. For small children, it means playing very quietly indoors or, better yet, at a school, a park, or somewhere else "far from the inn," as one *okami* joked. And for older children, it means not inviting friends over, except perhaps for a free bath. It means not disturbing guests with the sounds, bodies, and emotions of everyday home life, a lesson I learned as I helped carry our retired owner's body quietly across the Yamazakura lobby (see prologue). In other words, for the members of a ryokan family, hospitality means knowing when to be present and when to be absent.

### The Ryokan Trap

This convergence of home and workplace in time and space, along with its relative lack of privacy, makes some ryokan owners feel trapped. Managing a ryokan is a twenty-four-hour a day, year-round commitment. Most of the face-to-face hospitality occurs between 6:00 a.m. and 9:00 p.m., but someone needs to answer late-night requests or emergencies. These calls typically go directly to the owners' residence. They answer the 2:00 a.m. request for an extra blanket or the occasional desperate plea from a woman fleeing an abusive spouse and begging for the physical safety that will come with a job (see chapter 7). Busy inns like Yamazakura close only a few days a year for maintenance and major family events like weddings or funerals.

Employees like me liberated our bosses from much of the daily grind of hospitality, but they were still there. After all, what's a family business without the family around? Repeat guests often wanted to chat with our *okami* in the evening, and she seemed to enjoy the daily ritual of check-out, when she collected payment and bid guests farewell. It was an opportunity for her to display generosity by passing small souvenirs to children or giving her favorite customers a discount. Her constant presence and such small acts of kindness reminded guests whose family business it was. Meanwhile, her husband could rely on me and the other men to sweep the paths, scrub the baths, drive guests to the bus stop, and help park cars. But he didn't abandon us; he spent most days reading books in his residence and addressing problems like a sudden drop in water pressure.

Smaller inns like Arakawa's are busy in their own way. The more irregular the flow of guests, the more likely the owners do all the cleaning, serving, cooking, and driving, since they cannot afford to pay staff to just sit around on nights without guests. The owners are stuck, waiting and hoping someone will drop in without a reservation.

In either case, a ryokan immobilizes owners. It fixes them in place, since they cannot relocate the business. Plus, it fixes them in the profession. However, by being there every day the owners do more than just accept being stuck. As their daily routine gradually blends into a lifetime commitment to the family business, one might even say they embrace being stuck in place, since it enables them to honor ancestors, help build a community, and pass something significant to the next generation.

### The Immobile Ideal

Interestingly, an owner's embrace of being stuck in the ryokan contradicts a value long held in postwar Japanese society: social mobility. As Japan's economy steadily grew from the 1950s onward, a comfortable middle-class life was suddenly within reach for tens of millions more Japanese. Academic excellence, entrance into university, and employment in a good company or the public sector became an ideal route by which any child could achieve social mobility. This foundational promise of postwar Japan led many families, particularly mothers, to push their children to excel in school. Indeed, it is still considered a key component of a mother's carework, as women are often judged by their children's educational successes or failures.[3]

The same emphasis on social mobility would conflict with the ambitions of small family business owners like the Arakawas.[4] Educational excellence might threaten a ryokan's future. Who would take over if a child attended an elite university and accepted a coveted position in the Ministry of Foreign Affairs? Of course, Kuro-kawa's ryokan owners don't want their children to do poorly in school, and they are proud when their kids succeed. But at their core they value a different kind of success, which doesn't pass through a top university. It's more important to get some experience outside Kurokawa: to study and work elsewhere and gain some useful knowl-edge and skills, to learn how others (i.e., potential guests) think, and to hopefully find a spouse before returning home.

*Okami* understand the risks of failing to lure a successor back home. This has been the fate of at least two inns in Tsuetate, with the only viable successor of one becoming a doctor and the succes-sor of another becoming a schoolteacher. Each inn permanently closed when their owners were no longer physically able to manage the business. Now the buildings stand vacant, contributing to a land-scape of abandonment that is increasingly common in rural Japan. They are concrete reminders of the importance of succession to the couple at the heart of any family business.

### Policing Women's Work

At the heart of most family businesses is a married couple. In a ryokan they collaborate to keep the business running smoothly, but they play different roles and perform different tasks that are firmly embedded in Japan's gendered division of labor. He is called *shachō,* a gender-neutral term for "company president." He is the male head of household and de facto business owner. In short, he's "the boss." She is the *okami,* a gender-specific term sometimes used to mean "wife," but which also identifies a female business manager, or "proprietress."[5] In general, *shachō* is responsible for "men's work" (*otoko no shigoto*), typically work considered more masculine due to its location or its need for special tools or skills. This includes work done to the inn's exterior, like landscaping and building mainte-nance, but it also involves work done outside the inn, such as at-tending meetings of the local ryokan owners' guild. *Okami,* on the other hand, is responsible for "women's work" (*onna no shigoto*), which includes managing the household and caring for guests, chil-dren, and elderly family members.

In many ways, the *okami*'s interior work resembles the gendered division of labor found in most Japanese homes, where the typical husband is in paid employment outside the home and even a wife employed outside the home accepts responsibility for most of the physical and emotional labor required at home. National surveys often reveal gaping disparities between men and women in time spent on household chores and childcare, further reinforcing the "natural" divide between men's and women's work.

*Okami* and other ryokan staff police this divide. From the start of my research at Yamazakura, my novelty to both bosses and co-workers was not just my interest in the interior work and interior lives of *okami* and *nakai*, but my willingness to do "women's work." My willingness to run the vacuum cleaner, wipe a mirror, or wash towels was frequently met with surprise, particularly in the early months. When I did it well, my coworkers sometimes congratulated themselves for training a man. Initially some of my coworkers avoided working with me. Perhaps they thought I would get in their way or that they would have to clean up after me. Thankfully, that seldom happened, and soon they were happy for me to help them clean rooms and prepare for the next set of guests. Similarly, whenever I worked at other inns, female employees would remark to each other how good I was at tasks like dusting or laying out *futons*. Some of them may have even been questioning my masculinity.

One afternoon several months into my research I entered the dining room with a load of towels straight from the dryer. As I placed them on the floor and began folding them with a handful of coworkers, one of the *nakai* laughed and suddenly exclaimed that I would make a wonderful wife. I'm sure she meant it as a compliment, but she was clearly policing the boundaries of work that is appropriate for women and men.

Despite my willingness to blur these boundaries, there was one job I was never allowed to do at Yamazakura: serve food. And I heard of no men serving meals in ryokan elsewhere in Kurokawa. *Okami* and *nakai* justified this by labeling it "women's work," as if this answered the question. When pressed, some suggested that I probably didn't understand because I wasn't Japanese. Others explained that only women possessed the attractive figures and delicate fingers necessary for the job. Correctly carrying a tray, gliding across *tatami*, properly kneeling, and placing each dish in just the right place, just the right way, all while smiling and speaking pleasantly in front of guests: this was something they believed only women could do. More than one *okami* demonstrated by first plopping her teacup on the table as she imagined a man might, or perhaps as her husband does, before showing me the correct way: delicately holding back the sleeve of her blouse or kimono as she silently rested the cup on the table and slowly drew back her fully extended fingers. The difference was striking. Although a man might be able to precisely repeat this motion, the movement is so clearly feminine that the effect might make some guests uncomfortable, especially those who have also been socialized to recognize and police the boundaries between men's and women's work. Yamazakura found it safer to entrust the task of serving food only to women.

At the ryokan, this division of labor often boils down to sweat vs. makeup, and it reveals common beliefs about the appropriate spaces and practices of masculinity and femininity in Japan. Raking leaves, scrubbing baths, pruning bushes: such tasks done outside the ryokan involve physical exertion that deserves to be punctuated with a wipe of the brow. This is men's work, and many men who work outdoors wear a small towel around their necks precisely for this purpose. A man's sweat emphasizes how hard he is working.

Welcoming guests, serving tea and meals, and setting out the *futons* for the night all involve physical and emotional exertion. But sweating in front of a guest would ruin a woman's makeup and destroy the fantasy that "women's work," especially inside the home, is not work at all.

### The Fantasy of Non-work

This fantasy is built upon three intertwined beliefs about care and women's work. First, there is the idea that caring should be a self-less endeavor unmotivated by economic gain. Throughout the hospitality industry, customers gladly pay for their meals and accommodations, but no monetary price is attached to a warm smile or a helping hand. That would tarnish these acts of caring. Second, caring for the physical and emotional needs of others is believed to be something women do "naturally," as an extension of the caregiving that women are thought to be biologically programmed to do as potential (or actual) mothers. Finally, if such caring and caregiving comes naturally to women, it requires no special skills or training and cannot be seen as professional. Of course, these intertwined ideas lie at the heart of the long-held division, in Japan and elsewhere, between paid work outside the home and unpaid work inside the home. When mapped onto the ryokan, which typically doubles as the owners' residence, the labor of the *okami* and her female crew to make guests feel comfortable becomes repackaged as the *non*-work of hospitality. Indeed, sweating would make guests feel uncomfortable, since it would display the effort behind what should be effortless.

In spatial terms, then, *shachō* and other male employees are responsible for exteriors, while *okami* and a mostly female staff are responsible for interiors. Both *shachō* and *okami* derive their identity and authority from the spaces they manage: he manages a business due to his more public presence, while she manages a household due to her almost constant presence inside the inn. They also represent the inn to different publics. While *shachō* is the face of the inn to the community, *okami* is its face to guests. She spends more time in their presence, particularly in a small inn like Arakawa's, where she serves the meals. But even in a busier inn like Yamazakura, *okami* often stands behind the counter at check-in and bids customers farewell at check-out. In other words, she is *there*.

In this way, she resembles the ideal Japanese housewife, who is responsible for the carework that makes a house a home. This includes "being there" when her husband and children arrive home each day.[6] *Okami*'s presence in the pseudo-domestic space of the ryokan gives her authority and respect in the eyes of others. She is not an ambitious working woman and business manager, a role that might intimidate or alienate some guests. Instead, she is mother, wife, and household manager. As one *okami* put it, "Many Japanese lack a hometown in the countryside. I want my guests to feel at ease here, like they have returned home. [...] I'm the mother *(okaasan)* [...] who makes them feel comfortable."

Other *okami* echoed this language. When asked to define "*okami*," the most common response was "mother." This might not seem unusual for *okami* in their fifties or older, but even younger *okami* find "mother" a useful frame for conceptualizing their role. As one *okami* in her early thirties told me, "I'm a bit young, so maybe I don't fit the image [of a mother], but that's the feeling I try to portray." Like the ideal mother, she embodies the home through her constant presence. Immobilized in the family business, she waits for guests to return and treats them like family with her own unique form of hospitality.

### The Taste of Hospitality

When media talent Christel Takigawa made the final pitch for Tokyo's bid for the 2020 Summer Olympic Games, she highlighted something the other contenders lacked: hospitality. She memorably gestured each syllable of the Japanese word, slowing for emphasis: "*o-mo-te-na-shi.*" Visitors to Japan have long praised the quality of the service they encounter, whether in a five-star hotel or a neighborhood convenience store. Japanese hospitality is distinguished by its apparent sincerity, its selflessness, and its emphasis on anticipation, in which the host senses a guest's need before they do. Arakawa demonstrated her skill at anticipation when she offered to take our family photo before we asked. Likewise, I gradually became attuned to this skill by learning to do little things like turning around the slippers outside the baths and dining room so guests could easily step into them on their way between one space and another.

But the high standard of hospitality in Japan presents a challenge. If such sincerity, selflessness, and anticipation is found everywhere, how does any single ryokan stand out? In other words, in a country with tens of thousands of ryokan to choose from, all of whom supposedly feature the same "Japanese hospitality," how can a small inn like Arakawa's distinguish itself? How can it attract customers, stimulate word-of-mouth advertising, and encourage guests to keep returning for holidays and special family occasions like birthdays and anniversaries? It must foster its own unique style of hospitality. The survival of the family business depends on it.

There are subtle yet important differences in hospitality found in each ryokan. Beyond the obvious differences in location and building design, *okami* and employees say each inn has a unique taste, or flavor (*aji*). I did not really understand what they meant until I spent an afternoon with two coworkers at a café near Yamazakura. We chose a random weekday to break up our usual routine: eat lunch, retreat to our individual rooms, watch television or nap, and return for the 3:00 p.m. check-in. This was always time spent alone, and although we needed the rest, it had become boring. So at 1:00 p.m. we met at Mae's car and drove the short distance to the café.

As we walked from the parking lot toward the entrance I noticed subtle changes in Mae-chan. She seemed to straighten her back and speak more articulately than usual. When we stepped into the café the transition was complete. While seated at our table near the window, she did not laugh heartily or even smile as broadly as normal. She didn't crack any jokes about coworkers or hint at her fictitious affair with me. Where was the boisterous and slightly raunchy personality I had grown to love? She had been replaced by a refined twin.

A few minutes later the inn's *okami* entered the café. "Ahh, Maeda-san," she called, in place of the childish nickname (Mae-chan) we used. "Welcome. It has been so long. Thank you for stopping by." After chatting with us briefly, the *okami* left, and I asked Mae-chan to explain why she had transformed into a different person before my eyes.

Maeda had worked at this inn before Yamazakura. Naturally, she had adopted the mannerisms of her boss. When she moved to Yamazakura she did what the best *nakai* do: she molded herself to suit the taste of her new *okami*. In fact, as she later explained, she preferred the "taste" at this more refined ryokan. However, this clashed with the hospitality at our inn, which attracted a less wealthy and polished clientele. By modeling her behavior after her *okami*, Mae quickly blended in wherever she worked and provided guests the same form of hospitality her boss would give. Like an actress portraying a role, she gave me a concrete, if unintentional, lesson in what it means for each inn to have a distinctive taste.

Over time I came to notice other differences in each ryokan's taste. An inn's taste can be seen in the depth of a bow, the style of the décor, and the glow of a wooden floor. It can be felt in the sincerity of a smile or the heartiness of a laugh. Even a decision like whether or not to display a Christmas tree reveals the taste of the inn, and thus the taste of the *okami*. Depending on the guest, any given ryokan's hospitality may feel appropriately respectful or insincere and sycophantic. To another guest, the same hospitality may feel down to earth or downright rude.

On a more literal level, a ryokan's taste can also refer to its miso soup. This staple of Japanese cuisine usually consists of miso paste, fish stock, and some combination of vegetables, mushrooms, and/or tofu. It is less thick and hearty than a stew, but more substantial than a broth. Along with rice and pickled vegetables, miso soup is a staple of many home-cooked meals. Ryokan serve this trio as the penultimate course, just before dessert. It provides an unpretentious response to the extravagant, multi-course *kaiseki* meal that precedes it, and its timing at the end of the meal makes it the taste that lingers longest for guests.

This split in the ryokan meal reveals another gendered division of labor found in Japan, between male professional chefs and female home cooks. Most of the *kaiseki* meal involves complex ingredients and steps that require years of specialized training. This is the realm of men who graduate from culinary arts trade schools or spend years as apprentices in the kitchens of restaurants, hotels, and ryokan. Female professional chefs are rare in ryokan. In fact, I never met one, and several head chefs I met scoffed at the idea. On the other hand, the rice, pickled vegetables, and miso soup that conclude the ryokan meal are often made by the *okami* or another woman who works in the kitchen. For instance, my *okami* at Yamazakura cooked the guests' miso soup every night for her first decade on the job, before hiring a local woman in her late sixties to replace her. Other *okami* proudly told me that they still make the miso soup every night or several times a week, despite their busy schedules.

For *okami* who married into the business, getting the soup right was a vital part of their early training, but it was not the only interior work they had to learn. They also needed to learn to create a welcoming atmosphere for guests, from airing and fluffing the *futon*s to arranging flowers in the entrance. They had to learn how to cater to newlyweds and how to help guests celebrate birthdays and anniversaries. They also had to learn how to deal with guests who drank too much or tried to leave without paying. But the miso soup was the most literal way the taste of the family, specifically their mother-in-law, was passed to them and on to the next generation.

### Learning the Kubō Way

Kubō, *okami* of a small ryokan in Kurokawa, grew up in a farming family in a nearby village. As a child she watched her mother toil in the fields and at home, planting rice, cutting weeds, harvesting crops, raising children, cooking meals, cleaning the home, sewing, and whatever else was needed to care for her large family. It was like two full-time jobs. So when the eldest son of a souvenir shop owner in Kurokawa proposed marriage, Kubō jumped at the chance. She imagined she could escape to a more leisurely life. She was twenty-two years old.

A few months before the wedding, his parents purchased a ryokan. "I knew a little about Kurokawa Onsen," she admitted to me late one night in her inn's empty dining room, "but I didn't know anything about ryokan work." Her fiancée assured her that wouldn't be a problem. "He told me, 'You can sit around all day.'" I looked up from my notes and chuckled at the idea of an idle *okami*, especially a new bride. She didn't smile. "The opposite happened. He sat around while I worked," under the watchful eye of her new "bully" of a mother-in-law.

Kubō should not have been surprised. A new bride who moves in with her in-laws has long been a pitiable figure in Japan. She has the lowest status yet shoulders the greatest burden of caring for her new family. She is expected to wake first and sleep last, and she spends most of her day scrutinized by her mother-in-law, a figure of "virtually demonic character in Japanese folklore, fiction, and drama."[7] The expectations are greater in a family business.

Kubō needed to learn everything expected of a new wife and future *okami*, and she needed to learn it the "Kubō way." From the flavor of the miso soup she made each meal, to the way she cleaned the inn or spoke with guests, Kubō was expected to learn the taste of her new family. Her mother-in-law trained her the only way she knew how, by constantly criticizing her cooking, her sense of aesthetics, the way she moved in front of guests, even her personality. It was yet another form of interior work for Kubō; a long, demoralizing process in which her habits, desires, and tastes were disregarded and dismantled, before being slowly built up again in the way that suited the mother-in-law. Her mother-in-law could not afford to be kind and supportive. The reputation of the inn, the family, and the resort were on the line.

In those early days, the inn was only busy on weekends and holidays, so it could only afford a skeleton crew of full-time staff: a few chefs and *nakai*. On busy days Kubō hired local women, farmers like herself, to serve the evening meal or clean up after a large group of guests. Otherwise, most work fell on Kubō's shoulders. Even after giving birth to each of her four daughters, she was expected to quickly return to work. She was on her feet every day, caring for both family and guests, while her mother-in-law looked on from behind the scenes, correcting her errors and minding the grandchildren.

Today Kubō's inn is busy and profitable enough to spare her from the physically demanding work that consumed most of her twenties and thirties. She spends most days doing what she calls "backstage work" (*ura no shigoto*): managing her large staff and the inn's finances, plus cooking staff meals and even making the sweets served when guests arrive. She is both human resources manager— hiring and firing employees—and accountant—paying vendors and managing payroll—in a workday that ends at around 2:00 a.m. Like Arakawa, she is also the "face of the inn" (*ryokan no kao*), which means greeting guests in the lobby during check-in and check-out and answering the questions of curious foreign researchers like me.

"When will you stop being *okami*?" I asked near the end of our conversation. Kubō can only step aside when she trusts her replacement, so her most pressing interior work is training the next *okami*. This task has been complicated by her lack of a son, which she still considers a personal failure. A son is the natural heir for most ryokan. And if she had a son, she could repeat the pattern that worked on her: molding a daughter-in-law in her own image. Instead, Kubō had to convince one of her daughters to take over the inn, and that daughter had to find a husband willing to marry into the family, take the Kubō name, and become the official successor of both family and business. This arrangement will make Kubō's daughter the next *okami*.

Kubō stands at a crossroads. She wants to train her daughter, but she doesn't want to subject her to the same treatment she endured. Against her better judgment, she is easing her into the position. She will step aside, "Once they have a child." In the meantime, she wants her daughter to experience as little stress as possible, which may improve her chances of conceiving the next generation of owner. Unfortunately, this plan had not worked yet. "But it's been two and a half years (since they wed) and still no child."

"It's OK," I tried to assure her. "We've been married six years and still don't have children."

"Really?" she perked up. Given the intense pressure every *okami* feels to reproduce the family business into subsequent generations, most were curious about my own progress in this area.

"Yeah, it can take time. So once they have a child you'll quit?"

"I think I'll stop after the child gets fat" (*kodomo ga futottara;* or when the child is two to three years old). "I feel a bit sorry for her." She continued, "If she were my daughter-in-law (*yome*) I could leave everything to her (*mō makasete dōzotte hiku ne*). Since it's my daughter I can't do that. I can't just walk away. I feel sorry for her."

"Aren't you being easy on her?" I had heard from other *okami* that training under a tough mother-in-law was traumatic, but effective. The first few years in particular were a crucible of hardship that in retrospect were essential for learning the new family's taste, from its dishes and sense of humor to its aesthetic sensitivity. What seemed at the time like unnecessary cruelty by a mother-in-law developed the selflessness needed by an excellent hostess, as each new bride and young *okami* learned to always place the needs of others before her own. What better training for a daughter-in-law, wife, mother, and ryokan manager, whose value to her family (and business) rests in her ability to identify and care for the needs of both family members and strangers? Kubō recognized the value of this training and hinted that she would have done the same to a daughter-in-law. However, she did not wish to treat her own daughter so harshly. In other words, her empathy only extends to her own flesh and blood.

"I'm easy on her, but I have to be." She concluded our conversation by justifying her decision. "When I had kids my life never got any easier. I would feel very sorry for her if she had to go through that. So, I'll help out a bit." Indeed, it was the least one would expect from a woman who had spent a career caring for the needs of others.

### An Unwanted Job

I heard echoes of Kubō's story from at least twelve *okami* in and around Kurokawa. During the afternoon break or over late-night cups of green tea after their employees had gone to bed, they welcomed me into their inns and shared their stories, sometimes in what felt like a confessional. Women like Kubō who married into ryokan families recalled the shock of entering this unique world, with its myriad responsibilities to ancestors, in-laws, husbands, children, neighbors, strangers, and repeat customers, and the long struggle to learn their role and please their demanding mother-in-law. Others, like Kubō's daughter, who grew up in ryokan families, often admitted that they resisted taking over, since they knew its difficulties. However, they eventually accepted their fate and found a husband willing to join them in the enterprise. Despite their differences, all these women eventually accepted their *okami* responsibilities and set about reproducing both family and business.

Although each *okami*'s story of how she stepped into her role was unique, no one grew up wanting to be *okami*. It was a role you got stuck with, either because you married into a ryokan family or because you didn't marry out of one. One woman married the eldest son of a ryokan family when she was already thirty years old. In those days people still referred to a woman's marriage prospects with reference to a Christmas cake. Just as a Christmas cake cannot be sold after December 25, a woman over the age of twenty-five was considered past her prime. So when this *okami* and her future husband were set up on a date by their relatives and agreed to the match, she did not consider what she was getting into. "I didn't give it much thought," she admitted. "If I had really thought about it, I might not have come.

I mean, I grew up in a completely different situation in Kumamoto City." She (and both families) was just happy to finally be married.

Another *okami* was an only child, born after her parents moved to Kurokawa and opened an inn in their mid-forties. Unable to conceive until then, her parents long claimed she was born only because of the hot springs. Lacking siblings and feeling an obligation to Kurokawa itself, she chose not to marry out of the family, which would have threatened its future. Instead, she took over as *okami*.

All the *okami* I met recalled the endless hard work of their early years, when their inns were less busy. Like Arakawa today, they were responsible for most of the inn's interior work, which was physically and emotionally demanding. "I clearly remember waking every morning with back pain," one recalled. "My back hurt so much. It was tough; a really difficult job. I had to carry crates of beer bottles, that kind of stuff." She continued, "These days I don't do that anymore. Back then, the family had to do everything: *nakai,* check-in, phone reservations. My husband even made the meals. Now we have a professional chef!"

In addition to making the miso soup in her early years, my *okami* at Yamazakura cleaned rooms, laundered towels, and served meals. In fact, all of the *okami* I met in Kurokawa, most of whom began their training in the 1980s and early 1990s, said they began their careers by doing "everything," experiencing all the jobs needed to run an inn. This was necessary not only because they were not yet busy enough to hire the extra labor, but also because their mothers-in-law or mothers insisted they learn to do everything, in case they had to run their inns on their own. Some former *okami* had experienced a boom and bust cycle in the 1960s and 70s. Kurokawa's late eighties success was still new, and the senior *okami* knew it could be fleeting.

Over time, as their inns became busier, this new generation of *okami* hired more staff. These new employees took over the most physically taxing work and stood in for the *okami* in time-consuming tasks like serving meals. As one *okami* put it, "The job has gotten a lot easier physically, but the human relations and mental aspects have gotten much more difficult." In fact, she preferred when Kurokawa was less popular. She spent more time with her guests, and her children. In other words, she envies the life of *okami* like Arakawa, the woman in Tsuetate that opened this chapter. Perhaps she has forgotten the constant struggle to attract guests and the stress of staying afloat. Or perhaps she misses the immediacy of providing hospitality to her guests.

### Training in a New Era?

These days Kurokawa's *okami* spend less time climbing stairs and pushing vacuums than paying invoices, arranging work schedules, resolving employee disputes, and "being there" as the symbol of the inn. They handle correspondence, such as writing New Year's cards, and they attend meetings of the *okami* association. Some continue to cook staff meals or assist guests at check-in, but no one I met serves dinner, cleans toilets, or does laundry anymore. Their time is too precious, and they can afford to pay others to do this in their place.

Even as they continue to be tethered to the inn, many *okami* wish to professionalize the role, and some *okami* struggle with how to train their replacements. Like Kubō, other *okami* told me they value the adversity of their early years for molding them, but they are unsure how to create the same conditions amid Kurokawa's continued success. Unlike Arakawa, they no longer operate on the edge of survival, forced to work long hours and make sacrifices in the present to safeguard the future of the family business. How can they prepare the next *okami* for this new reality? And should they?

Sakai, the *okami* at Yamazakura, decided to outsource the training of her replacement. Like Kubō, she grew up in a nearby village, but she eagerly moved to Kumamoto City after high school and took a job in retail. She loved the freedom and convenience of living in the big city and never imagined returning to the countryside. So she was as surprised as anyone when she fell for a handsome young man from Kurokawa. She played the dutiful daughter-in-law, waiting on her new family and learning the trade of this unfamiliar industry. She and her husband worked ten years under the direction of his parents and slowly raised the standard of the inn, until the younger couple took over as *shachō* and *okami*.

Along the way, they raised three talented daughters who continue to provide immense joy in their lives. But they never had a son, which she, and some in-laws, still considers a personal failure. After years of collective hand-wringing among family members, one of the daughters agreed to take over the inn. However, Sakai did not feel up to the challenge of training her. So, she asked the *okami* of a well-regarded ryokan in Kyoto to undertake the task.

Sitting in her claustrophobic office behind the lobby, she explained that, like Kubō, she fears she will be too soft on her daughter. With guilt in her voice, she explained all the ways she spoiled her daughter for almost three decades, from private high school tuition and study abroad, to rent and food and gasoline money for years after university. Why would she stop now? Sakai credits her mother-in-law with shaping her into the *okami* she is today, but she doesn't know how to train an *okami* except through the harsh tactics she endured. And she is unwilling to repeat this process. How will her daughter learn to endure in the face of criticism from guests? How will she learn the humility and strength needed to deal with customers who demand too much, are rude to her employees, or refuse to pay? How will she learn to navigate the many obstacles that come with running a family business?

Importantly, despite decades in the position and the experience of hosting over fifteen thousand guests a year, Sakai doesn't consider herself a "professional." This leads her to doubt her tastes, especially in the face of outside experts who offer advice on hospitality, cuisine, and interior design; in other words, all the aspects that make a ryokan stand out. In fact, during my time at Yamazakura, Sakai hired two such experts for short stints, one of whom led a mandatory customer service training session roundly criticized by my colleagues. They simply couldn't understand why our *okami* trusted these outsiders, who had never worked in a ryokan, over her own instincts.

Sakai feels her hospitality is good enough for the customers around Kyushu who comprise most of her regular guests. But as Kurokawa has gained national attention and even attracted visitors from overseas, she worries she may be unable to satisfy this broader spectrum of potentially more demanding guests.

She calls herself "just a housewife" (*tada no shufu*), which offers her a useful model for imagining her role and making her relatable to others. She is not a professional businesswoman focused on the bottom line. She is a humble wife and mother who cares for her guests as any Japanese woman would in her own home. Indeed, this persona of the rural housewife is part of her charm, her *aji*. But this attitude also means she doesn't think she has marketable skills to teach others. So, her daughter will spend up to a year training under the firm hand of a stranger, who will provide the hard lessons and specialized training the younger *okami* needs to guide the ryokan in the future.

Sakai and many of her peers in Kurokawa recognize that the role of the *okami* seems to be shifting. Even as they value their own harsh training for providing them the hard lessons that shaped them, they understand that the next generation of *okami* needs to learn different skills, some of which they are unable to teach. It's not only that Sakai and Kubō don't want to put their daughters through the humiliation and strain they endured, but that the family business has changed so much in a generation that their knowledge and experience may no longer be useful.

### No Success Without Succession
While some of their responsibilities have changed, all *okami* know they still must ensure succession. Sadly, women like Kubō who only raised daughters often blame themselves for not having a son, or they worry excessively about a lack of grandchildren. For them, having a son and training a daughter-in-law is the "normal" (*atarimae*) way to fulfil this obligation. Why else raise three or more daughters (one family I met had five daughters) in a country where most families have two children or fewer? Indeed, the question of succession loomed large over all *okami* in ways that I did not perceive in their husbands. Yet again, we see a gendered division of labor; in this case, the emotional and physical labor of bearing a successor to the family business. It is the often unbearable weight that can come from not producing a son, and therefore being considered a failure in your womanly duty, while peers proudly parade their sons. But the weight of succession is not carried by *okami* alone. As I explain in the next chapter, their children carry it, too.

# Chapter 5

# How to Succeed in Business

Murakami always knew he would take over the family business. It was not his dream. It was his obligation. I met him in the autumn of 2006 in the lobby of his family inn, Fujimisō. I recognized him as a member of the next generation of owners who had recently returned to Kurokawa. He recognized me as the odd foreigner researching ryokan.

A few days later we went to dinner. He picked me up dressed in black jeans and a rock concert t-shirt. To my surprise, he was joined by Ayako, a young woman who was working the front desk at Fujimisō the day we met. They had worked in a Tokyo restaurant several years before and had been friends ever since. When he returned to Kurokawa, he offered her a job. It was nothing romantic, they insisted, they were just friends and colleagues.

After months working with people decades my senior it was refreshing to speak to folks near my age. We talked about movies, bands, and our favorite baths around Kurokawa. We even scheduled a karaoke session later in the month. He asked what I thought about working in a ryokan. I asked about his recent move back home.

Murakami first left Kurokawa after high school to attend a two-year culinary institute in Tokyo. He stayed on after getting his certificate and worked a series of low-paying jobs in bars and restaurants around Tokyo. Like many young people, he lived a precarious existence, earning just enough to pay the bills and devoting his free time to dating and playing in a rock band. Unlike most of his friends, he didn't have to build a career or save money for the future. The family business was always waiting for him. Around the time he turned thirty, his parents said he had been away long enough.

"I had a lot of fun in Tokyo, and I didn't want to return to 'the sticks' (*inaka*)."

"So why did you?"

"I didn't have a choice," he answered quickly. Then he sat up in his chair and continued in a slightly deeper voice, "I'm the eldest son (*chōnan desu*)."

I struggled to restrain my laughter. The carefree rocker had suddenly matured a decade. He seemed to be mocking his own seriousness, but he didn't crack a smile. I said, "Whoa, that was a quick change! Being *chōnan* must be serious business."

He smiled and looked around the table for an explanation. "What did I do? Did I really change?"

"Yes!!" Ayako and I replied.

He paused and laughed. "I guess '*chōnan*' is a powerful word."

He asked about my siblings. I'm the youngest of four, I explained, with two older stepbrothers and an older sister. He sat back as this information washed over him. He said this explained why I could live in Japan, have an international marriage, and pursue my professional interests without any concern for what happened back home. I shared none of his obligations. Murakami grew up knowing he would be Fujimisō's next *shachō*. "That's why I never studied in school," he joked. "There was no point!" Even when he was "playing" in Tokyo, he knew he would eventually return to his *furusato*, take over as head of household and inherit the family business.

### A Daughter's Dilemma

Unlike Murakami, Masako never planned to take over Yamanoyado. As a child, the only aspect of the ryokan industry she enjoyed was her father's landscaping work: tending the grounds and planning the gardens. But she soon learned that was "man's work," and not possible for her future. She never wanted her mother's position. "I'm not good at interacting with people, with customers, so I never thought I'd be *okami*." That position would go to her youngest sister. So Masako left for university, assuming she would not live in Kurokawa again.

Her parents stopped trying for a son after their third daughter was born. They were pleasantly surprised when the youngest expressed interest in taking over the inn at an early age. Since I first met them, her parents had told me the same rehearsed succession plan: their youngest daughter loved everything about the ryokan, so after university and a few years of work experience she would take over the family business. Importantly, she would bring a husband, they assured me, who would join the family register as adopted son-in-law (*muko yōshi*) and eventual head of household. Then the cycle would continue, with the couple managing the inn and passing it to one of their children, ideally their eldest son.

In the year before I moved Kurokawa, that plan changed. The youngest daughter began to lose her naïve excitement about ryokan life, just as she entered a prestigious high school in Fukuoka. At the same time, Masako found herself jobless and unsure what to do with her life. She approached her parents and offered them a deal. If they supported her dream to study English in the United States for a year, she would accept the burden of taking over the ryokan. Given the growing number of non-Japanese guests who spoke English, she argued, she could gain a valuable skill while setting their minds at ease about who would succeed them. After weeks of deliberation, her parents agreed.

My wife and I invited Masako for dinner a few weeks before she left for the US. We chatted about her sudden change of life plan at our dining table. She was excited about her upcoming trip. "I always wanted to improve my English, and I realize this is my last chance." She spoke of her upcoming time abroad like it was her last bit of freedom before the toil of ryokan life, and she admitted to being more nervous about becoming the next *okami* than living overseas. She worried about her lack of work experience and dreaded working with customers and managing staff, which require the kind of people skills she has always lacked. However, she is trying to be optimistic. She thinks her parents have spoiled her for too long. Taking over the ryokan will end her reliance on them and give her life direction. Perhaps they will finally treat her like an adult.

### Succession as Responsibility and Burden

A façade of Japanese tradition has been literally landscaped into existence in Kurokawa. This landscape work produces a time-less *furusato*, or hometown, aesthetic that Japanese and non-Japanese tourists seek. Moreover, it solidifies the position of individuals and families as "locals" who are responsible for Kurokawa: they are both credited with its success and burdened with its future. This results in spatially nested responsibilities for locals who own family businesses. They must maintain the village, manage their inns, and produce competent successors.

Ryokan owners in and around Kurokawa are under tremendous pressure not only to keep tourists coming in the door, but also to keep their households and communities intact. They are not corporations lured to the area by tax incentives, inexpensive land, or cheap labor. Most of them grew up in the hamlet and struggled in difficult times. Today they are monumentally successful in an unpredictable industry. But everything could change tomorrow. Another scandal like the one involving the Ai Ladies Hotel could turn visitors away. In the meantime, ryokan owners have to worry about more than the future of the business. They embody their company's successes and failures, and they hope to pass their inns to the next generation. Kurokawa's ryokan have been successful enough to lure successors home, providing a vehicle for local families to sustain their communities and households, and bucking the trend of rural depopulation and economic decline found elsewhere. But it is not straightforward or easy to determine who will take over or when they will be ready.

The return of Murakami and Masako to Kurokawa to take over their respective family businesses introduces the role of succession work in the production of fixity found in the ryokan world. The continuity of both the family line and a ryokan's personalized form of hospitality help an inn feel fixed in time and space, a home away from home. While most landscape and hospitality work is highly visible, selecting and preparing a successor requires anxious, extended, behind-the-scenes work by families and communities.

### Choosing a Successor

What characteristics make an ideal successor, and how do families cope with exceptions? How does a successor train, and when should owners step aside for the next generation? The answers to these questions help explain the importance of succession in making the ryokan feel fixed in time and space, and they show how gendered forms of labor are mapped onto ryokan space. For some families, the choice of successor is straightforward, dictated by practical reasons and social norms. For others, the decision is more complicated, compounded by geography and gender. As I show, a disproportionate amount of this physical and emotional labor falls to the *okami*, who must worry about bearing and raising the next generation inn owner, on top of her existing responsibilities of managing both the household and the business.

### Eldest sons

Most ryokan owners consider an eldest son, or *chōnan*, like Murakami the ideal successor. In some ways this is no surprise, since succession by eldest son to head of the household is the norm in Japan today.[1] This was not always the case. Prior to implementation of the Meiji Civil Code (1898), inheritance practices and household (*ie*) forms differed greatly based on region (e.g., Eastern vs. Western Japan) and status (e.g., samurai vs. commoners). That changed when the inheritance pattern of the former samurai class became instituted as the preferred method for all.[2] While exceptions continue today, the eldest son is especially preferable when land, tools, skills, artistic knowledge, or other tangible and intangible resources are passed down, such as in family enterprises based in the arts (tea ceremony, pottery, traditional theatre) or primary industries (farming, fishing, forestry). Ryokan fit here, since they also pass assets like property, buildings, landscaped gardens, access to hot springs, bedding, furniture, dishes, and professional cooking equipment, as well as generations' worth of business knowledge, connections, experience, reputation, and even repeat customers. Succession by the eldest son is considered ideal in most ryokan families, even those without sons, because it is straightforward. There is no need to convince a child who resists or negotiate with multiple children who want to take over (or who want to avoid taking over). An eldest son like Murakami grows up knowing his duty, while other children, both male and female, grow up untethered by geography or duty. They can live anywhere or pursue any career, with the knowledge, of course, that they cannot rely on the safety net of the family business.[3]

Taniguchi, the fifty-year-old *okami* at Furuya, was one of many inn owners, both male and female, who stressed this succession ideal. We met one wintry afternoon at her inn a few hours before check-in. She welcomed me in the lobby and quickly led me down a narrow corridor to a nondescript door at the back of the inn, which opened to a three-room apartment where she lived with her husband and two children. Over a pot of English breakfast tea and carefully peeled apple slices, we discussed the ryokan's history, her role in its daily operation, her employees, and the inn's future. When asked who would take over the ryokan following her retirement, she took me to the next room, where she introduced her seventeen-year-old son. He looked up briefly from a book. He was preparing for a university entrance exam and didn't seem to appreciate the distraction.

Taniguchi beamed as she explained that he was the first son born in the family in over one hundred years. A lack of boys in the previous four generations had caused her family great stress and embarrassment. As the oldest of four girls, she grew up hearing family, friends, and neighbors lament the challenge they faced in finding a suitable husband and successor of the family business for one of the daughters. When Taniguchi gave birth to a daughter, people worried the cycle would continue. A decade later she bore the miracle seated before us, sparking celebrations and marking the end of the family's ill fortune. Taniguchi's immense personal pride at being the first woman in the family to accomplish this feat in a century was obvious.

Clearly embarrassed by his mother's tale of family strife and ultimate triumph, the young would-be successor buried his head in his book. When I asked if he looked forward to taking over the inn someday, Taniguchi laughed and answered for him. "He doesn't care about the ryokan." Like Murakami, he had no choice in the matter. It was his duty as *chōnan* (eldest son). Later I learned that his older sister actually *wants* to take over the business, but the family insists on passing it to her uninterested brother instead.

This ideal of the eldest son as successor places intense pressure on ryokan families to produce a male heir and on eldest sons to accept the duty. However, a disproportionate burden falls on the emotions and bodies of *okami*. Ryokan owners, male and female, current and retired, frequently told me the most important job of an *okami* was to bear a son. Some even joked that once she accomplishes this, she can retire. A successful couple may try for another child, sometimes as insurance, but in general, they can stop at one if it's a son. On the other hand, *okami* who do not bear a son may continue trying long past the national average. Among the dozens of ryokan families I knew in Kurokawa and around the country, those with sons tended to have only one or two children, while those without a son had three, four, or even five daughters. Those *okami* often blame themselves for being unable to produce a son. In a country that averages fewer than two children per family, the prevalence of so many daughters clearly indicates the high value placed on sons as ryokan successors and the intense physical and emotional labor that falls on *okami* to produce the ideal heir.

### Multiple daughters

Families with multiple daughters but no son lack a natural successor. This can make the decision complicated. Some parents prefer the eldest daughter, or *chōjo*, but this may not always be best, given the many factors that can affect the decision. For instance, the eventual successor must marry, since a ryokan is expected to have at its core a husband and wife who will produce an heir of their own. A daughter who does not marry for personal or professional reasons is therefore not ideal. At the same time, a ryokan daughter must do more than just find a spouse. She must find a man willing to marry into her family, take her last name, and eventually become head of her household. This means marrying someone who is not already *his* family's heir, like an only child or an only son, since he cannot head two households. According to several *okami* the ideal son-in-law is a second or third son. Unfortunately, Japan's low birthrate and decreasing population makes a second or third son increasingly difficult to find.

Geography further complicates the picture, placing an extra burden on women successors in a place like Kurokawa. In other families, succession can be done from a distance. A man may marry into his wife's family as an adopted son-in-law while the couple continues to live in another city or even overseas. However, marrying into a ryokan family involves a spatial commitment: just as a woman marrying into a ryokan family must uproot herself from her professional and personal commitments elsewhere, an adopted son-in-law must move to the inn. This often means cutting his career midstream and relocating to a remote location like Kurokawa, a sacrifice that many ryokan families worry that few men are willing to make.

Given all these issues, succession is a source of constant anxiety for some ryokan families, particularly the *okami*, who bear the greatest burden for producing a son. They spend inordinate time and energy stressing about who their daughters are dating, and who will be willing and able to eventually move back home. One *okami* worried when her eldest daughter dated an only child. To make matters worse, his family owned a company. If they married, the couple would have to choose one family business over the other, and he was likely to prefer to succeed his own family business in Nagasaki. The ryokan would lose this daughter as potential successor and be forced to convince one of her sisters to take over instead. Occasionally such pressures break up young couples, whose obligations pull them in different directions regardless of their love for one another.

Families without a son often consider the unique prospects of each daughter before deciding which one will succeed them in the family business. Such negotiations are part of the ongoing succession work at ryokan around Japan, which is essential for the continuity of the family and business, but remains hidden from guests.

### Only daughters

Succession in families without a son causes more stress and involves more negotiation. However, a family with an only daughter can inspire the same sense of duty to take over. This is especially the case in family enterprises with geographically fixed assets, such as land, structures, access to natural resources, and community or commercial reputation. The only daughter of a colleague at Yamazakura provides an example of a child just as obligated to become successor as a *chōnan* like Murakami.

When I began working with Sakamoto in 2006, he was a full-time ryokan employee and part-time farmer in his late fifties. He had lived his entire life in the same home, twenty minutes from Kurokawa. His father died around the time he graduated from middle school, and as the eldest son, Sakamoto left school at age fifteen to take over the family farm. He married in his thirties, and his wife moved in with him and his mother. Years later, when they had all but given up hope, they were finally blessed with a daughter.

When I met Sakamoto, his daughter was only twelve years old. However, he and his wife had already planned her professional life and eventual trajectory back to them. He confidently told me that she would graduate from the local high school, attend nursing school in Kumamoto City, work in the city for a few years, marry by age twenty-five, then return home with her husband, who would take over the farm while she worked at the local hospital. While still physically active in their early seventies, Sakamoto's wife would care for the inevitable grandchildren while he taught the husband how to manage their fields and forests. Eventually, his daughter's nursing degree and work experience would enable the couple to age with dignity and die peacefully at home under her care.

Sakamoto never stated this arrangement as a wish or ambition. He didn't even say his daughter agreed with this plan. Instead, he laid out her future matter-of-factly as we washed dishes, shoveled snow, and cleaned baths. It felt as though he were trying to state this vision frequently enough to conjure it into reality. Each time, I pestered him with questions such as, what if she doesn't want to be a nurse, or return home, or marry, or have children? For Sakamoto, my questions confirmed my own lack of family obligations, and my inability to understand this aspect of Japanese society. His daughter's *desires* were irrelevant. What mattered were her *obligations*. Maintaining the family line and home trumped her wishes. He had accepted his role as successor at a young age. Why should his only daughter be any different?

### No children

Couples without children face other problems. In order to continue the family and the business, couples must adopt. However, a couple does not usually adopt a child. Instead, they add a young adult to the household registry as an adopted son. The first choice is usually a relative, such as a nephew or cousin who also happens to be the second or third son in his own family. A successful family enterprise offers an attractive option for a young man to enter as successor, however he still must fulfill the obligations of any successor: perform rituals and pray for the new family's ancestors, maintain the family home and grave, care for his adopted parents in their old age, marry, and produce a successor of his own. While rare, there is history of this practice among Kurokawa's ryokan. One owner, now in her sixties, mentioned that her father became her inn's successor as an adopted son, as did the successor in the generation before him. She and her sisters were the first children naturally born to the inn in three generations. They did not have a brother, so she (the eldest daughter) married a man who became an adopted son-in-law, took the family name, and eventually became the head of household.

Succession is a serious issue in Japanese families, particularly those with family enterprises, long histories, and fixed assets. Despite attempts to eliminate gender bias in Japanese society in workplaces, politics, and elsewhere, these cases show that sons are preferred successors and thus more valuable than daughters. All ryokan owners I spoke with, including those without sons, admitted that the ideal successor is a son, since it makes succession straightforward and an eldest son is most likely to accept the obligation. Murakami visibly carries the burden and pride of this ideal when he adjusts both posture and voice to physically shoulder his responsibility as *chōnan*, while *okami* without a son often speak of their daughters with worry in their eyes and guilt in their voices. As the cases above show, the lack of a son complicates succession for families, which must 1) find the best option among multiple daughters, as in Masako's case; 2) convince an only daughter to accept the responsibility, like Sakamoto's daughter; or 3) adopt an adult son to continue the family line in a childless family. Choosing a successor is a vital step to ensuring the continuity of an inn and the family line that runs it; however, this is only the first step in the succession process.

### Preparing for Succession

Even when there is a son to take over a family business, a family often struggles with how to prepare him to take over, whether or not he will marry, whether his bride will make a suitable *okami*, if/when the young couple will produce a successor, and when to step aside. All of these aspects of what I call "succession work" show the challenges ryokan owners in Kurokawa face when passing the family business to the next generation. Foremost is the issue of geography, which provides a successor with the experience and perspective necessary to run a ryokan, while also tethering them to place and potentially limiting their ability to marry.

### *Preparation*

Succession work is a long process. Growing up in an inn exposes one to the challenges, restrictions, and rewards of ryokan life. Years spent in the ryokan at a young age make this way of life seem normal. However, the road to succession also must lead away from the ryokan. It is vital that a successor also live and work away from home. In ryokan around Kurokawa, families send their successors to universities or trade schools, and they encourage them to remain in cities like Tokyo, Osaka, and Fukuoka for several years of work experience. Some of Kurokawa's young successors studied hotel management or even worked in the service industry, while others have been construction supervisors, lab technicians, and more. The specific subject, degree, and job experience seems to matter less than the experience of living outside Kurokawa. Ryokan owners argue that time away from home is the only thing that can inspire appreciation of the village, and the ryokan as a particular institution. As owners put it, they want their children to return home with the eyes of a tourist. As parents, ryokan owners also want to spoil their children a bit and let them "play" in the city (as they did when they were young). Such parental generosity is obvious in Masako's opportunity to study in the United States and Murakami's extended "play" in Tokyo. Parents understand the burdens of managing an inn and want their children to enjoy some freedom before returning home.

When it comes time to return home, some owners try to make the prospect attractive through investments in the inn or living quarters. For example, when Murakami's parents insisted he return, he proposed a major remodel of the inn, which he argued would raise the inn's profile. They agreed, hoping to make his transition easier. During our meal, he excitedly showed me cellphone photos of the progress and invited me to visit again when the work was finished. Although he always knew he would return, this redesign meant the time was right.

Other families remodel the existing living quarters or build a new home off-site for the young couple, in order to ease their transition back home. This differs from past generations in Kurokawa, when successors and their spouses moved into the living quarters with the current owners. In fact, many of the *okami* currently aged fifty to seventy recall the stress of living and working under the demanding eye of their mothers-in-law, who was suddenly under the same roof. This particularly traumatic element of succession work had some value, but current *okami* hope to offer their daughters-in-law (or less frequently, sons-in-law) a warmer welcome by providing the young couple its own space. Of course, such generosity is limited to inns that can afford it and is less likely in ryokan outside popular tourist destinations like Kurokawa.

Families may prepare the way for successors to return, but these are not innocent gifts. They cleverly bind successors more tightly to their obligations. For instance, giving Murakami his dream design pressures him to remain at the inn and maintain it for the next generation. Moreover, his parents paid for the renovation with a loan that will eventually transfer to Murakami, which will financially tie him to the inn. Similarly, the gift of a renovated or separate living space carries the unspoken expectation that a young couple will quickly start a family. While previous generations moved into cramped quarters with their in-laws, today's successors cannot delay or avoid their obligation of continuing the family line due a lack of privacy or extra stress of living under the same roof. Again, the burden of such succession work falls primarily on women, as any delay or inability in becoming pregnant becomes seen as her fault.

After returning home, a successor should learn and experience every aspect of the ryokan's operation. While growing up at the inn, he or she may have helped during holidays or busy weekends. However, the successor likely has not worked in the inn for a decade or more, and his or her spouse probably only experienced a ryokan as a guest. In theory, acting as front desk clerk, *nakai* (for women), and handyman/driver (for men) enables the couple to train new employees, correct staff errors, pitch in during busy times, or even run the inn on their own if guest numbers drop dramatically.

The generation of *okami* and *shachō* currently prepping their children to take over experienced this type of on-the-job training. They recount moving back to Kurokawa in the 1980s, when family members still did most the work themselves, always under the watchful and demanding eyes of their parents (or in-laws). *Okami* who married into ryokan families, in particular, recall the terrible stress of these years, when their every move at work and home was criticized by a mother-in-law until they reached her standard. This often-tense relationship appears elsewhere in Japanese society, whenever a woman physically moves into her husband's family home. Although less common today, the continued prevalence of this practice in family enterprises is sometimes blamed for the difficulty of young successors to find spouses. Japan's relative affluence and the increased number of women in careers means young women today can afford to be particular when it comes to marriage, and to avoid a situation in which they may live under the thumb of a mother-in-law.

Despite claims of the need for all successors (and spouses) in Kurokawa to undergo a crash course in ryokan work in preparation for managing the inn, I heard of few new owners who actually delivered on the promise. According to staff at inns around the resort, young successors may help in the kitchen or lay out *futons* when inns are especially busy, but in general they do not experience the same long monotonous workday as staff, nor do they experience it for a prolonged period. Instead, they spend long stretches of the day attending meetings, running errands by car, working on the inn's social media presence (webpage, blog, Facebook and Twitter accounts), and doing other tasks that staff consider unimportant and useless in relieving their immediate workload. In the past, successors may have been doing all the work or sweating alongside staff, but Kurokawa's ongoing success means most successors don't have to.

Masako suggests another form of preparation: training at another ryokan. After she returns home from the United States, she will work three to four months in a ryokan in Kyoto. This is no ploy to delay her inevitable return to Kurokawa. "My parents are spoiling me now, before I leave for the United States. If I return in a year and start working here right away, I'm afraid they will spoil me again. I need to go somewhere else to train." Eventually, she will come back home and take over the family business, but she wants to work elsewhere first and get hired on her own merits. "I don't want my parents to make a request on my behalf. I want to participate in a job hunt like everyone else. All my friends share 'tales of suffering' (kurōbanashi) on the job hunt. But not me. I've had a lot of part-time jobs, but never a real job hunt." Masako believes this set of tribulations—the job hunt, the grueling work at a busy inn, the experience of working under the thumb of a demanding okami—will finally convince her parents she is mature enough to take over.

Each family is unique in determining how and when to give a successor full responsibility for the ryokan. Some owners may be tired of the job and anxious to retire. Others may enjoy it and delay stepping aside. They may provide advice to the successor and come out to greet repeat guests for years, slowly receding into the background. The former shachō at Yamazakura, for instance, continued to make his presence felt among staff after his retirement by eating lunch and dinner with them in the kitchen.

A key factor in a successor's preparedness is his or her maturity. Legal adulthood in Japan comes at age twenty; however, many Japanese believe university students are not yet adults. Others feel maturity only comes when one secures full-time employment, marries, or has a child. Despite this lack or agreement, there seem to be some key features among ryokan successors in Kurokawa. First, one must spend time studying and living away from home. Next, one must understand the sacrifices of past generations of owners, both in keeping businesses afloat in hard times and revitalizing the village from the 1980s onwards, as I recounted in chapter 2. The next generation of owners knows this heroic narrative and is quick to share it with others. In fact, nearly every year from 2012 to 2019, I have taken my students to meet members of Kurokawa's Seinenbu, or young adults' association, populated by successors in their twenties and thirties. Each year I ask them to explain their plans for the resort's future, but first they dutifully repeat the narrative of their parents' work. They clearly respect this story and are careful to not undermine it. As one member put it, "We must not cut the trees our parents planted," an apt metaphor for both the literal landscaping and the communal spirit developed by their forefathers. The young people's challenge is how to plant their own trees, so to speak, without damaging the landscape or reputation of the village. These young successors freely admit to being spoiled while growing up, and in some cases even into their late twenties, thanks to the economic success of their family enterprises. Now, they wish to demonstrate their maturity by facing their own challenges.

Young successors like Murakami and Masako may attend university, train at other inns, work elsewhere in the service industry, and even spend years working alongside their parents in order to gain perspective and experience that should help them do their jobs. But from the perspective of many ryokan owners, they will not be truly ready to take over until they are married. Indeed, for some families marriage is the clearest sign of a successor's maturity. Unfortunately, young people from Kurokawa and successors in family enterprises throughout Japan face challenges to marriage because of their location and the expectations that come with marrying into a family enterprise.

### Marriage
In all family enterprises with geographically fixed assets that are passed down (land, structures, resources, local reputation), successors are expected to move back to the family home around the time of marriage. Such households can have three, and sometimes four, generations living under one roof. Multi-generation cohabitation is relatively rare in Japan today, due to the postwar increase in the number of urban and suburban households, the smaller size of these dwellings, and a shift toward the preference of the nuclear family.[4] However, the practice of multi-generation cohabitation remains prevalent in many small family enterprises in both rural (among farmers, fishermen) and urban areas (medical clinics, hair salons, restaurants, convenience stores), where businesses routinely pass from one generation to another.

Of course, if the family enterprise is failing or unattractive, it may be abandoned, as happened with many farms beginning in the

1960s. As I noted in chapter 2, young people who departed the countryside for education and work opportunities in the cities often did not return to take over family farms and other enterprises. This slow evacuation of the countryside was a key factor in producing the rural nostalgia that eventually fueled success in places like Kurokawa, but it has not made living in the countryside any more attractive. In fact, some of the same aspects that appeal to tourists—slow pace of life, lack of industry, location of Japanese traditional values—deter potential residents. Most Japanese people today wish to keep the countryside at a safe distance: close enough for a short escape, but not so close that one lives surrounded by rice fields.[5] While this relationship with the countryside may benefit business in Kurokawa, it negatively impacts the marriage prospects of successors like Murakami and Masako.

Successors of family enterprises in rural areas struggle with a refusal by many young people to move to the countryside. Although this can affect both male and female successors, the media has portrayed it as an issue that impacts the eldest sons of rural families in particular and rural society in general. Life in the countryside does not appeal to many young people for a variety of reasons, including the slow pace of life, the lack of employment opportunities that suit their education levels and interests, and the prevalence of conservative social values and complex social relations.

Young women are usually blamed for refusing to consider life in the countryside. The implication is that they are selfish, superficial, and spoiled. They care too much about brand name goods and the conveniences of city life to appreciate the pace and simple pleasures of village life. They are too focused on personal ambitions and careers to contribute to a family and community through marriage. In media depictions, the victims of young women's selfishness are not only the young successors responsible for perpetuating their families, but also their local communities and ultimately, the Japanese countryside. Without spouses, these young men (and in families with no sons, young women) cannot fulfill their obligations.

To combat this "farming village marriage problem" (*nōson kekkon mondai*), local authorities around Japan have devised matchmaking schemes to expose young women from the cities to life in the country. Agricultural activities like fruit-picking and rice-planting have introduced young female urbanites to single male farmers in the hopes of showing the charms of rural life and creating some sparks. The desperation underlying such programs highlights the fact that while many Japanese may be nostalgic for rural landscapes and excited about visiting them on holiday, most do not want to live or work in them permanently. Rural avoidance has been blamed for contributing to population decline in rural areas, even leading some rural men to use matchmaking agencies to find spouses overseas from places like China and the Philippines.[6]

Such extreme measures to find a spouse reveal the pressures facing successors of family enterprises to fulfill their obligations and the ways that the location of home can be an obstacle. Even when dating, successors may struggle with how much to disclose about where they come from, or their plans to return. While in Tokyo, Murakami wondered whether or not to tell people about his predetermined future, and now that he has returned home without a girlfriend or wife, he (and particularly his mother) worries it will be difficult to find a spouse. He even jokes about using an international marriage broker, like several farmers around Kurokawa have done. However, he knows that his parents would disapprove, since they don't consider a non-Japanese wife a suitable *okami*.

Another *chōnan* chose to keep his obligation to return to Kurokawa a secret when dating. According to his wife, originally from a city in northern Kyushu, he only mentioned that his parents lived in a village in Kumamoto. She knew he was the eldest son, but she assumed they would spend their lives in Fukuoka and visit his *furusato* during the holidays. "I imagined some small village surrounded by rice fields," she recalled one afternoon at her inn. "But there isn't even a real convenience store. There's nothing here." More importantly, she did not know they would be expected to live with his family and run the business. "He never said a thing [about the inn]." It took a few years to get over the shock, but she eventually grew to enjoy the position. However, she still cannot believe her husband tricked her by not revealing his obligation.

These stories reveal some of the challenges successors face when trying to fulfill their obligations and in particular, how the location of their home makes their task more difficult. Given these obstacles, it is not surprising that successors and their families utilize deception (keeping one's future a secret), incentives (like private living space or a new home), and other techniques to perpetuate the ryokan and the family line.

Six years after we first met, I caught up with Murakami. He had been working continuously at his inn, learning all facets of the business. However, his parents were still in control. I asked when he would take over. "Mother wants me to find a wife first. Once I marry, my parents say they will retire." His long and incomplete succession work reveals many of the challenges facing successors in Japan today, not only in Kurokawa, but also specific to those in rural areas and in small family enterprises. The multiple obligations placed on a successor risk outweighing the potential rewards that may come from succession. Indeed, finding a spouse willing to move to the countryside, take on the role of *okami* or *shachō* (as adopted son-in-law), and produce the next generation successor creates formidable challenges compounded by geography and the different expectations of single young men and women. The permanence associated with the ryokan relies on successors skillfully navigating obstacles that are often beyond their control.

## Chapter 6

# A Day in the Life

Ryokan owners frequently called their business a home (*ie*) and referred to their staff as family (*kazoku*). But owners and their employees lived in different worlds, with different social and economic circumstances, different obligations, and different futures. In the first half of this book, I explained the national and regional context for the landscape work done in Kurokawa. I also discussed the interior carework done by each *okami*, which includes establishing her unique flavor (*aji*) of hospitality and doing the generational work associated with succession. All of that work is essential for maintaining the family business.

In this chapter I move deeper into the backstage regions of the ryokan and shift attention to the everyday work of ryokan employees, most of whom lack the long-term financial and social stability of their bosses. This narrows our scope in both space and time, from the nationally symbolic, multi-generational work of ryokan owners, to the microgeographies of the everyday—even the minute-by-minute—work of *nakai*, front desk clerks, drivers, and cooks. When busy ryokan mobilize hospitality, these are the bodies on the front lines, standing in for their bosses and ultimately helping reproduce a family and business that does not belong to them.

Ryokan owners and their employees work within different time frames. Owners think seasonally, annually, even generationally about staffing decisions and when to replace towels, *yukata*, dishes, brochures, and even themselves. Could aging *tatami* mats or *futons* last another year or two? Could the owners replace the bath stools on New Year's Day as is customary, or should they wait another year? When should they create a new brochure or update the website? When could they remodel or even rebuild the inn? Which child would take over as the next owner? Who would they marry, and would they have grandchildren? In other words, ryokan owners have both the freedom and responsibility to do long-term, generational work.

Employees think more in terms of minutes and hours. My co-workers and I followed a general schedule—arrive by 7:30 a.m., serve breakfast from 8:00 a.m., wash dishes at 8:30 a.m., tea break at 9:30 a.m., clean rooms and baths at 10:00 a.m., lunch at 12:30 p.m., break from 12:45 p.m., welcome guests from 3:00 p.m., serve dinner from 6:00 p.m., wash dishes at 7:00 p.m., prepare the dining room for breakfast around 8:30 p.m., and finish around 9:00 p.m. However, that routine was frequently interrupted by things that had to be done immediately: when a guest called to make a reservation or to request a ride from the bus stop; when a family arrived in the parking lot to check in; when a guest requested another flask of sake; when a couple left their room after dinner, providing us a narrow window to tidy their room, move their table, and lay out their *futons* and pillows for the night. Such hospitable moments punctuated the day, often providing a much needed break from another task and reaffirming why we were here in the first place: to serve our guests.

Sometimes these moments interrupted another task. When the front desk called to the kitchen to request shuttle service, I abruptly stopped washing dishes, dried my hands, changed shoes, and ran up the driveway. Within a minute I returned to the inn entrance with the company van. I waited patiently with the van door open and smiled as two Korean women in their 20s, dressed in *yukata*, stepped inside. I asked where they would like to go, waited until they were ready to depart, and eased out of the driveway. As I drove slowly through the village, the stack of dishes, and Kazuko's stress level, grew in the back of my mind. Hurry up. Slow down. One immediate task—driving guests to another inn so they could try its bath—took precedent over a less immediate one—washing dishes.

At other times, guests interrupted the monotony of waiting. For instance, I spent many afternoons in the parking lot waiting for guests to arrive. My job was simple: greet everyone, carry luggage and accompany guests to the front desk, and protect the limited number of parking spaces reserved for overnight guests by directing other visitors—like those just using the bath—to a second parking lot. Sometimes guests arrived at a regular pace, every five to ten minutes, giving me ample time to welcome each group, help them park, and walk with them to the front desk. At other times, three cars arrived at once, causing a minor traffic jam in our narrow lot. And sometimes I waited an hour before anyone arrived, with nothing to do but sweep each acorn as it fell onto the dark asphalt. When a car finally pulled in, I was often as relieved to see our guests as they were to reach the end of their journey. Such moments reminded me what mattered most: satisfying our guests' immediate needs. We were bodies in motion, on call, and at rest, working around the un-predictable, unknowable needs of strangers.

In this chapter I pivot from ryokan owners to ryokan employees. I introduce the routines and unpredictable interruptions of the typi-cally atypical ryokan workday. Ryokan work requires flexibility. Ryokan workers follow a rough schedule that could be interrupted at any moment, depending on the needs of guests. We don't know what might lie around the corner, but we must always smile and carry on, in order to provide the best possible hospitality in place of our bosses. In this chapter I weave together two timelines—a daily sched-ule and twelve months of fieldnotes from 2006 and 2007—to give a sense of the regular and irregular rhythms of the ryokan workday, the spaces and technologies of our work, the joys and frustrations of mobilizing hospitality, and the people that kept the place running through their physical and emotional labor.

### 6:50 a.m.—The Daily Commute

Sakamoto's workday began at 6:50 when he left home in the company van. It could carry up to nine guests, but Sakamoto also used it to commute to work, picking up three or four colleagues along the way. Most were women without a driver's license, who lived between Sakamoto's house and Yamazakura. Everyone needed to be at their designated spot on time—Takeda in front of her home at 7:00, Nakagawa next to her apartment block at 7:05, me near the Higo Bank branch at 7:10, and Eguchi in front of her home at 7:15—or we would all be late. Thankfully, there was no time clock, no morning staff meeting, and no penalty for arriving a few minutes late. Time was flexible at Yamazakura.

When we arrived at the inn around 7:30, Sakamoto dropped the van key at the front desk and began his morning rounds, check-ing the large outdoor and indoor baths. He tested the temperature and looked for damage and pests (dead insects, spiderwebs), before lighting a fire in the *irori* (open hearth around which guests often chatted). At some point, he stopped in the kitchen to eat a bowl of rice and miso soup. Amid this general routine he was always on call and vulnerable to interruption. After heavy snowfall or strong winds, he might need to clear debris from the baths, sweep snow from the paths, or spread de-icing agent to prevent falls. Or he might be suddenly called by the front desk to run an errand or drive guests to the bus stop. A guest might also stop Sakamoto in mid-stride to ask a question or request he take their photo. At that moment nothing mattered but helping the guest. There was no end to the tasks that *could* be done at any time at the ryokan, but no matter how busy we were, the guest standing in front of us always came first. In fact, guests often provided a much-needed break in an otherwise nonstop workday. For Sakamoto and the rest of us at Yamazakura, every day was full of such routines and interruptions.

### 7:30 a.m.—August 1, 2006—The Kitchen

I entered Yamazakura on my first day of work not through the lobby, but through the kitchen. This was the door for deliveries of meat, poultry, fish, vegetables, and fresh flowers, and it was the door for employees. The kitchen was much less inviting an entrance than the lobby. Instead of a highly polished wooden floor glowing in the morning sunlight and smelling of cut flowers, freshly brewed coffee, or the smoke of a charcoal brazier, the kitchen floor was a gray laminate material scarred by years of wear, dull in the dim fluorescent light. Long slashes caused by dropped knives and metal dragged across it gave the floor a well-worn character, while hinting at food lodged in the cracks for years.

From the doorway, the room was wider than it was deep. It was split down the middle by a path that led to a sliding door that opened into the heart of the inn. Everything behind this sliding door was the inn's backstage and closed to guests. On the left side of the path was a long workstation with a table, an industrial dishwasher, and a sink. I recognized the dishwasher immediately. I had used a similar model at a Pizza Hut during my first part-time job in high school. It was a stainless steel box with a handle that when lowered, shot jets of hot water at a square plastic tray loaded with dishes. After about two minutes the cycle was complete, and one raised the handle and pulled the tray out the other side. The dishes were too hot to touch, and any food stuck on a dish before it went into the machine was likely baked on the surface. Therefore, every dish needed to be carefully washed by hand first. The machine merely rinsed them clean.

Behind the long workstation on the left side of the room were several tiny spaces wrapped around a walk-in refrigerator. One space had a large sink, where vegetables and rice were washed before cooking. In another space was another sink used for fresh flowers and a two-burner gas range. What little space remained included a table with a microwave and two large electric rice cookers; large enough to serve fifty guests. Two women worked in this cramped side of the room: Kazuko, in her late fifties, and Takeda, in her early seventies. Takeda worked from 7:30 a.m. to 4:30 p.m. most days and focused on two tasks: making meals for the staff and preparing rice, miso soup, and pickled vegetables (*tsukemono*) for guests. Kazuko worked from 6:30 a.m. to 9:00 p.m. and assisted with the staff meals, which were usually high-calorie dishes like curried rice, hashed beef rice, and Japanese hamburg steak, plus miso soup, and a vegetable dish. She also washed dishes for three-plus hours and laundered the guests' bath towels every day.

The right side of the room was a brighter, airier space with two long stainless-steel tables in the center and a walk-in freezer on one side. Along one wall was another sink, a fish broiler, a tempura station, and more gas ranges. This side of the room belonged to the three male chefs who only prepared guest meals. In one corner was a small desk where the head chef sat and smoked between courses, while planning future dishes. His punch-perm haircut and gruff appearance made him look like a middle-aged gangster moonlighting as a chef, but his skills at preparing the complex *kaiseki* meal were undeniable.

The whole room smelled like stale food and cigarettes. This was partly because half of each meal was prepared hours in advance, chilled, then set out in order to reach room temperature prior to serving. There was simply not enough space, time, or manpower to prepare the intricate dinner any other way. Another source of the stale odor was the empty boxes that served as makeshift garbage cans around the room. They absorbed the kitchen smells—grilling, deep frying, steaming, stewing, pickling, tobacco—for weeks or months at a time, until they became damp enough to threaten their structural integrity. Then they were replaced with a new empty box that would eventually suffer the same fate.

This kitchen was my work and research base for the next twelve months; a cramped space with uncomfortable stools, dim fluorescent lighting, the rhythmic grinding of the dishwasher, and an endless parade of smells—from freshly made tempura to the heavy sweetness of the curry made for the staff lunch. Without a dedicated break room, this was also the space where most employees paused between tasks. It was the ideal location to observe ryokan work. But I knew from the first day that I could not stand back and watch. Amid a chronic shortage of workers, I was a body that needed to be mobilized to provide hospitality.

### 8:00 a.m.—August 8, 2006—The Pantry

Breakfast began at 8:00 in the large dining room on the first floor. While three or four *nakai* served the meal, a few people put away *futons* and tidied rooms. At 7:50, after I finished my own breakfast of rice and miso soup, Eguchi had asked me to join her in the second-floor pantry, where we waited for guests to leave their rooms. It was a tight space for two people, especially relative strangers like us. I am not a very tall man, but I am larger than the *nakai* Eguchi normally shared this space with, so it may have felt more uncomfortable than usual. But she did not seem to mind. We had been working together nearly a week, and she seemed to enjoy watching me do "women's work." Like ryokan owners, Eguchi believed in a strict gendered division of labor and took a certain pride in training a man to do these tasks well.

The pantry had a sink and a small table for resting food trays, flower vases, and pots of hot water used for making tea. Shelves on one end held extra sheets, towels, *yukata*, matches, ashtrays, and other essential items. On the other end of the room was a dumb-waiter, an essential link between the kitchen below and the guest-rooms on the second floor. The *nakai* used it constantly each evening, sending dinner trays up and dirty dishes back down. Sometimes they even called the kitchen to ask us to send up bottles of beer and fresh flasks of sake, to save them the trouble of taking the stairs. The pantry was a congested staging ground for each course before it was served. It was also a space of retreat; a quiet escape where one could close the door and not be bothered by any guest or coworker. Sometimes it was the only place to have a moment's rest all evening.

At 8:00 a.m., the pantry provided Eguchi and me a break from the bustle below, as we waited for guests to leave their rooms for breakfast. We chatted about the sweltering day to come while listening for the click of a lock and a door sliding open. We would then leave the pantry and walk toward the sound, trying not to surprise the guest stepping into the hallway. We greeted them and asked if they were going to breakfast, and if so, if we could put away their bedding. Once they were out of sight, we grabbed the master keys and opened the door.

The job was simple: remove the pillowcases and the sheets from the *futons* and comforters *(kakebuton)*. Replace the comforter covers based on the number of guests scheduled to stay in the room later that night. Next, place all the bedding in the closet and move the table and floor cushions *(zabuton)* back to the center of the room. Finally, wash the teapot and teacups and replace the pot of hot water so guests could make a fresh pot of tea when they returned from breakfast. The aim was to make the room look as inviting and tidy as when they had arrived the previous day. We worked quickly, careful not to disturb anything valuable. If we found something in the bedsheets, like a wristwatch, we carefully placed it on the table so guests would find it before they checked out.

The entire process could take less than five minutes, but I was still learning how to deftly slide my hands into the sheet to find the corners of the comforter. Then, mirroring each other, we crossed one arm over the other and neatly pulled the entire sheet over the comforter in one smooth motion. Finally, we folded it in fourths and placed it in the closet. One week into the work, I still sometimes got my arms crossed and had to endure Eguchi's impatient sideways glance as she waited for me to find the corners. But when I did it correctly, it felt almost like we were dancing, as we spread our arms wide, fluffed the comforter, wrapped it in a fresh new shell, stepped toward each other, and turned to place the finished product delicately in the closet.

It was satisfying to restore order to a room in under five minutes. These were precious moments when our bodies were occupied but our minds were free; rare quiet moments away from the bustle of the kitchen and the threat of a guest interrupting with a request. However, the feeling never lasted long, as we soon heard another door open down the hallway. One of us would drop what we were doing and chase down the next guest. Then we would repeat the process, eventually finishing all rooms by around 8:45.

### 8:30 a.m.—August 20, 2006—Washing Dishes

It was supposed to be my day off. I had been working nearly every day for three weeks, and I was getting tired. After only five days I already had a sore lower back, stiff shoulders, and a phlegmy cough

I couldn't shake. My feet were tired from standing up to twelve hours a day. And my hands were a wreck: they were wrinkled from washing dishes and scrubbing baths, blistered from rubbing the sharp edges of the wooden food trays, and constantly cramping from squeezing the garden hose nozzle to drench the paths in a cool mist each afternoon. By the third week only my cough was gone, and we had just endured one of Japan's busiest travel periods of the year, Obon. I needed a day off, but I felt too guilty to take it.

For the past few days, Kazuko had been sulking. She needed to take off this morning to attend her son's school function and felt guilty that her absence would leave Takeda, the grandmotherly cook whom everyone loved, washing the breakfast dishes of over forty guests. It was usually a three-person job. Kazuko and I washed while Takeda sorted and stored the dry dishes in a dozen different locations. With both of us scheduled to be gone, how would Takeda cope? Kazuko's guilt was contagious, so I decided to come in only long enough to help Takeda with the breakfast dishes. In those early weeks I was still living on site, so I only had to throw on my uniform and walk thirty seconds to the kitchen. When I arrived at 8:30, Takeda was already bent over the sink, a tray of dirty dishes stacked beside her. I stepped up to the tray and said good morning. She quickly replied and scrubbed the next dish without missing a beat.

By 8:30 some guests had nearly finished breakfast, and the *nakai* were returning from the dining room with serving trays laden with empty dishes. Each *nakai* would pass the tray to me or place it on a table nearby. The *nakai* would remove toothpicks, chopsticks, tissues, or other burnable items from the tray, before grabbing a clean tray and returning to the dining room to collect more. In the meantime, I dumped the uneaten food—grilled fish, eggs, rice, *nattō* (fermented beans), and miso soup—into a large plastic sieve and gently slid the empty dish into the sink of hot water beside me. I was careful not to splash water on Kazuko or Takeda, who cleaned each dish and placed it in the dishwasher. After I removed all the dishes from a tray, I wiped it clean and dry so it was ready to be taken back to the dining room for another load. The work was unpredictable. Sometimes we waited up to ten minutes between trays of empty dishes, as *nakai* chatted with guests or refilled their rice container out of our sight in the dining room. At other times *nakai* returned with five or six trays at a time, causing a sudden flurry of activity. Washing breakfast dishes often meant standing in one place for an hour, which led to both a sore back and a growing disgust as all the uneaten food slowly mixed into an unrecognizable slurry. This was the unglamorous side of ryokan work.

Like changing the *futons*, washing dishes was simple, repetitive, and potentially dull. But there were magical moments, too. There was a simple pleasure in emptying one tray of dirty dishes precisely as a *nakai* returned from the dining room with a full one. The trick was to time it so that I caught her attention as I held up the first tray and began wiping it, clearing the space in front of me so she could slide her full tray there and not on a table in the other room. Then, in the ten seconds it took her to remove the burnable trash, I finished wiping the tray and passed it to her seamlessly, so that she could avoid leaning over to pick up a clean tray to take back to the dining room. No words were exchanged. My reward was a smile of acknowledgement and the indescribably satisfying sensation of being part of a well-oiled machine.

I do not want to romanticize the manual labor of the ryokan, but just as our time did not flow at an even pace but was punctuated by unpredictable bursts of activity, the potential drudgery of simple tasks like washing dishes and replacing comforters occasionally included moments of elation at being a member of a smoothly running team. A busy working kitchen has a buzz. It is like static electricity being generated from the many bodies swirling past each other in a narrow space. When everyone senses each other and anticipates their movements, there is an unspoken sense of camaraderie, of being part of something larger than oneself.

On this day, I felt that sensation with Takeda and the *nakai*, who knew we were short-handed and pitched in more than usual. After an hour of non-stop movement I pulled the last set of dishes out of the dishwasher to let them cool. Takeda gave me a quick "*Gokurōsama*" (thanks for the hard work; lit. You must be tired) and said she would put away those dishes later. First, it was time for tea.

### 9:30 a.m.—September 17, 2006—Morning Tea Break

The flurry of activity surrounding breakfast usually lasted from 8:00 to 9:30, when we in the kitchen washed the final dishes and the *nakai* wiped all the tables in the dining room and stored the floor cushions for the day. Once this was complete, we met in the dining room to share a cup of green tea and rest. When I say "we," I only mean the women working behind the scenes in the kitchen and guestrooms, plus me. The front staff was busy checking out our guests, and the men—the three male chefs and two drivers/handymen—continued working. At 9:30 the chefs were already doing prep work for dinner, and the other men were usually carrying luggage to the parking lot, driving guests to the bus stop, or cleaning baths. Plus, they would not have felt welcome at the tea. They did not get along with most of the *nakai,* and the feeling was mutual.

There was no daily staff meeting at Yamazakura, unlike other ryokan I visited. However, the 9:30 tea break was a vital time for exchanging information. While the front desk staff handled all reservations and knew who we were hosting weeks or months in advance, the break offered the *nakai* their first glimpse of who would be staying that night and who they would serve at dinner. Based on the number of *nakai* working that day and the number of guests in each room, the *nakai* would then collectively decide which three or four rooms they would cover (Fig. 9). This collective decision only took a minute or two, since there was no supervisor, and most people claimed no

FIGURE 9. Deciding room assignments at the morning meeting. Photo by author.

preference for where they worked. It was a lottery anyway, since the guests were so varied. During the remaining time, Suzuki sat in the garden and smoked, Eguchi studied the guest list, and everyone chatted about the previous night's guests: what fashions women had been wearing when they arrived, how much makeup an elementary school student from Osaka had been wearing, or how drunk a guest had become.

What to an outsider might have sounded like gossip was often potentially useful information. For example, despite being divorced, Eguchi always wore her wedding band at work. This came in handy one night when she was still waiting on three men at 9:30, who asked her to join them for a drink after work. At our tea break the next day she explained how she had thanked them for the offer, but lightly touched her ring and apologized, saying she needed to get home to her husband. The lie was useful in two ways: the guests promptly stopped their flirtations, and they chipped in to help her finish quickly, by stacking the remaining dinner dishes on her tray. They even told her they would lay out their *futons* by themselves. Such tales were shared for comedic effect, but they could also be lessons other *nakai* might use in the future.

Today the conversation focused on Typhoon #13, which was expected to hit Kurokawa with heavy winds and rain later that evening. Someone heard from the front desk that airlines had canceled flights in and out of Kumamoto Airport after 2:00 p.m. Many of our guests had flown from Tokyo, Nagoya, or Osaka and rented a car to reach Yamazakura, so someone wondered if any of last night's guests would be back for another night or if some of tonight's guests might have to cancel. Also, a group of thirty guests scheduled for lunch tomorrow had already canceled, leaving a sudden surplus of meat, seafood, and vegetables. Perhaps this was for the best, some suggested, since the typhoon might disrupt tomorrow's food deliveries. Today's morning meeting left us with more unpredictability than usual.

As we stirred at 10:00 a.m. to begin cleaning the guestrooms, Keiko appeared at the door with unanticipated news: *Okami* was sending the commuters among us home for the day. She didn't want us to get stuck at the inn, so Sakamoto would pull the van to the entrance in a few minutes and take us all home. By this time, I had moved to an apartment fifteen minutes from the inn, so this applied to me, too. With five of us leaving early, I worried about the burden on those left behind, but Sakamoto assured me there were enough employees who stayed in the company dormitory to take our place. Even if they were scheduled to have today off, how could they refuse if *Okami* requested their assistance? They had been primed to be flexible, both to suit the everyday needs of guests and the longer-term needs of their bosses. Since they lived so close to the inn, they were nearly trapped in this situation.

### 10:00 a.m.—October 28, 2006—Cleaning Guestrooms

10:00 a.m. was the most predictable time of day. It was when all guests checked out. Only rarely did guests stay more than one night (usually couples from the US or Europe), and since such guests often explored the surrounding area during the day, we could start cleaning rooms without disturbing anyone at 10:00 a.m. At Yamazakura, each *nakai* cleaned the rooms where she would serve dinner later that evening. Some *nakai* told me this made them feel that they were already caring for their guests hours before they arrived. Others took the cleaning less seriously. It was just another in a long list of jobs that had to be done.

On my first day at Yamazakura, Eguchi trained me just as she had been taught: one task at a time. My first task was to prepare the *yukata*. I gathered all the used *yukata*, tied them in a bundle, and carried them to a storage area where they would be collected later by the dry-cleaning company. Then I gathered the *yukata* sashes. Eguchi demonstrated how to tightly wind one into a star pattern, before telling me to make stars of the remaining sashes in the six rooms we were cleaning. I also needed to check the guest list to determine the correct number and color of sashes and *yukata* for each room, which was based on the number of men and women. When I finally finished, Eguchi walked to each closet and checked my work. From that point forward, she expected me to remember what to do when she asked me to prepare the *yukata*. Then, she set about teaching me another task.

In the early days I usually assisted two *nakai* as they cleaned six rooms between them. While I slowly prepared the *yukata* and vacuumed, they washed and replaced all of the glasses and tea cups, wiped all surfaces of the vanity, replaced the towels and pillow cases, emptied the garbage, replaced the amenities (hairbrush, shaver, ear buds), wiped the table, dusted the *tokonoma* and all paper doors, cleaned the windows, and cleaned the toilet. As I became quicker and more competent, I learned all of these jobs, one at a time, until I could be trusted to clean a room by myself.

There was no established routine for cleaning a room. Sachiko preferred working systematically from the left side of the room to the right. Mae-chan kept a checklist in her head. In fact, she wanted to introduce a paper checklist for everyone, but Suzuki and some others opposed the idea. Most *nakai* worked less systematically, but regardless of their method, they typically finished cleaning their rooms by 12:15. That said, it was impossible to predict precisely when one would finish. Some days we finished at 11:40; other days, at 1:30.

Some rooms barely needed tidying: there was nothing in the trash, no cigarettes in the ashtray, and the teapot had not been used. Sometimes the only sign that a guest had stayed was a neat pile of *yukata* in the corner, two damp towels draped on the drying rack, and a 1000-yen note wrapped in a tissue in the center of the table as a tip. It might take only twenty minutes to clean such a room, instead of the average forty-five minutes, which meant I might finish three rooms by noon and then help someone else in need.

Other rooms looked like they had been destroyed on purpose. There was trash—tissues, food wrappers, cigarette butts, bottle caps, empty cans and bottles, shopping bags, condoms, torn underwear—scattered everywhere. Birthday cake rubbed into the *tatami* mat, beer splashed on the mirror. These were the rooms that guests asked us to not tidy during breakfast, and as soon as we opened the door after check-out, we knew why. Sometimes I wanted to close the door and walk away. This was another source of everyday unpredictability in the ryokan. You never knew what you might find behind the guest-room door. But it was no use getting upset at strangers who had already departed. We just made the room as inviting as possible for the next guests who would arrive in a matter of hours.

By late October I kept pace with my colleagues and felt like a useful member of the team. On this day, Eguchi and I cleaned a block of six rooms together. Three of them would be Eguchi's that evening, one would be Sachiko's, and the remaining two would be empty. Some *nakai* preferred to work alone, but Eguchi and I had developed a routine to split the tasks. First, I piled the dirty towels from all six rooms in the hall, so Kazuko could easily collect them on her way to the laundry room. This saved her the trouble of entering each room and stepping around us as we worked. Then I collected and sorted the *yukata* and garbage and took both downstairs. While I did this, Eguchi rolled the *yukata* sashes and hung the *haori* (coat worn over a *yukata*) in each closet. Next, I put all the dirty teacups and beer glasses on trays so Eguchi could take them to the pantry to wash. Then I put on all twelve clean pillowcases. Next I wiped the sinks and mirrors in each room and replaced the toiletries.

I was about to begin dusting my first room when it struck me: Eguchi was dragging her feet. Normally, we would have put on the pillowcases together and finished everything but the dusting, vacuuming, and cleaning toilets by around 11:15. Today, she was still washing teacups and beer glasses, and she hadn't begun to change the flowers. At this pace, we might not finish by 12:30, and I might be stuck dusting and vacuuming all six rooms, something I had never seen anyone else do. Usually this strenuous task was split among the *nakai*. Plus, today's rooms were tidy to begin with, and two of them were going to be empty. "What is taking her so long?" I thought.

Sachiko joined us a few minutes later, after finishing her two other rooms elsewhere, but this did not seem to speed the work. I expected one of them to pop into my room to grab the duster at any moment, but no one came. At 11:45, when I began dusting the third room, I spotted Eguchi leaning against the dry mop in the hallway, talking to Sachiko as she cleaned a toilet. In the past Sachiko had scolded me for chatting instead of working, but today I held my tongue. I was still the newest member of the team and lowest in the hierarchy.

While I stewed inside, it dawned on me that Eguchi and Sachiko might be utilizing a classic "weapon of the weak," James Scott's term for the ways people subtly push back against those who hold power over them.[1] Scott argues most resistance is not open, violent, or organized. It is usually invisible, harmless, and disorganized. However, it can be effective. At Yamazakura there was no clear outlet for expressing dissatisfaction with the working conditions, plus most of my *nakai* coworkers were in rather precarious personal circumstances (chapter 7) and would not have risked directly complaining to *Okami* about anything. Plus, direct confrontation would have been unusual culturally speaking. In fact, some *nakai* had been excited by my arrival in August not because I would lighten the workload, but because I might provide an avenue for their concerns to reach *Okami*. Instead, it seemed that on this particular day Eguchi and

Sachiko were slowing their work pace in order to remind *Okami* that we were still understaffed.

I started working at Yamazakura at the beginning of August, when we were fully booked every night, despite having two fewer *nakai* than in recent years. This might explain why *Okami* was eager for me to begin. She may have hoped I would help reduce some of the load for the rest of the staff, and in particular the pressure to hire more *nakai*. In those early days in August we worked as quickly as possible but never finished cleaning rooms by 12:30. Part of the slow pace was due to my inexperience and the time it took to train me. We were exhausted every day, working at a pace that seemed unhealthy and unsustainable.

As the months passed, two things happened. First, we had slightly fewer guests as summer turned to autumn. Second, I became better at the job. I thought I was helping my colleagues by working faster. However, at our recent morning tea breaks some *nakai* worried out loud that *Okami* was no longer searching for a new *nakai*. On a day like today, when the rooms were relatively clean to begin with, Eguchi and Sachiko seemed to be stretching out the work so it would last until well past our usual lunch time. Better yet, if we finished later than usual, word might get back to *Okami*—possibly through me—and keep pressure on her to search for a new *nakai*. Mobilizing hospitality at a slower pace appeared to be the only way for my co-workers to express their continued need for additional labor support and manage the unpredictability of their days.

### 10:00 a.m.—November 22, 2006—Cleaning Baths

While the *nakai* cleaned rooms, the drivers cleaned Yamazakura's many baths. The 1980s brought a shift in hot springs guests from large groups like companies on worker retreats, to couples who desired more privacy. In response, ryokan around Japan built more guestrooms with private baths. The same occurred in Kurokawa. Such rooms come at a premium, of course, because they require more space and maintenance. An older inn with a small footprint cannot install private baths without a complete remodel, or without removing one room to build an attached bath. Yamazakura was built in an era when ryokan only had one or two large baths, in which all guests bathed communally, only separated by sex. Over the years Yamazakura expanded to include a wing of rooms with private baths, each of which had to be cleaned daily.

More ryokan meant more work. Each of these rooms was larger than those in the main building and had a separate changing room for its bath, which also meant more cleaning. The rooms' distance from the main building meant more walking, with *nakai* carrying trays of food farther from the kitchen. Because there were stairs along the way, they could not use a cart, and everything had to be carried by hand. More halls meant more floors to sweep. Plus, the hall was partially outdoors, which meant coping with wind, rain, snow, heat, and cold, all while trying to remain presentable to guests. These halls also attracted spiderwebs and dead moths that had to be cleared several times a day. Ryokan guests wanted to be surrounded by nature, but only to a point. And of course, more baths meant more time and bodies scrubbing them.

When I began in August there were two drivers responsible for this task. Anytime one of them had the day off or had to drive guests to the bus stop, I scrubbed in his place. The process began as soon as possible each morning, since some baths took several hours to refill with their constant trickle of hot springs water. Once guests checked out of a room with a bath, one of us got a call from the front desk. We went to the room and began by opening the windows and pulling the plug. While the bath drained, we used a deck brush and a hose to scrub and rinse all the wood, stone, and concrete surfaces. We checked the level of the shampoo and liquid soap containers, and once the bath was empty, we stepped inside and scrubbed it, too, while avoiding the scalding water that continued to flow. Then we replaced the plug, closed the windows, and moved to the next bath, repeating the thirty to forty-minute process for each bath during the next two or three hours. Two people could easily finish all the baths by noon if there were no interruptions.

But every morning was unpredictable. One day a group coming for lunch needed to be picked up in Oguni at 11:30. This meant Sakamoto cleaned baths until 11:00, and Morita, the other driver and handyman, suddenly shouldered a double burden for at least an hour. On another day in November two Korean women walked from the village center to take a bath. When they finished, the front desk staff worried they might catch a cold from the cool autumn air, so they offered them a ride back to the town center. Anytime the front desk offered someone a ride, it was one of us men who did it. So, I rested my deck brush against the wall, confident it would still be there when I returned in thirty minutes.

Because of the unpredictability of the day, the drivers felt as understaffed as the *nakai*. Their lunch was often interrupted by an errand, and sometimes they had to wait more than an hour at a bus stop because a guest missed their original bus. In late-October they seemed to get some relief when *Okami* hired a local man in his fifties to work part-time. An additional body would make it easier for the drivers to schedule a day off or plan ahead, such as for days with multiple groups of non-Japanese guests, who tended to arrive by bus and thus needed to be collected from one of several nearby bus stops. Unfortunately, this new driver only lasted a day. The hours he spent hunched over scrubbing baths and washing dishes were too hard on his back. The next day he arrived and apologized to *Okami* and *Shachō* before driving away and leaving us all deflated.

Several weeks later *Okami* hired another new driver, a man in his mid-thirties from Yokohama. Ogata had managed a local café until it closed for the winter. He jumped at the opportunity to work at Yamazakura. A week into his new job, Ogata already fit comfortably into the team. He had a warm smile, a strong back, and a driver's license, the most important raw materials for a driver and bath scrubber. Guests seemed to like him, and he worked quickly. In fact, *nakai* soon complained about the other drivers. If Ogata could clean four baths in ninety minutes and then volunteer to help clean a guestroom, what were the other two men doing? Perhaps, like Eguchi and Sachiko, they were stretching out their work in order to subtly convince *Okami* they needed another hand. But Ogata was a quick study. He soon learned how to sneak a quick break away from the prying eyes of others, by departing for a bus stop pick-up a few minutes earlier than necessary or driving back to the inn particularly slowly so guests could enjoy the ride. What may have seemed to guests like a genuine interest in their journey and a desire to orientate them to the village was also a way to slow the day's routine and avoid whatever work was waiting back at the inn. Whether in the van or in a guestroom, we all manipulated time in this way.

Thanks to Ogata I no longer felt caught between helping the *nakai* and the drivers. On particularly busy days in my first few months, both sides pleaded for my assistance. With Ogata here, I could concentrate on helping the *nakai*, while still scrubbing baths when necessary. On this day in late November, I spent most of the morning cleaning guestrooms. However, when I saw Sakamoto depart at 11:30 to drive guests somewhere, I realized the *nakai* could finish their rooms on time without me and decided to clean Saka-moto's remaining two baths. For the first time, I could feel the benefit of having an extra set of hands.

### 12:30—Lunch

At some inns I visited, all the employees ate meals together. Called *makanai,* the employee meal can be a time of bonding and informal training through sharing war stories. It can also be a time when people discuss hobbies and things other than work, making connections that can last beyond their time in the company. In any society, sharing a meal is significant. It is a moment of gathering as a collective. The same applies in Japan, where coworkers eat together at important ceremonies at the end and beginning of the year, and where meals are still considered an important part of the routine of family life.

At Yamazakura, Kazuko and Takeda prepared lunch so it could be ready as early as 11:30 or reheated and eaten any time after that. However, we never ate as a unit. This would have been physically impossible because of a lack of stools, and we would have struggled to squeeze around the tables in the kitchen. Of course, if our bosses thought eating together was important, they could have redesigned the kitchen and made it possible. Regardless, it was clear that many of my colleagues did not wish to eat together in the first place.

Some people ate in haste so they could start their break as quickly as possible. Others purposefully delayed eating to avoid the rush and to eat at a more leisurely pace. Some coworkers planned their mornings so they would finish simultaneously and eat together, while others purposefully avoided eating with specific individuals. For instance, Kazuko never ate with Morita, even if it meant wolfing down the last of her curry so she could avoid sitting at the table with him. Regardless of the impression we gave our guests through our collective hospitality, we were no big, happy family.

### 1:00 p.m.—December 31, 2006—The Laundry Room

Everyone spent the morning preparing for the New Year. There were new flower arrangements in all the rooms, along with *kagami mochi* resting on pieces of paper. Above the front entrance hung twisted rope and paper wreaths. We placed newly designed *yukata* in every room and new slippers in one of the private villas. The rarest sight was *Okami* and *Shachō* working feverishly throughout the day.

It was only the second time I had seen *Okami* working anywhere but her office or the front desk, and only the third time I had seen *Shachō* working at all. He was typically in the residence or away from the inn at a meeting. Today, *Okami* spent hours arranging flowers in massive vases in the lobby and the dining room, while *Shachō* put cleaning solution around the baths, placed new wooden stools and rinsing tubs in all the baths, and hung seasonal decorations. The real treat of the day was our *makanai*: sukiyaki for lunch and sushi for dinner. We also received small gifts from the retired owners. The holiday seemed to put everyone in a good mood. Moods had also improved since *Okami* hired a new *nakai* in late November. It was a small victory for the *nakai* who had been shorthanded for so long.

With the additional driver and *nakai*, I finally caught my breath and reconsidered my role in the ryokan. From the beginning, I had wanted to dive in; to experience the training, the obligations, the camaraderie, the routines, and the interruptions of working at a ryokan. I felt that only by putting my body and mind through what my colleagues experienced could I understand the work required behind the scenes to make guests feel at home in the ryokan. And since the start of August I had done just that. I had worked twenty-four days or more each month, completing the same long shifts as most of my coworkers, from 7:30 a.m. to 10:00 p.m. or later. I often got home at 10:30 or 11:00 p.m., wrote fieldnotes for two hours or longer, then slept until 6:30 and started all over again. It was more physically and emotionally exhausting than I had ever imagined.

By the end of November, I began to question the logic of suffering for the sake of hospitality. Why was I ignoring my back pain, burning my fingertips on the hot dishes, spending most days dehydrated, and delaying using the toilet? Why had I developed a twitch in my left eye, or failed to take time to visit the doctor? Had this been my family, and my business, my physical pain and the endless days would have made more sense. Who was I suffering for?

I was suffering for my colleagues. I relished hearing Sachiko exclaim, "Oh, you're so helpful!" (*Aa, tasukarimasu*) when I unexpectedly arrived to help her clean a guestroom, instead of stretching out a task elsewhere to end precisely at lunch. And I often sacrificed toilet breaks so that Kazuko and I could maintain our dishwashing rhythm. I ignored my pain and discomfort for the sense of camaraderie that came from "helping" my colleagues.

I was suffering for my guests. When I picked up a couple from

Canada at the bus stop, I felt a sudden sense of responsibility to care for them throughout their stay. In the two days that followed, I skipped lunch to drive them around the village and constantly worried about their meals. They indicated only upon arrival that they were vegetarians, so I considered it my duty to explain their food restrictions to the head chef. I even suggested dishes they might enjoy, despite the fact that I had no place in the ryokan's professional kitchen. I could not explain why I cared so much about these strangers, as much as I would have cared for my own family. I wanted them to fall in love with Yamazakura and to remember their stay for the rest of their lives. When they left and thanked me for all I had done, I felt my suffering had been worth it.

I was suffering for myself. I wanted to be considered competent by my colleagues, not some mascot for the inn or someone to rely on only when a non-Japanese guest checked in. Plus, I had internalized the work ethic of my colleagues, which seemed to revolve around quiet perseverance. Most of them were members of a postwar generation that had been raised to value suffering in silence, especially in the workplace, even if it led to physical and mental strain. Collectively, one could argue that this spirit of quiet perseverance was partly responsible for the nation's healthy postwar economic growth. But it has left a heavy toll on many people, who now live with a culture of work that accepts suffering as unavoidable. In fact, several of my colleagues felt that accepting poor working conditions, including mandatory overtime, was an essential part of becoming an adult.

It's no wonder that the person most respected by my colleagues during my first month at Yamazakura was Saitō Yūki, a high school baseball player who became a symbol of perseverance (*gaman*) during the 2006 summer national baseball tournament. During the two-week tournament he threw the most innings (69) and pitches (948) in tournament history, almost single-handedly leading his team to the National Championship. Despite his obvious exhaustion and overuse by his coach, he persevered, making him a national hero and the main topic of conversation at the ryokan for weeks. With this young man as role model, it often seemed that my colleagues tolerated our long hours and shorthanded work environment as a badge of honor. Complaints flowed during the morning tea break, in the pantry, and during my nightly bath with the driver Sakamoto. But over time they seemed less like problems to be solved than a list of tribulations that provided evidence of our hard work.

I had felt the physical pain of the work, as well as the emotional frustration at slow coworkers, absent management, and demanding guests. I had cultivated a spirit of perseverance in myself. But by the end of November I felt that I had suffered enough. It was time to adjust my schedule and carve more time for myself. Instead of 7:30 a.m.–9:00 p.m., I negotiated with *Okami* to work 7:30 a.m.–6:00 p.m., with no afternoon break. In retrospect, I was still working too much, but I felt it was a small victory that gave me more control over my time. Instead of an unpredictable break in the middle of the day and uncertainty about what time I would get home at night, my new schedule ensured I would finish at 6:00. With my new schedule, I spent my afternoons washing the dishes of any lunch guests, collecting early arriving guests from the bus stop, and doing my most time-sensitive task: laundry.

Laundry began at 10:00, when I collected the bath towels from each room and carried them to the makeshift space that served as the laundry room. The ceiling was made of translucent plastic panels. This let in the warmth of the sun in warmer months, but created a frigid workplace in the winter. The space lacked insulation and felt nearly like being outdoors. Every day I washed up to fifty large bath towels in two machines designed to hold ten at a time. Therefore, I had to spend hours running back and forth between the laundry room and wherever else I was working. As soon as the first two loads finished, I started two more loads, moved six wet towels into each of the two small dryers, and hung the remaining wet towels on bamboo drying poles in the center of the room. Laundry was one of the most predictable tasks at Yamazakura, since everything was on a timer. However, it was frustrating because the equipment was not suited to the task. We were using household appliances for a business.

We all had a space to escape at the ryokan. The *nakai* had the pantry and the guestrooms, where they could stretch out their tasks out of the sight of others. The drivers had the van and the baths to work without spying eyes. I had the laundry room. It was my space to write notes and rest, since no one ever bothered me there. But between loads I was expected to do other jobs, like clean rooms before lunch and help at the front desk after lunch. Afternoons before check-in were the slowest time of the day. I welcomed visitors who arrived to use our outdoor baths, helped address thank you cards to guests from overseas and answer emails written in English, or picked up guests from the bus stop. But I usually sat quietly, stuck waiting for something to do between loads of laundry, while the two women at the front desk answered phones and did paperwork.

### 2:00 p.m.—January 4, 2007—The Van

Once my final load of laundry was in the dryer, I moved outside to sweep the paths, from the parking lot past the inn entrance to the outdoor baths. In warmer months, I also sprayed the paths, plus the surrounding trees and bushes, with a gentle mist. Like splashing water on the sidewalk in front of a shop in the city, spraying the paths controlled dust and made everything glisten. On especially hot days, the water kept the path cool as guests walked from their cars to the inn entrance. We wanted their first impression of Yamazakura to be a cool, inviting tunnel of greenery, transporting them to another world.

The task of spraying the paths required great concentration, since the hose was a potential tripping hazard for guests and other staff. Plus, squeezing the nozzle continuously for twenty to thirty minutes often led to hand cramps. In the winter months, I was happy to no longer spray paths or wrestle the long hose back into its tiny storage space when finished. Instead, I often spread deicing agent on the paths, and after a rainy day, I would line the paths with open umbrellas that dried in the sun.

On this afternoon in early January, the front desk called me just as I was removing a warm bundle of towels from the dryer. I was asked to prepare the van. Two young women staying last night and tonight wanted to go bath-hopping. I thought I would drop them in the town center, where they could walk around and explore more than a dozen inns. But they asked me to drive them to an inn nearly fifteen minutes away. I happily complied. This was one of the unadvertised services we provided, which was necessary in a village with no taxi service. Driving them across the village felt decadent, as though I was abandoning my other work. But mobilizing hospitality meant focusing my attention on the guest in front of me. Nothing else mattered.

The conversation during the drive was predictable. They asked why I was working here and remarked how fortunate I was to be surrounded by nature. I asked where they were from and why they were visiting Kurokawa. They were friends who met in university and who were now working and living in Kyoto. This was a reunion and a rare holiday for both of them. They chose Kurokawa because of its well-known baths, and they were extremely satisfied so far. When we finally arrived at the entrance of the ryokan on the other side of the village, they said they would finish in thirty minutes. This left me in a holding pattern, with nothing to do but wait in the parking lot. Thanks to Yamazakura's exceptional hospitality I had an unexpected break in the middle of an otherwise hectic day. Much like the pantry and the laundry room, the van provided an escape from the unpredictable workday, beyond the judgmental eyes of my colleagues.

### 6:00 p.m.—March 4, 2007—Washing Dinner Dishes

By early March I was still working during the days, helping in the evenings only when needed. Today was one of those times. One of the drivers had recently quit, leaving Ogata, the newest member, and Sakamoto, who worked full-time at Yamazakura and ran his family farm. Today Sakamoto was burning his fields, an essential part of the annual agricultural cycle at the end of winter. Sakamoto had been preparing for weeks and had repeatedly reminded everyone that he would not work this day. So, for the first night in nearly a month I returned to assist with Yamazakura's dinner service.

Along with the bath, dinner is arguably the most important element at any ryokan. The *kaiseki* meal takes all day to prepare, but each element must be served at precisely the right moment and temperature. Each ingredient is carefully sourced, by local farmers whenever possible, and the result resembles a work of art. It is composed of uniquely shaped dishes of different materials, depths, and sizes spread before each guest in seemingly endless variety. The impact can be profound, sparking curiosity about each item, squeals of excitement, and photos from all angles. While guests pay for their room and our service, most of the cost of a ryokan stay is wrapped up in the food. The more expensive the ryokan, the more expensive the ingredients for dinner (Figures 10 and 11).

Our guests consumed the multi-sensory show of the ryokan dinner in the comfort of their rooms, as their personal *nakai* presented a parade of delicacies over the course of one or two hours. The timing of this procession depended entirely on the guests: how quickly they ate and how many questions they asked. Backstage in the kitchen, we were a ballet of bodies prepping serving trays laden with unique plates and bowls for each dish, decorated with seasonal garnishes like leaves and grasses. The moment a piece of tempura

FIGURE 10. Assembling the *kaiseki* dinner for a large party of guests in the dining room. Photo by author.

FIGURE 11. Clearing dirty dishes after dinner. Photo by author.

was laid upon a blood-red maple leaf, it was rushed out of the kitchen with all the seriousness and immediacy of an organ transplant.

A small whiteboard hung above the long workstation in the middle the kitchen. This was the nerve center of the ryokan's back-stage area. It indicated all the information the chefs and *nakai* needed to prepare and deliver an average of forty *kaiseki* meals each evening. Each guestroom was listed by name (e.g., Pine, Camellia), and at 9:00 a.m. every morning someone from the front desk wrote the details for the day: the number of guests in each room, the price of the meal, and any dietary restrictions (e.g., no meat). There were two tiers of meal at Yamazakura: the standard meal and a more expensive option, which included add-ons like a higher grade of beef grilled at the table. This information on the whiteboard provided the chefs enough details to begin their preparations each morning. Then as guests checked in throughout the afternoon, each *nakai* returned to the kitchen and wrote their guests' requested dinner time—6:00, 6:30, or 7:00—under the name of each room, as well as any changes, like a last-minute cancellation.

From one glance at the whiteboard we could guess how the evening might proceed; whether the work would flow steadily or spike at a certain time. We knew when we could help each other without being asked. For instance, someone with a few minutes to spare at 6:30 might notice a group of six people about to start dinner, and without a word from anyone, they would place six plates on two trays, ready to hold the grilled sweetfish (*ayu*) that the chefs would place under the burner at any moment. Based on the board we knew that if most guests ate at 6:00 p.m., we might have a spike in work from 6:15 to 7:00 p.m., followed by a trickle, until the final dish was washed and the kitchen floor mopped as early as 8:30 p.m. We also knew that just one group of six guests eating at 7:00 p.m. could drag out our night, slowed by alcohol and a request for the final course of rice and miso soup finally—mercifully—at 9:30 p.m. On such a night we would be lucky to turn out the kitchen lights and head to the bath at 10:30 p.m.

From 6:00 p.m. onward, we had to remain flexible, ready to spring into action. As soon as guests finished their dinner, it set off a flurry of activity—extra *nakai* arriving to help clear dishes from the room, followed by a wave of dirty dishes flowing into the kitchen. Without the whiteboard we would be lost, but it could not prepare us for the inevitable unpredictability of every evening.

Two of the most common evening interruptions, which dis-
lodged me from my spot at the kitchen sink, were driving guests to a
bath at another inn and laying out *futons* in the guestrooms. On this
particular evening in March, I was asked to do neither. No guests left
the inn after dinner, and the *nakai* handled the *futons* themselves.
This meant we could concentrate on washing dishes. There were also
no dramas, like the time I accidentally threw two celebratory sea
bream carcasses in the food waste bin and then spent twenty minutes
picking through the uneaten food of forty guests in order to find ten
toothpicks that had been holding the fish in its display position. On
this day in March, all forty guests checked in before 5:30 and most
of them ate dinner at 6:00 or 6:30. By 7:30 p.m., most guests were
finished eating, and we were barreling through the bulk of the dirty
dishes. The *nakai* were already setting up the breakfast tables in the
dining room by 8:00, and I finished mopping the floor at 8:30 p.m.
Within five minutes I was showering, thoroughly washing off the
workday before slipping into the bath. One of our guests was already
enjoying a post-dinner soak, and we quickly struck up a conversation. On most nights we finished work so late that our guests were
settled in their rooms by the time we bathed. In hindsight, my colleagues would have been fine without my labor today. But no one
could have predicted that when the day began. Unpredictability was
the norm at the ryokan.

### August 4, 2007—Closing Time

My last day at Yamazakura came just over a year after my first.
It was a busy summer day, with over forty guests. Keiko from the
front desk had called a few days in advance to ask if I could cover
for Sakamoto, who had to travel to Kumamoto City for his daughter's
school event. I only worked in the afternoon, from 3:00 to closing. I
spent most of the afternoon in the parking lot welcoming guests, and
I drove one couple to the town center. He was from Shikoku; she
from Okinawa. They were meeting in the middle for a few days. They
had hoped to stay in Kurokawa but found all the inns fully booked.
They had walked to Yamazakura, so I offered to drive them back to
the town center, where they could continue their hunt for accommodations. I considered it my last chance to go beyond what was necessary, mobilizing hospitality even when unnecessary. They were
not technically our guests, after all, and they could have walked back
to town. However, with a little effort, I could show them how much

Yamazakura cared, which might make a lasting impression and convince them to return some day. It also made me feel good to be generous with my time and break up the monotony of my afternoon. Anything for a guest.

Over the previous few months, I had gradually reduced my working days to less than once a week, as I began spending more time working at other inns and interviewing their owners, their next generation of owners, and their employees. I still felt connected to my colleagues at Yamazakura and even joined the company trip to South Korea in June. Unfortunately, many of my coworkers still lacked any connection to each other, and three days in Seoul did not change that. When my final day came in August, I could still sense the internal rivalries between some *nakai,* plus the general animosity between the men and the women, with both sides still accusing the other of laziness and poor hospitality.

Perhaps a stronger sense of direction from our bosses would have alleviated these internal divisions that were invisible to our guests. However, we were largely left alone. *Shachō* and *Okami* seemed too preoccupied with their longer-term work to worry about the minute-by-minute work of hospitality. That work fell on our tired shoulders. Sometimes my colleagues wore their physical and mental exhaustion like a badge of honor, silently accepting it as the normal condition for any employee in Japan. After all, this was how they had been raised. Other times they engaged in clever tactics like foot-dragging with the hope of triggering change. In the end, such weapons of the weak seemed to work, since *Okami* had hired another new driver and *nakai* earlier that summer.

But there was no long-term solution to ease the physical and emotional labor of hospitality. In fact, if my colleagues agreed on anything, it would have been that hospitality should be exhausting. Exhaustion was the only way to know you did everything possible to make a guest feel at home.

A year is a long time in a ryokan. Seasons change, employees come and go, and thousands of guests cross the lobby seeking a temporary escape from their everyday lives. In the next chapter I turn a microscopic lens on the employees who arguably bear the greatest burden of caring for these guests: the *nakai.* They are responsible for a handful of guests for the entirety of their stay. But knowing the long hours of the ryokan workday and the expectation of Japanese women to care for their own family members at home begs the question: who are these women who can devote so much time to caring for the needs of strangers? In the next chapter I explore the circumstances that led some of my coworkers to the ryokan industry and explain how the ryokan has become a last resort for women pushed to the peripheries of Japanese society.

## Chapter 7

# Women without Homes

The *nakai* lottery began at 3:00 p.m., when guests started checking in at Yamazakura. Each morning after checkout we spent two hours cleaning the hallways and guestrooms. In each room we changed the pillowcases and *futon* covers and set out the appropriate number and color of *yukata* and toiletries based on what little we knew about our new guests: the name on the reservation and the number of men, women, and children in each room. Besides that, they were a mystery. What time would they arrive? Would they be young, old, friendly, rude? What time would they want dinner? Would the kids be cute or monstrous? If it were a foreign name, would they speak any Japanese? More importantly, would we make a personal connection that led to a heartfelt thank you card and years of repeat visits, or would we spend the evening rushing back and forth to the kitchen to refill sake bottles for the unappreciative? At 3:00 p.m. anything was possible.

On a chilly December afternoon, I sat on the floor of the large dining hall with two women. Between us lay a mound of towels I had just pulled from the dryer. Their warmth on our fingertips seemed to trigger our small talk about the dropping temperatures outside and the coming winter. Two other women carried chilled dishes from the kitchen and sorted them onto serving trays, where they would gradually reach room temperature before dinner. At the front of the room, Eguchi knelt before the large alcove, arranging seasonal grasses and bare branches in a massive vase that would accentuate tomorrow's breakfast, served in this room.

Once guests started arriving, we would be on our feet and on the move until at least 9:00 p.m., with little time to use the toilet, grab a cigarette, gossip about our guests, or complain about each other. So we worked slowly and deliberately, trying to look busy as we waited for the phone to ring. After all, no one wanted to look idle and risk being given some thankless task like tidying the linen closet.

When the first call came at 3:45, Suzuki set down her tray and answered the phone. "Pine!" she called to the rest of us. Komura recognized the room as one of hers and dropped a towel in mid-fold. She struggled to her feet, rubbed life into her sixty-four-year-old legs, and walked to the table with the guest list. Scanning it she said to no one in particular, "Pine. A couple. Name is Tanaka. I wonder if they are married?" She removed some lint from her uniform and checked her hair and makeup in the mirror. Then she slid open the door and walked to the lobby to meet her guests. It was showtime.

Over the next few hours Komura embodied the idea of flexible labor. She would be on the move all evening, carrying food between the kitchen and her three or four guestrooms. She would also shape-shift to suit her guests. She might be an entertainer, pouring drinks and enlivening the meal with conversation. Or a tour guide, answering questions about the best local spots to visit the next day. She might be a babysitter, playing rock-scissors-paper to entertain a child. Or she might blend into the background, delivering each course and removing empty dishes as invisibly as possible, careful to not disturb the icy silence of a lovers' quarrel. Her hospitality would vary as much as her guests—former classmates meeting for a reunion after years apart, colleagues on a team-building trip, families celebrating a birthday or wedding anniversary, couples of all ages and varieties, from newlyweds and retirees, to apparent extramarital affairs. However, her goal remained the same: provide hospitality and make strangers feel at home.

### Home-less Women

The *okami* is the co-owner and woman at the center of the family business that is the ryokan. She internalizes Japan's gendered geography of home and accepts responsibility for what happens inside the ryokan. This includes managing the taste (*aji*) of its hospitality (*omotenashi*), which means deciding its décor and hiring and firing staff. But in busy ryokan like those in Kurokawa, the *okami* does not personally show guests to their rooms, serve them dinner, or clean up after them. There is not enough of her to go around. In other words, the *okami* is not the body of hospitality. That job falls to women like Komura, Maeda, and Suzuki. They provide a protective layer between the *okami* and her guests, producing and feeling the tourist encounter in a way their bosses do not: hearts swelling with pride at a compliment; faces flushing in embarrassment when a guest does not speak Japanese; fists clenching at an insult or an unreasonable request.

Ryokan hospitality is so intimate and time-consuming, so physically and emotionally demanding, that any *okami* with more than a handful of guests must mobilize a specialized labor force that will care for guests in her place; a group of women untethered to the space that both defines and devalues their labor. Put simply, the ryokan needs women without a home. Not destitute per se, but without a household of members who need the physical and emotional labor of these women. After all, if my coworkers were taking care of strangers every evening at Yamazakura, they could not be taking care of husbands, children, parents-in-law, or grandchildren at home. In this way, my coworkers complicated the common image of a Japanese woman devoted to and defined by her place in the home, an image that applies so powerfully to *okami* (chapter 4). My coworkers were free from such domestic responsibilities. But they were stuck in a different kind of domestic trap, in which the only work they could find comprised what a coworker called, "exactly what I did as a housewife" (*shufu no koto to mattaku issho*).

In this chapter I introduce these "women without a home": the *nakai*. Their job is to make guests feel at home, while they belong to neither the family nor the business. Nearly all the dozens of *nakai* I worked with and met around Kurokawa were transplants from distant cities and towns who would never call Kurokawa home. They lived in company dormitories or rented apartments in neighboring villages. Many had worked at other ryokan, flowing through the industry in search of a steady job, decent accommodations, a conflict-free work environment, and for some, escape from an abusive man. Divorced, separated, widowed, and unmarried, what they shared was what they lacked: a home whose family members needed their everyday "around the body care," which is expected of most Japanese women of a certain age.[1] This left them the time and energy to provide this care for strangers, via the ryokan's intimate, time-consuming, Japanese-style hospitality. But their freedom made many of them vulnerable. They were susceptible to the demands of their bosses, with no permanent roof over their heads, little job security, and a looming sense that today could be their last. The *okami* could simply say, "Don't come in tomorrow" (*ashita konakute ii*), making a *nakai* jobless.

The recent success of Kurokawa's ryokan has been sustained by the strong arms, warm smiles, flexible personalities, and vulnerable lives of women like Suzuki, the woman I featured in the prologue who escaped her abusive husband by working at an inn. Without the physical and emotional labor of such women, Yamazakura and thousands of busy ryokan like it around the country would come to a standstill. In this chapter I share how my *nakai* coworkers ended up in the ryokan industry and what the work meant to them. I found no common path to the ryokan, but most *nakai* did not plan to work there. It just sort of happened, in many cases following economic and personal struggle, and a lack of other options. In the end, working as a *nakai* left my coworkers both free and stuck. Without the responsibilities of home, they had more potential mobility than most women in Japan. However, they were trapped in a dead-end job, haunted by the feeling that with no skills, career, or job prospects, they had nowhere else to go. Indeed, for many *nakai*—like their bosses—the ryokan was their last resort.

### Maeda: Never Part of the Plan

Most inns have an experienced *nakai* who guides new employees, helps plan the daily and monthly work schedule, and communicates between a busy *okami* and her team of *nakai*. When I arrived at Yamazakura in 2006, this was Maeda (whom we usually called "Mae-chan," with the informal "chan" suffix, instead of the typical more polite "san"). She had been at the inn more than six years and had become one of its veterans. *Nakai* turnover at ryokan can be high, since many are part-timers without contracts or temps on fixed contracts of three months or six months. New employees might arrive at any time, so it is important to have a veteran on hand to ensure consistency in the taste *(aji)* of the inn's hospitality. After all, even an experienced *nakai* needs to learn the idiosyncrasies of each new workplace. At Yamazakura, Maeda was the only full-time regular employee *(seishain)* in a sea of part-time *nakai*, making her valuable for passing on the inn's taste.

Maeda constantly strove to improve the inn's service, and I could feel her dedication to her craft every time she reminded me to wipe the serving trays to a high shine while I washed the dishes, or when she praised me for getting the bath towels so clean and fluffy. She insisted guests would notice such details, and these details would make a lasting impression. Her professionalism, attention to detail, communication skills, and ability to anticipate the needs of her guests made it seem like she had spent her career in the ryokan industry. In fact, she was relatively new to the *ryokan,* and this world was never part of her plan.

"After high school [in the mid-1960s] I worked in accounting for a large company," she explained one afternoon during our break. We sat at a low table in an empty guest room, my voice recorder between us as she mapped her path to Yamazakura. She sat upright and looked nervous, glancing at the recording device. She must have seen the concern on my face, because she suddenly assured me everything was OK. In fact, she was excited to help with the research. She said it made her feel important. Now that we were finally doing more than chatting idly while laying out *futons,* she was ready and took her role in my research seriously.

"I was good at my job," she continued, "the first person trained to use the latest adding machine. It was a huge, complex machine that I used to calculate the monthly payroll." She was the only staff member to receive special training on the new machine, an upgrade from the abacus she used previously. She beamed at the memory, especially of being a respected member of the company. "I was the only woman in a company of around a hundred men, who treated me like a younger sister. When I told them I would marry, they were upset. They wanted me to stay." She managed to hold out a few more years, until her second child was born. At that point, the pressure to quit from her husband and his family was too strong.

Maeda's coworkers may have wanted her to stay, but they probably were not surprised she "retired" from the company at such a young age. It did not matter how fulfilling she found the work, how valuable she was to the company, or whether she would have preferred to keep her job. Both Maeda and her coworkers understood that she was expected to dedicate herself full-time to her husband and their two children at home. This was the normal trajectory for a young woman like Maeda, at least among couples who could survive on a husband's salary alone.[2] Maeda felt she had no choice but to follow the same path.

Her brief career occurred in an era marked by the continuous entry of educated, hard-working young women like her into the workforce, then swiftly into the home. When they married in their early- to mid-twenties and left their full-time jobs, they were replaced by young female high school and junior college graduates only too willing to accept equally low wages and few opportunities for career advancement. After all, many of them expected to quickly marry and "retire" from paid work, too. Despite their absence from the workplace, though, full-time "professional housewives" (*sengyō shufu*) like Maeda remained integral to the postwar Japanese economy, and they were supported by corporations and the state through spousal benefits, tax incentives, and more.[3] The lifetime employment system, which became widespread during the Income-Doubling 1960s and continued in the decades that followed as a cornerstone of Japan's employment picture, provided the salary and benefits that enabled women like Maeda to leave paid employment and manage the home. It demanded long working hours and dedication to the company by their husbands, but it could not function without the unpaid labor of women at home. They cooked meals, cleaned, did laundry, raised children, and did all the other household management tasks that kept the family running smoothly and kept the husband working smoothly.[4]

Eventually many housewives returned to the workforce, often after their children entered elementary school. As their children grew and educational and other household expenses increased, some families needed a second income, while many women also wanted the challenge, satisfaction, and sociality of paid employment. Over the decades, this trend led to an M-curve that still characterizes female employment in Japan today.[5] However, most women who returned to paid employment did so only as part-timers, in positions that enabled them to retain the home as their primary responsibility. In fact, women often chose jobs more for the location and ability to balance the work with their domestic duties than the content or the skills involved. Finding work near the home was important because it allowed women to put home and family first, such as collecting a sick child from school. This tendency to return to paid employment while putting the home first remains common in Japan today. Indeed, Goldstein-Gidoni has shown that housewives who return to work still consider it best if their husbands do not even notice they are working. In other words, it's best if the quality of their housework remains constant, the children don't suffer because of her absence, and the wives are "at the threshold to send him off in the morning and to welcome him back late in the evening."[6] The same gendered geography that compels an *okami* to "be there" to greet her guests as they arrive for check-in each afternoon tethers mothers and wives to the home even after they return to paid employment.

Maeda returned to paid work sooner than most, and not out of choice, but because her marriage ended soon after her second child was born. The trigger was her husband's gambling. She admitted that before the wedding, "My parents warned me he was the wrong man. They even tried to arrange a marriage for me. But I was stubborn and in love." She even went so far as to slip out the bathroom window of a restaurant while dressed in a kimono during a date her parents had arranged. Maeda's parents found husbands for each of her sisters. "My sisters all cried at their weddings because they didn't want to marry those men. But now they have all become very close to their husbands, while I'm the only one crying." With a bittersweet smile she added, "They were right. I was an idiot (*baka*). I always regret giving up that job and marrying him." Decades later, Maeda still could not separate the regret of her failed marriage from the regret of losing her career. She abandoned a rewarding job for him, and the choice has haunted her ever since.

### Set Adrift, Seeking Permanence

Following her divorce, Maeda was set adrift with her children. She worked a series of part-time jobs before eventually finding full-time work as a golf caddy, a job that paid well and like ryokan work, was popular among divorced women. Maeda enjoyed being active, meeting new people, and working outdoors, but the heavy bags and constant walking eventually became a burden. In some ways, her caddy experience prepared her for *nakai* work. She is still on her feet all day. Now she carries grilled fish and fresh towels instead of golf clubs.

Maeda found her first *nakai* position in a job ad magazine in the mid-1990s. "My kids had left home, and I was wondering what to do, since I would be lonely at night." She liked the idea of meeting new people and staying active, and she did not want to be alone in an empty apartment. Plus, the pay sounded better than most jobs she was qualified for. That's what led her to Kurokawa. She enjoyed the work and made friends quickly, but she soon became frustrated by the job's lack of permanence. She wanted to become a full-time regular employee. It would mean more job security, better pay, insurance, and a pension, all the benefits she had enjoyed in her first job and expected by so many male employees in Japan over the decades. "I asked my manager [...], but he told me it would take a few years" to become a full-time employee. "So I told him, 'I quit!'"

Unfortunately, Maeda did not have a backup plan. "A friend at the inn said, 'If you go home you'll only be lonely. You should find another job *somewhere*'" (*ie ni kaettemo sabishii dake kara*, dokka de *mata shigoto wo mitsuketa hō ga ii yo*). Maeda interviewed at another inn the next day. Most *okami* in Kurokawa are constantly seeking staff due to high turnover, and Maeda found a new job quickly. It seemed perfect. It was full-time, with good pay and benefits. Plus, Maeda's new *okami* was highly regarded in Kurokawa and around Kyushu for her high service standards. She even hired a hospitality instructor from a vocational school in Kumamoto City who offered the employees a monthly training session. This former flight attendant made employees do enunciation drills and ran them through real-life scenarios and role-play exercises in which they apologized to guests and politely declined unreasonable requests. Instead of simply passing along what her mother-in-law taught her, this *okami* aimed to professionalize her staff, and Maeda soaked it up. Sadly, she had to quit within a year of arriving because she "could not get along" (*dōshitemo awanakatta*) with a male colleague. I pressed for more details, but she simply said she had no choice. According to *okami* and ryokan staff around Kurokawa, personalities often clash in the cramped, high-stress environment of a busy ryokan, and sometimes quitting is the only way to deal with a coworker who is annoying, stubborn, nosy, or inappropriate.

Maeda soon moved on to her third *nakai* job in two years, this one also without a contract. Plus, it had shorter hours and lower pay. Maeda had come to Kurokawa to work and earn as much as possible. "I'm alone," she explained, "so I don't have anything to do" (*hitori dakara nani mo suru koto ga nai*). She would rather be working. Eventually, Yamazakura's owners, who heard about Maeda from other owners, offered her the permanence she desired: a regular full-time position with better pay, benefits, full-time hours, and a room in the dormitory. She remained there ever since.

Maeda never planned to work in a ryokan, but it offered her a second chance at a rewarding career. And she excelled at her job. She often shared with me the letters, gifts, and photographs sent by her guests, thanking her for making their stay special. When repeat guests called to make a reservation, they often asked for Maeda by name, and she seemed to truly love the job. "The best part of the job is meeting different people every day," she told me, "all coming from different places." She did her best to meet their needs. On her days off she often checked out nearby restaurants and cafes, in case guests asked for recommendations, and she read the newspaper daily to keep up on national and world events. "Whatever happens in the world, I need to be able to join the conversation. I think that's good for me." It seemed that to Maeda hospitality was not selfless work, as *okami* often frame it, but an opportunity for self-improvement.

Still, the ryokan was not where Maeda thought she would be at this stage of her life. Near the end of our conversation, she circled back to her first accounting job, which she still regretted abandoning. In fact, despite her experience and skill in hospitality, she would prefer to work in accounting. "But I have been away too long. I have no skills. I am embarrassed to say I don't even know how to use a computer." Like other women in Japan who have spent years out of regular paid employment, Maeda struggled to imagine that domestic chores, raising children, managing a household, and working part-time jobs in unrelated fields constituted anything but unskilled work. Indeed, despite her efforts at professionalization, Maeda considered the position of *nakai* a step down, a last resort for women like her who had no opportunity to return to "skilled" employment and no other options.

### Nishihara: Liberating Work

Most of the *nakai* I worked with and met around Kurokawa were divorced. Their reasons were many, including financial troubles, alcohol, extramarital affairs, and physical abuse, but the overall narrative was universal: they were escaping toxic husbands. Most *nakai* I knew had a very low opinion of men: they were selfish, unreliable, threatening, and useless around the home. They spent money they didn't have and made promises they couldn't keep. In fact, I often wondered if the women were so kind to me in part because their husbands had set the bar so low. Any interest I showed in their lives or assistance I gave in the workplace was often praised and repaid with snacks, cups of tea, and expressions of surprised but grateful thanks. These women may not have expected (or wanted) marriage to include the same kind of compatibility, equality, and romantic love often expected in the West. Indeed, anthropologist Amy Borovoy argues that the Japanese idea of marriage commonly consists of "a compatible division of labor that does not hinge on sexual attraction or shared interests."[7] However, my coworkers expected financial stability, some level of marital fidelity, and a safe home. When their husbands could not meet these minimum standards, the women left.

The ryokan was a logical destination, and their arrival seemed like a win-win for both the women and their bosses. These separated or divorced women already had experience caring for the emotional and physical needs of others. Once they left their husbands, they were free to care for ryokan guests instead. At the same time, the ryokan provided the women a roof over their heads and the opportunity to earn a living, even if they had been out of paid employment for decades. One *nakai* explained bluntly: the position of *nakai* meant she could finally live without a man. No one at Yamazakura praised the ryokan for its liberating potential more than Nishihara.

Nishihara, aged forty-eight, joined our team in late 2006, a few months after I arrived. She had worked elsewhere in Kurokawa before wanting a change, so she called the *okami* at Yamazakura out of the blue. She interviewed and started the next day. Nishihara was soon a favorite among the *nakai*. She worked hard and could take a joke. During a morning tea break about six weeks after she arrived, everyone suddenly decided to stuff their empty candy wrappers in Nishihara's pockets and down the back of her uniform. Just some random silliness to pass the time. Another morning when Nishihara asked me to join her upstairs to put away the *futon*, Maeda feigned jealousy, calling out, "No affairs with anyone but me, Chris! I'll tell your wife." Nishihara laughed, clearly in on the joke. Plus, she arrived just when we were feeling stretched thin. Having an extra hand on deck meant each *nakai* could look after two or three rooms each night instead of three or four. This increased the time they could spend with their guests. We could clean the rooms at a more relaxed pace and enjoy a longer break. Finally, it made it easier for *nakai* to schedule a day off. Personally, Nishihara's arrival helped me understand why everyone was so happy to welcome me months before. One extra body made a world of difference.

Like most *nakai* I met, Nishihara initially hesitated to reveal much about herself, so I let her ask the questions. It was all part of the give-and-take of working together and building trust. Anytime we worked together Nishihara peppered me with questions about my wife, my family, my research, even my finances. Finally in March 2007 she offered to sit for an interview and share her story. Her only condition was that we meet outside the ryokan and on her day off. I got the feeling she wanted to ensure our conversation was not overheard by any snoopy coworkers. We met in a nearby village at a rustic farmhouse that had been converted to a café. It was yet another nostalgia-themed business inspired by Kurokawa's success. I arrived a few minutes early and found a quiet corner, where Nishihara soon joined me. After some small talk about how we spent our days off, I asked how she first started working as a *nakai*. Like many *nakai* I met, she spoke of youthful mistakes and missed opportunities, but she described the ryokan as a sanctuary when she had no other options.

Nishihara had her first child at the age of twenty. "It was a mistake," she admitted, but they married three years later. Her husband was the second son in his family, but because his older brother lived elsewhere, the young couple was expected to move in with his parents. This situation was unbearable for Nishihara because her new mother-in-law doubted their child's legitimacy. She thought another man might be the father. Eventually the couple had a second child, but the relationship soon fell apart. They divorced, and with no money or job, Nishihara moved back to her parents' home with her eldest son, who was six at the time. Her ex-husband later remarried and the new couple treated his second son as their own; the family's legitimate heir. Her family torn apart and her future uncertain, Nishihara was lost.

"Because I married so young, I didn't have any career or training. I didn't even have a driver's license." Like many women in postwar Japan, Nishihara had chosen marriage over career. In fact, it never really seemed like she had a choice. She relied on her husband for his income, while he relied on her to raise their children and manage the home. This was the standard arrangement, and it worked—economically, socially—for many. But what happens when this arrangement falls apart? Where does a woman go when she leaves the relative stability of marriage?

Nishihara needed a job that did not require any special training or education. It also needed on-site housing (because she could not drive) and the potential to save enough money to study or train for a real career. The location also mattered to Nishihara. She wanted to be far enough from her parents' home so she could become self-reliant, but close enough to visit her son, whom she left in her parents' care.

She found all she needed at a ryokan. After several years as a *nakai*, Nishihara earned her driver's license and enough money to begin nursing school. She graduated a few years later, but full-time employment in the field eluded her. Before arriving at Yamazakura she had cobbled together one- or two-year stints in elderly care facilities, random offices, and five different ryokan and hotels around Kyushu. Even at Yamazakura she was just a part-timer, without a contract and with little prospect for a permanent position.

The ryokan may not have been Nishihara's first job choice, but she seemed to enjoy it. At Yamazakura, I often saw her chatting and laughing with guests in the hallways and at breakfast. And she got along with most of the staff, with the exception of the male drivers. She occasionally walked back and forth to the dormitory with Komura, and Suzuki and Maeda sometimes stroked her hair during the morning tea break like a younger sister. However, her precarious situation weighed heavily on her. Years of moving around Kyushu had left her with no savings, no steady career, and no permanent home. She lacked the comfort and security she expected at this stage in life. The only silver lining was her dorm room ("It's tiny, but it's mine") and her independence. She proudly told me, "This job has a dorm and three meals, so I don't need a man. That is very liberating" (*Kono shigoto de wa, sanshoku, ryō mo atte, otoko wa hitsuyō ga nai. Hijō ni kaihō desu*).

Nishihara's sense of liberation was tempered by her lack of options. Like many divorced *nakai* I met, she felt liberation because she no longer had to rely on and care for a husband. At the same time, she lacked the stability of a home or career and had to rely instead on her boss, for both her income and a room in the dormitory. She had left behind friends, neighbors, and family to take this position deep in the Kumamoto countryside, where she was surrounded by strangers who all had seniority over her. She was in no position to complain about anything. Nishihara approached problems at work with a good-natured futility. When I asked what she would like to change about the job (pay, hours, responsibilities?), she smiled and said that answering my question wouldn't change anything anyway, so why bother? As the newest staff member, even thinking about what she might change was a waste of time. She was just happy to have a job.

Divorced women like Maeda and Nishihara were particularly vulnerable to exploitation by ryokan owners, since they had few other options. They felt so grateful for the job that they hardly complained about anything: pay, unexpected overtime, scheduling conflicts, bullying by coworkers, staff meals, or employee housing. One *okami* openly admitted that she preferred hiring divorced women precisely because they seldom complained. It was only in the past few years that her *nakai* had begun requesting private dormitory rooms. Until then, this *okami* could squeeze three or more women into a single room. Women who were only separated (not divorced), on the other hand, were far less predictable. They might abandon the ryokan and return to their husbands without notice. According to some *okami*, another unpredictable pool of *nakai* labor was women in their late teens and twenties who had not yet married or had children. They complained the most, about long hours, bullying by coworkers, the size and condition of their housing, and the lack of any clear guidelines on how to do their jobs. Some *okami* reasoned that these young women complained precisely because they had not yet been married or raised children. They had not yet learned to ignore their own needs and focus all their energy on the needs of others. Divorced women, on the other hand, needed little training to provide the kind of warm, homelike hospitality expected in the ryokan. What was left unsaid was the fact that divorced women were also ideal employees because they had nowhere else to go. They were trapped.

Like many divorced *nakai*, Nishihara was both mobile and stuck. Unlike most Japanese women her age, she did not need to "be there" for anyone. There was no husband, no children, no other relatives she was expected to care for at home. She was free to work all day, and she was free to move across the country at a moment's notice if she liked. However, she had failed to find permanent employment and felt unqualified for any position besides *nakai*. She had nowhere else to go, and her gratitude to her *okami* made her likely to stick around. Her liberation came with a catch: she was trapped in a dead-end job.

### Help Wanted: Precarious Women

Another vulnerable population long associated with *nakai* work is single mothers, whether divorced like Nishihara, or unmarried. While Nishihara's parents helped raise her son while she worked, other single mothers purposefully search for ryokan that can meet their special needs. In the prologue I mentioned Suzuki, who fled an abusive husband with her youngest child in tow. She soon found work at a large ryokan hotel that provided childcare while she worked. And she was not alone. Many of her coworkers were young single mothers who needed both the job and the childcare it provided. In general, very few Japanese companies provide childcare. In fact, the lack of childcare remains a key reason why many women leave paid employment to raise a child, delay marriage, delay having children, or do not have children at all.

On the surface, any company that provides childcare to its employees, particularly single mothers, may appear forward-thinking and generous. But this benefit reveals another way ryokan may take advantage of vulnerable women. Take Kagaya Ryokan, for instance. Located in Ishikawa Prefecture, for decades it has been considered one of the finest ryokan in the country. In addition to its food and atmosphere, its hospitality is often highlighted as outstanding. How does it consistently rate so high in this category? One key is that each *nakai* oversees only one room per night. Like Arakawa, the *okami* in Tsuetate who spent her evening answering our questions and timing our meal to suit the flow of the conversation, the *nakai* at Kagaya can devote themselves fully to their guests. Contrast this with Yamazakura, where each *nakai* oversees two to four rooms and constantly rushes from one to the next. Each Kagaya *nakai* has the time to inquire about her guests' travel plans, share the history of the inn, and explain the source of all the ingredients of the dishes served at dinner and breakfast. She can accommodate special requests from the kitchen and ensure a birthday cake is ready with candles at just the right moment to carry into the guestroom. Her dedication and attention are uninterrupted, which is only the result of her attention not being elsewhere.

Industry expert Doi Kyūtarō traces Kagaya's success to its 1970s decision to create "a work environment that puts single mother employees at ease" (*boshi katei no jūgyōin ga anshin shiteiru hatarakeru kankyō*).[8] This included twenty-four-hour care for children aged one through the end of elementary school. This left *nakai* free to worry about their guests, instead of their children. Kagaya understood that single mothers without a permanent home were some of the only women mobile enough to relocate from anywhere in Japan to a dormitory located in this remote stretch of the Noto peninsula, and only steps from the workplace. Mobile and stuck. Finally, unlike married women who might choose to work only when convenient in order to supplement the family income, single mothers were the sole breadwinners and had to accommodate the long, unpredictable ryokan schedule, which requires working from breakfast to sometimes well past midnight. Like other ryokan that provide childcare, Kagaya's decision was not so much that of a benevolent and generous employer as a shrewd choice that enabled it to attract a pliant workforce and mobilize as much hospitality from it as possible.

Not every *nakai* I met or worked with was divorced or a single mother. There were widows living on small pensions, women in their forties and fifties who had never married, and women in their late teens and twenties who had not yet married. One *nakai* had worked in retail for almost two decades before being forced to resign because her company thought she was too old for the position. She eventually found work in a ryokan, where her age was not a liability. Some young *nakai* were new university graduates who had failed to find a regular full-time position, like the French literature major who accepted a six-month contract in Kurokawa through a dispatch agency, which she felt gave her time to find something more permanent and relevant to her degree. The common thread among most *nakai* I met was that they fell into the position by accident or out of desperation, when they felt they were out of options.

### Takahashi: Debtor's Prison

When I met Takahashi in 2006, she was in her early fifties and already had an eighteen-year career as a *nakai*. She was a no-nonsense worker; polite to everyone, but with no time for gossip. She wanted to work as quickly and efficiently as possible, and she was often impatient with colleagues who cleaned too slowly or did careless things like poorly arranging dishes on a tray, which meant more trips to the kitchen. But in front of guests, she was the picture of sweetness, with an easy smile and a willingness to go out of her way to meet their needs.

Like many of her colleagues, Takahashi never intended to become a *nakai*. She was raised a farmer, married a farmer, and thought she would die a farmer. As she explained one afternoon during our break, the ryokan was her last resort to escape crippling debt. Takahashi's journey to the ryokan began with the death of her father-in-law, whose family had farmed in Kurokawa for generations. When he died, he left behind a wife (his third) and considerable personal debt. Takahashi's mother-in-law wanted to distance herself from the debt. She also wanted to be compensated for decades of work as housewife and farmer. "I worked for this family for thirty years," Takahashi recalled her saying. "I want out. Give me everything."

"We only had some fields and the residence," Takahashi explained. Giving up these properties would leave Takahashi and her husband homeless and without a livelihood. "The case went through mediation and a trial," she continued. Eventually, the mother-in-law got the fields while Takahashi and her husband, the eldest son, retained the family home. "But we still had to pay the debts. Plus, we had two young children." The couple was desperate. They had survived by growing rice and cucumbers for market. Now most of their land was gone; payment for the mother-in-law's decades of domestic labor. The couple tried everything to make ends meet, even driving a small bus to transport guests from distant train stations to Kurokawa's ryokan.

Eventually some neighbors who owned a ryokan paid their debts. But this act of kindness left the couple with a new lender and still no regular income. They had run out of options. "We decided, 'Let's work there [at the neighbor's ryokan],' and we quit being farmers" (*Watashitachi ga jā soko itte hatarakō to iu koto de ne, mō ohyakushō wa yamete*). It was a heavy decision. Takahashi and her husband were not simply switching jobs. They were abandoning an identity passed through their families for generations. They would no longer be farmers, literally one of the "hundred names" (*hyakushō*). Instead, they would work for someone else, waiting on guests in the ryokan industry.

### Balancing Work and Home

It took seven years for the couple to work off the debt, during which Takahashi creatively balanced her responsibilities at work and home. "I would pick up the kids from nursery school [and later elementary school] and go straight to work. They ate dinner and took a bath at the inn [while I worked]. The bath was their playground," she laughed. It was not ideal, but she had no choice. "Guests would always ask the staff, 'There are two unaccompanied kids playing in the bath. Are they OK?'" Luckily, her coworkers helped whenever possible by watching her kids during short breaks. "Then at 9:00 p.m., I would lay them in the back of our van in the parking lot. We always had a van in those days so we could put a *futon* in the back. At 9:00 I would say 'Go sleep in the van!' After work I would drive home with the kids still asleep in the back."

Takahashi was not homeless in the same way as her coworkers. She lived with her husband and children, and she still did the laundry, cleaned the house, and tended her garden outside work hours. But like her coworkers, Takahashi was free from some of the most time-consuming daily physical labor of caring for others, including preparing meals and the evening bath. These she cleverly outsourced to the inn. Even her husband's job at the ryokan spared Takahashi the pressure of cooking his meals, since he ate with his coworkers.

I felt exhausted listening to Takahashi, imagining the sacrifices she made to repay that debt. Did she ever want to quit? "Never," she replied immediately, in a serious tone. "We had to pay back that loan every month, and the job was the only way we could do it. Neighbors would ask when we would break, but I was determined to [pay the debt and] start over. Because of that determination, I never disliked the job."

Their debt finally paid, Takahashi and her husband could stop working at their neighbor's ryokan. However, they realized they could not afford to leave the industry. Their children would soon begin middle school and the costs of education and other necessities would increase. They still needed a steady income, and there were few other job opportunities in the area besides tourism. Takahashi's husband remained at the first ryokan as driver and handyman, while she moved to an inn across town, with slightly less pay but fewer hours. This meant more time at home. However, once her youngest child graduated from high school, she shifted to Yamazakura, which had longer hours and higher pay. With the kids gone and her husband still bathing and eating most meals at work, Takahashi could afford to spend less time at home.

When I first met her in 2006, Takahashi was still working fifty hours a week cleaning rooms and serving meals to strangers. She still needed the income, but she also enjoyed meeting new people every day. She took seriously the responsibility of caring for these strangers, who traveled from afar to experience *her* hospitality. She did not initially want to work as a *nakai*. Like her coworkers, circumstances beyond her control gave her few options. She may have been still living at home with her husband, but she was also stuck in the ryokan.

### The Hospitality Dividend

Ryokan like Yamazakura and Kagaya did not create the conditions that pushed so many women into the open arms of the industry. They didn't make it normal for women in Japan to abandon their careers to raise a child, which kept them out of paid employment and financially dependent on their husbands for so many years. Ryokan didn't create the expectation that the home should be the center of a woman's world, leading those who eventually return to paid employment to choose a job close to home over one that utilized their skills and expertise. Ryokan didn't create an employment environment in which women past a certain age are discriminated against in hiring and retainment, leading to fewer work options in their thirties and beyond. Ryokan didn't make Japanese men feel justified leaving most of the physical and emotional labor of the home to women, and they didn't make it common for divorced and separated women to leave their homes. They did not create a society that pushes single mothers to the margins and leaves them desperately few options.

Japan's ryokan did not create the conditions that drove so many *nakai* to the margins and into a job that was never part of the plan. However, they welcomed these women with open arms and reaped a "hospitality dividend" by employing them. These women who have fallen through the cracks and been made precarious by Japanese society largely self-recruit, often require little training, and tend to not complain about the work, due to the gratitude they feel toward their *okami*. The *okami* answered the *nakai*'s phone call in the middle of the night, interviewed her, and provided a job and a place to live in a time of need. "I would never work elsewhere," said Suzuki. "*Okami*-san is like a god (*kamisama mitai*). She has helped me so much. I returned to my husband several times, but he treats me badly every time, and I come back. I simply call, and *Okami*-san invites me back to work." In a world where they lack a place to call home, the ryokan provided these women a last resort.

From the perspective of our guests, all the women at Yamazakura—free from the responsibilities of home and alike in their hard-luck paths to the ryokan—worked together smoothly. Every room looked spotless. Every dish arrived on time. Every need was anticipated and cared for. Given their shared marginalization in Japanese society, one might think the *nakai* at Yamazakura would support each other both in the workplace and beyond. But behind the scenes, rivalries simmered for years and backbiting was rampant. Anyone gone for the day was fair game for gossip ("I don't think she ever leaves her [dormitory] room. She just sits and smokes all day."), joyful mockery ("Why is it so quiet and peaceful today? I wonder why, I wonder why? Could it be because so-and-so is gone today?"), and speculation ("I wonder where she goes on her day off? She leaves the dorm early in the morning and doesn't return until late at night").

This disconnect between a public façade of seamless cooperation and the backstage reality of personal grudges and petty gossip is not unusual in any ryokan, or any workplace for that matter. The backstage tensions at Yamazakura were interesting not because they took place in the otherwise relaxing and rejuvenating space of the ryokan, but because they stemmed from contrasting beliefs about how to mobilize hospitality.

# Chapter 8

# Professional Care?

Yamazakura was eerily quiet. It was 11:00 a.m., and the inn should have been buzzing. My wife and I stepped into the lobby expecting to hear vacuums rolling on *tatami* mats and the thump-thump-thumping of slippers hurrying across wooden floors. It was my favorite time of the day, when everyone paused the quiet and subdued performance that was necessary in front of guests, and instead just worked. During my short research visit in 2004, I had grown to love the messy process of resetting the ryokan for each day's new slate of guests. It was one of the reasons I wanted to return, to do this backstage work and experience the rhythms of the ryokan for a longer period.

But first I needed a uniform. Only then would I legitimately belong behind the scenes in the ryokan. Before I learned about the responsibilities and burdens of ryokan owners (chapter 4) and their children (chapter 5), or the daily routines (chapter 6) or life stories of the *nakai* who became my coworkers and friends (chapter 7), I needed to sort out some details, like when to start, where to stay, and what to wear. So, in late July 2006, we returned to Yamazakura well after the final guest would have checked out, only to find the inn quiet.

A voice called from behind the front desk, "*Irasshaimase!*" It was the polite "welcome" used by all businesses to greet visitors and potential customers. "Are you here to take a—oh, you surprised me!" Akahoshi's head had popped up from behind the desk. She smiled and laughed. "I didn't recognize you right away! I thought you were guests here to take a bath." Then she corrected herself, this time using the welcome usually reserved for family members arriving home: "*Okaerinasai!*" Akahoshi had grown up nearby and worked the front desk for more than five years. She recognized us immediately. Turning toward the back office, she called, "*Okami*-san, Chris and Hisako are here!"

"What? Who is it?" *Okami*-san asked, waving aside the short curtain that separated her office from the front desk area and stepping toward us. "Oh! You're finally here! Welcome!" She swept into the lobby, radiating a smile that had sent off countless satisfied guests over the years. We felt genuinely welcome. I corresponded with her husband during the previous year to arrange my research and called when we reached Kumamoto a few weeks before. I was pleased to finally enter the lobby and see *Okami*-san's smile.

We talked briefly about our families and our health, then sorted out the details of our stay. Eventually I asked what had been bothering me. "Why is it so quiet today? Where is everyone?"

"In a few months we will host a very important guest. Everything must be perfect. So we hired a hospitality expert to provide training sessions (*kenshū*). Everyone has to attend, even the head chef," she added with a hint of embarrassment, as if the chef were above professionalization. She motioned to the dining room and invited me to peek in from the hall. Outside the doors I found two perfectly straight rows of colorful slippers—a hodgepodge of colors and sizes that clearly belonged to the nearly twenty staff members who worked in Yamazakura's guestrooms, front desk, kitchen, and parking lot. Between these was a small space, an unobstructed path with a single pair of guest slippers. These clearly belonged to the expert. The staff had literally made way for their guest, as though demonstrating to him their preexisting knowledge.

Through a sliver between the doors I glimpsed a small bald man seated at the front of the room. He spoke uninterrupted. The women—*nakai*, front desk staff, and cooks—sat attentively on their heels and took notes. They acted as if they were absorbing his every word, and he looked pleased to oblige. Even the men—chefs and drivers—sat quietly, appearing to pay attention.

I had not yet officially begun my research and one of my central understandings about the ryokan was falling apart. I had not yet heard of formal hospitality training at a small family inn like Yamazakura. Two years before, the *nakai* here told me their only training consisted of a few days of working alongside a coworker, followed by the occasional correction of a mistake. That was enough. After all, as Eguchi and Suzuki explained, they were not professionals. They were just women doing womanly things: serving, cleaning, caring.

Today's training session sparked many questions: Had the quality of service declined, and did Yamazakura's staff really need professionalization, or did this special guest require service they could not provide? If the model for ryokan hospitality was supposed to be the *okami* (chapter 4), would an outside "expert" undermine her authority? More broadly, might this *kenshū* signal recognition of the ryokan's physical and emotional labor as professional skills?

I could not stay long. We had to run more errands before moving to this tiny village. Plus, I felt awkward eavesdropping at the door. I was certain my new colleagues would tell me everything they learned when I started a few days later, given their undivided attention and the importance of this event to *Okami*-san.

On my first day of work I washed a mountain of breakfast dishes before joining the *nakai* and female cooks in the dining room for the first of many morning tea breaks. My lower back was already sore from an hour spent hunched over the sink. All I wanted was to lie on the inviting *tatami* floor for the twenty minutes that remained of the break, but I decided to ask Eguchi what she learned at the *kenshū*.

"Nothing," she said with a wave of her hand. "It was a waste of time and money" (*jikan to okane wo mottainai*).

Takahashi added, "He only told us things we already knew."

"*Okami*-san is excited about him and the *kenshū* right now," Eguchi continued, "but she will forget all about him and his advice in few months." The others seemed to agree.

Shimada later confessed, "He was no one special, just some old guy (*tada no ojisan*). Thanks to him we probably will not receive any bonus this year."

"We're all veterans," Suzuki insisted. "*Okami*-san has never organized a *kenshū* before. Why start now? Just because of the VIP? I don't understand it at all."

I was surprised by their reactions, especially since the *nakai* had given the expert their undivided attention during the *kenshū*. In hindsight, they had been the perfect hosts: making him feel welcome, regardless of their feelings. Most of the *nakai* were surprised and even insulted by the *kenshū*. Why had *Okami* invited a man with no ryokan experience into their workplace, to tell them how to do their jobs?

In this chapter I explore these reactions through our preparations for the visit of our VIP guest and its aftermath. More generally, I explore tensions among *okami* and *nakai* around Kurokawa regarding the professionalization of hospitality. Some valued it, while others thought it undermined the very soul of the ryokan. As I show, these tensions surrounded more than hospitality. They struck at the heart of what it means to be a working woman in Japan today.

### Mobilizing Hospitality

As I have repeatedly mentioned in this book, Kurokawa's ryokan owners need to mobilize hospitality to succeed. The popularity of each family business has outstripped the family's ability to care for its guests, therefore all of Kurokawa's ryokan have hired non-family employees. However, how each *okami* mobilized her staff differed, based on personal preference and her feelings about the professionalization of hospitality.

For some *okami,* mobilizing hospitality simply meant hiring enough women to do the work in her place. They believed that women, and Japanese women in particular, were "naturally" (*shizen ni*) adept at caring for the physical and emotional needs of others. Therefore, nearly any woman would do. Ideally, she had been a wife or mother, experience that would have reinforced society's expectations that women should care for others and put their own needs last. Importantly, these *okami* felt a *nakai* did not need any experience in the service industry, or a ryokan, nor did she need much training beyond basic advice about her posture or the patter she used when leading guests from the lobby to their room. Other things, like how to open and close a door, or how to gently place a dish on a table, could be learned from a colleague. But for the most part, these *okami,* which included Yamazakura's co-owner, trusted that a *nakai*'s instincts and experiences *as a woman* adequately prepared her to care for strangers.

In fact, some *okami* preferred *nakai* with no previous ryokan experience. As I explained in chapter 4, many people still believe each ryokan's "flavor" emanates from the personality, postures, and gestures of a single person: the *okami*. In this context, a *nakai*'s past work experience could become more than worthless; it could become an obstacle to adjusting to "the way" (*yarikata*) of the new inn. It is no wonder that many *nakai* told me the first advice they received when switching from one ryokan to another was to forget everything they had learned.

One *okami* solved this problem by hiring fresh high school graduates. She felt that like a young daughter-in-law, an inexperienced eighteen-year-old could be more easily molded in her image. As she doted on a pair of young employees in the lobby one afternoon, she praised how "clean" and "pure" (*kirei*) they were, since they had no work experience and no bad habits for her to break. Employees who had worked elsewhere always think they have a better way of doing things, so their experience gets in the way. "These two have cute, smiling faces, so they'll do fine," she explained, suggesting that their smiles indicated their malleability in her hands. "But it will take about three years to become good at their jobs," during which she will watch them like a hawk as they work with customers, and she corrects every mistake as soon as possible. For this *okami*, mobilizing hospitality required a hands-on approach, with her fully in charge of both the form and the training.

Both types of *okami*—those who hired mature *nakai* and trusted their socialization as Japanese women to maintain the inn's hospitality, and those who hired inexperienced *nakai* and trusted only themselves as trainers—saw little value in professional hospitality training like the *kenshū* at Yamazakura. They believed such events diluted the flavor of hospitality they were trying to produce. More importantly, professionalization undermined the spirit of the ryokan. They believed ryokan, especially those set in a *furusato* landscape like Kurokawa, should provide a warmer, less polished form of hospitality than that found on a Japan Airlines flight or at a hotel in Tokyo. In the eyes of these *okami*, and even some *nakai*, *kenshū* threatened to standardize hospitality and thus minimize the diversity of flavors found among ryokan. Professionalized hospitality just did not belong in a place like Kurokawa.

For other *okami*, mobilizing hospitality meant hiring experts to provide regular courses that would help their employees hone and build their skills. They thought that modeling the inn's hospitality on their personality was too old-fashioned. When they took over day-to-day management of the family business decades ago, they hired local women to work part-time during busy seasons, confident they would treat guests with appropriate hometown hospitality. However, as their inns became more popular and guest expectations increased, they felt that the lessons from their mothers-in-law or mothers were inadequate. So, they turned to outside experts.

These different ways of mobilizing hospitality around Kurokawa revealed a tension around professional development. Some *okami* believed in the value of professionalization and arranged regular training sessions for their employees. Some even convinced the Kurokawa Ryokan Association, the *kumiai*, to provide monthly sessions that any Kurokawa employee could attend at no cost. Other *okami* refused to organize such sessions and even preferred that their employees not attend the free *kumiai* sessions. *Nakai* were also split on the topic of professional development. Some enthusiastically attended these free *kumiai* sessions, relishing the opportunity for skills development and career growth, as well as the chance to make friends with employees at other inns. Other *nakai* considered the lessons a waste of time. This is important because it speaks to the ways different women valued, or devalued, their own labor, particularly in the space of the ryokan. The pending arrival of Yamazakura's VIP guest brought to light this tension surrounding professional development for both my *okami* and my colleagues.

### Ryokan Reform

I started working at Yamazakura precisely as it began preparing to host a very special guest. I thought I would have a front-row seat to the professionalization of ryokan hospitality and experience it myself. But as Eguchi made clear on my first day, Yamazakura was not about to undergo a hospitality revolution. In fact, as the weeks passed, and the event drew nearer, no one spoke of the training or the upcoming visit. And no one seemed to change their work habits in any discernible way. My coworkers were too busy caring for the guests in front of them each day to care about a single guest in what seemed like the distant future.

Yet all around us, the inn was being transformed. The owners repainted the building exterior and replaced part of the roof. They replaced all sixty *tatami* mats in the dining hall and refurbished the sliding doors in every room that would be used during the visit. They also purchased new dishes that would be used only on that day, plus new bedding and a one-of-a-kind *yukata* specially designed for the guest of honor. Aside from these infrastructure upgrades and special item purchases, *Okami* and *Shachō* hired a small team of specialists to advise them and record the event, including a photographer, a young female chef to help create the dinner menu, and a hospitality expert to hold training sessions. One colleague who had seen some of the receipts for these purchases guessed the preparations for this single night might cost the ryokan up to ten million yen, or nearly a hundred thousand US dollars. It was a massive investment that was consuming Yamazakura's owners, but it seemed completely absent from my colleagues' minds.

Near the end of August, I stopped by the front office to ask *Okami* about the upcoming visit. She explained how Yamazakura ended up in this unique position. A local public servant had called earlier in the summer, explaining that a VIP guest would attend an event in Kumamoto in October and wished to spend the night at a nearby hot springs. After three other ryokan declined the opportunity to host, Yamazakura got the call. *Okami* felt she could not refuse, not because of pressure from town hall, but because it would be a first for Yamazakura and a rare honor.

However, she was concerned. Yamazakura was known for its unpretentious *furusato* charm, which extended beyond its architecture to its hospitality. *Okami* was proud of this fact. She had purposefully hired a team of mature women whom she believed could provide hospitality that suited this area and matched her personality, and she had never felt the need to organize hospitality training sessions. The women learned from each other and seemed to excel at their jobs. The ryokan's incredible success over the decades was sufficient evidence of the value of their hospitality. However, Ogawa-san, an acquaintance of *Shachō* who learned of the VIP visit, sowed doubt in her mind. What did they know about hosting such an elite guest? Yamazakura's easygoing rural hospitality might be deemed inadequate, or even rude. *Okami* did not want to bring shame on the family business, the rest of Kurokawa, or the village of Minami-Oguni, so she and *Shachō* began their reforms. The usual gendered division of labor applied: *Shachō* was responsible for how the ryokan looked, while *Okami* was responsible for reforming how the ryokan felt. This included hiring an expert to "skill up" her *nakai* for the big day.

Why couldn't *Okami* do it herself? With a guilty glance at the floor, she said she was too nice (*yasashisugiru*) to her staff to demand they make the necessary changes, such as using more humble language or enunciating their words. Being nice was useful at times, especially when *Okami* needed to ask her employees to work on their scheduled day off. But it made her appear weak in the eyes of her employees. She needed to hire an outside expert to do what she could not.

### The Second *Kenshū*

The second *kenshū* took place in early September, exactly one month between the first session and the VIP visit. It was held on a weekday morning at 10:00, when we would normally start cleaning guestrooms. Instead, we had to sacrifice our afternoon break and clean after lunch. This already irritated some coworkers. Then they learned that unlike the first *kenshū*, which demanded everyone attend, the second *kenshū* would only be for the *nakai* and the front staff. "The men [drivers] need training more than we do!" exclaimed one *nakai* who thought all men were naturally less hospitable than women. After finishing the breakfast dishes, we skipped our morning tea break and prepared the dining room. We arranged three rows of tables to face a single table at the front of the room, where the expert would sit.

The speaker, Furukawa, began by reminding us of his credentials. He had worked over thirty years as a "hotel man," gradually moving from bellhop to manager, before starting his own service-focused consulting firm. While he had no experience working in a ryokan, that did not seem to matter. He was being paid to raise the quality of our hospitality, which to him meant introducing a more standardized (read: hotel) form of hospitality into ryokan space. The idea that each ryokan had its own unique flavor, or that the ryokan was appealing precisely because it featured a more homely form of hospitality, did not seem to concern him.

Next, Furukawa led exercises to standardize our greetings. We took turns reciting phrases of welcome, understanding, and apology, which he called the "Seven Major Hospitality Phrases" (*sekkyaku nana daiyōgo*) (see below). We repeated them as a group and individually, until he was satisfied. Then we stood in two lines and practiced smiling, reciting these phrases, and bowing to one another. In trying to standardize our speech, I could sense the individuality of each *nakai* being replaced with an almost robotic voice. Komura-san, our oldest *nakai*, struggled to enunciate her words, blaming her uneven teeth. Several *nakai* who had grown up in the area had to train themselves to avoid using the local dialect. Furukawa aimed to "fix" all such unique qualities for the sake of standardization and professional development.

| | |
|---|---|
| *Irasshaimase* | Welcome |
| *Kashikomarimashita* | Yes (I understand / I will take care of it) |
| *Shōshō omachi kudasaimase* | Just a moment please |
| *Taihen omatase shimashita* | I'm sorry to have kept you waiting |
| *Shitsurei itashimasu* | Excuse me |
| *Mōshiwake gozaimasen* | I'm sorry / I apologize |
| *Arigatō gozaimashita* | Thank you very much |

Furukawa also provided spatial advice, like how to greet a guest in the hallway (always stop, step to the side, and bow slightly so they can pass) and how to properly approach and open a guestroom door. It was the first time I had learned some of these things, and it occurred to me that I could have used this sort of training in my first few days on the job. However, during the two-hour session Furukawa seemed intent on doing more than training the *nakai* to enunciate their words. He wanted to alter how they used their bodies as instruments of hospitality.

### Permanently Hospitable Bodies

*Nakai* spend hours each day engaged in physical and emotional labor: kneeling and standing as if on repeat, all while trying to "read the room," to determine whether their guests want someone to blend into the background, someone to play along with their racy jokes, or someone to tell them about the excellent pizza restaurant located nearby. A good *nakai* could be all of these when necessary, but she could not be "on" all the time. In front of guests, she could move quietly through the hallways and doorways, careful not to disturb a family argument or the laughter of a college reunion. She could be nearly invisible when necessary. But when we cleaned guestrooms each morning we moved differently through space. We walked quickly and loudly. We slid open doors and closets with a swift and satisfying single movement. We threw open the windows to try to get rid of the smell of tobacco and sometimes exclaimed loudly enough to attract colleagues when we found a particularly disgusting mess. It felt good to make some noise, to whack a *futon* in the sunlight and watch the dust rise and blow away.

Similarly, when the *nakai* returned from their afternoon break each day, they folded towels, organized dinner trays, filled containers with pickled plums, and other tasks to keep their hands busy, all while chatting about celebrities, local bargains, or recent memorable guests. Some carefully studied the daily list of guest names, memorizing each one and speculating on their relationships (family? married? dating? friends?) and why they were here (anniversary? birthday? company trip?). They smoked, gossiped, or told jokes to embarrass me; anything to delay putting on their *nakai* smile until necessary.[1] When the call finally came from the front desk, they could be ready in an instant. But it was only by distracting themselves with other things and by conserving their hospitable selves that they could welcome their guests in the lobby with genuine excitement.

In the *kenshū*, Furukawa proposed new routines to replace these tactics of physical and emotional conservation and release. He passed out a list of questions: "At the start of the day, do you begin with facial warmups? How many times a day do you look at yourself in the mirror? At the start of the day, are you carrying a notebook, pen, matches, and a small plastic bag?" He asked if we opened our mouths wide and did pronunciation exercises every day. Then he distributed a list of vocal exercises and tongue twisters that he suggested we keep in our uniforms so we could practice in our free moments throughout the day. In other words, instead of gossip in the pantry between courses or sneaking a cigarette next to the river, he suggested the *nakai* practice smiling in the mirror. He did not expect us to answer his questions or to discuss them with each other. The questions were simply a pedagogical device used to suggest a new mental and physical routine that would transform us to think and behave in a new way throughout the day. Furukawa's ultimate purpose seemed to be to standardize our hospitality by making us permanently hospitable bodies.

After the session, several *nakai* repeated their complaints from the first *kenshū*: it was a waste of time and money, plus they had more ryokan work experience than the so-called expert. Their complaints were also spatial: the attitudes, language, and manners Furukawa suggested did not belong in the ryokan. He was trying to change the way the *nakai* bowed, spoke, and interacted with guests, but he did not seem to understand that a ryokan was supposed to *feel* different from a hotel. It was supposed to feel more relaxed (*yawarakai*, lit. soft, flexible). It was supposed to feel more like home. The *nakai* complained because Furukawa was applying his experience *as a man* in the businesslike space of the hotel to their experiences *as women* in a space they considered more feminine and personal. Here, gender intersected with geography, as they often compared the physical and emotional work of caring for guests in the ryokan to caring for family members in the home. They were doing work that resembled their experiences as wives and mothers; work that they associated with domestic space and which they felt came naturally. Instead of perceiving the *kenshū* as a way to build employment skills, some of my colleagues saw it as a failed attempt to codify and standardize feelings and behaviors they thought should come naturally.

### The VIP Visit

The day of the VIP visit began with confusion and frustration. We were starved for information, including what time our guest would arrive. Of course, it was normal for us to not know when our guests would arrive, but we had enough experience to anticipate the general flow of a normal evening, and we knew how to kill time and conserve energy within that flow. Today was not normal.

During the breakfast rush we were told there would be a morning meeting at 11:00, during our usual cleaning time. But we did not know if we should begin cleaning, then stop for the meeting, or just wait until it began. Could we attend the meeting sweaty? What would Furukawa say, especially after reminding us to check our appearance in the mirror all day? During our 9:30 tea break, we heard the meeting might begin earlier, so we delayed cleaning. As we waited in the dining room, *Okami* suddenly popped in and out. Then, *Shachō* and Furukawa entered and everyone cleared a space at the front of the room. *Shachō* opened the meeting by thanking us for our hard work. It was the first time I had heard him address the entire staff in the two months since I arrived. Then Furukawa took over. He thanked us and said we would make history today. "You're probably all very nervous, because out of twenty-four inns in Kurokawa, Yamazakura was chosen. The weather is beautiful and thanks to all the preparations, it will be a great day. As of tomorrow, this will be a new Yamazakura." Then he released us and asked us to prepare for rehearsal at 4:00.

Because of our delayed start, we finished cleaning around 1:15, then returned again at 3:00. However, after folding the towels we realized there was nothing to do. So we sat around and chatted in what felt like the most decadent and wasteful fashion. We were not even pretending to do work while killing time. Finally, at 4:00 we assembled in front of the inn, where Furukawa instructed the *nakai* and female cooks to form a line. I had only seen this kind of formal ryokan welcoming line on television, and it looked out of place in this *furusato* landscape. Furukawa directed the rehearsal, instructing *Shachō* what to say, how to walk, and where to stand. It was uncomfortable to watch our boss fumble through his lines, like a nervous schoolboy practicing a speech. When the car arrived, *Shachō* would step forward and greet our guest. We would bow as he introduced himself, giving his name and position as owner of the inn. Then he would invite the guest to follow him to the lobby to meet *Okami* and his parents (the former owners). *Shachō* was visibly nervous and lit a cigarette as soon as the rehearsal finished.

During the next few hours we tried to kill time constructively. Morita watered the paths for a second time. I swept spider webs in the garden. At 6:15 a white station wagon raced into the parking lot. It was the prefectural police, informing us the group would arrive in three minutes. At 6:20 five black cars arrived. Our guest of honor stepped out and gave a slight bow, before walking to the waiting line of *Shachō* and the staff. *Shachō* gave his brief introductions flawlessly, and once the formalities were finished, we all rushed inside to try to look busy. As we walked back to the kitchen one coworker told me under her breath that regular guests were better. They were far less trouble.

Dinner began at 7:10 in the dining room for our guest-of-honor and the small party of special guests. At the same time, a handful of others, including the security personnel, were served in their rooms. With fewer than ten guests, I had little to do. Before Takahashi served each course, I carefully passed the dish from the chef to the photographer, then to Takahashi. When Takahashi returned from the dining room I washed and dried each dish by hand, since we decided to avoid using the noisy automatic dishwasher. Plus, this special set of newly purchased dishes was too precious to trust to the machine.

At 8:30 p.m., Maeda, the former golf caddy and lead *nakai* at Yamazakura, asked me to help her prepare the guest bedding. Time was moving at a glacial pace, so I was happy to be occupied with a new task. As we went through our paces, I noticed she was visibly upset. The slightest prompt revealed the reason. For weeks she believed she would have the honor of serving dinner. After all, she was the head *nakai*. However, just this morning *Okami* gave the responsibility to Takahashi, the *nakai* who had worked her way out of her family's debt. As we laid out the bedding in the room of Ogawa, *Shachō*'s acquaintance and the mastermind behind this VIP visit, Maeda wondered if he had changed *Okami*'s mind. Maeda said she looked forward to the day when Ogawa would no longer interfere at Yamazakura. She tried to estimate the expense of hiring him to advise on this event, including his free night's stay, but she stopped midway, too angry to complete her calculations. Maeda even blamed Ogawa for her lack of summer bonus, since his plan led to the hiring of the hospitality expert, a photographer, and more. She said she could almost imagine her money going directly into his pocket. It was the most upset I had seen her, and it was completely out of character. This day was turning out to be unforgettable for the wrong reasons.

We ended work well past 10:00 p.m. On the ride home, our driver Sakamoto estimated we had worked over fourteen hours, with no overtime pay and a shorter break than usual. The biggest insult of the night, though, was that the staff dinner consisted of only a fried egg and a rice ball for each of us, which we all complained about for days. The next morning began earlier than normal, at 7:00 a.m., with the guests having an early breakfast, before departing by 9:00. As soon as the cars were out sight *Shachō* and Furukawa thanked us for our hard work and assured us a new day had dawned at Yamazakura.

Within a week, things had returned to normal. No one mentioned the *kenshū*, or what they had learned, or even the VIP visit. I saw no difference in how *nakai* spoke with guests or spent their breaks. I did not see anyone practicing their smiles in the mirror or carrying tongue-twisters in their pockets. In other words, Eguchi was correct: *Okami*'s enthusiasm for the outside expert was only temporary. Furukawa had already been forgotten.

**Learning the Basics**

While everyone seemed to be blocking Furukawa from their memory, I soon learned that the underlying tensions surrounding the professionalization of ryokan hospitality that surfaced in preparation for the VIP visit had been boiling beneath the surface at Yamazakura for years. The loudest complaints about Furukawa's *kenshū*, and professional development in general, had come from Eguchi and Suzuki. However, I had let these loud voices drown out the others. In fact, several *nakai* believed in the value of professional development and wanted more events like it.

I learned this from Maeda a few weeks after the VIP visit. Although she did not mention the visit itself, she told me about her own struggles to professionalize her colleagues since the day she arrived. At one point in our conversation about her path to the ryokan, Maeda described the training regimen she endured at another inn in Kurokawa. "First, I spent a month shadowing an experienced *nakai* (*senpai*). Then, my *senpai* tested to see if I was ready to work alone by pretending to be a guest, whom I led from the lobby to the room." Maeda said she practiced over and over until her *senpai* decided she was ready to work alone. I mentioned that this sounded very difficult, but she did not complain about the experience. In fact, she spoke of it fondly. She cherished the professionalization offered by her former employer and the professional crew she worked with. Management took these women seriously and helped them develop into skilled professionals.

When I asked how that experience compared to Yamazakura, she hesitated. "Sorry to start bad-mouthing," (*waruguchi ni narukedo gomen ne*), Maeda finally said, "but when I started I was told, 'when you're here, do things the Yamazakura way (*koko no yarikata*).' But this place doesn't have a way (*koko no yarikata wa nai to omou*). I thought the basics of the service industry were the same everywhere, so I was shocked when I got here." She continued, "The maids (*nakai*) here, they really don't understand the service industry (*koko no meidosan wa hontō no sābisugyō wo shiranai to omotteru*) [...] Some of them are old, but they still don't know the basics." As I soon learned, Maeda had been struggling to teach some of her colleagues "the basics" since she arrived at Yamazakura six years before.

Her first order of business was the bathrooms. "When I started working here, some people wiped the sink with a [clean] towel and then put it out for guests to use, without washing it!" she said with disgust. She thought a lack of proper equipment might be to blame. "There were no buckets for cleaning the bathrooms, so I told *Okami*, 'This is not right. Please buy buckets.'" Maeda got her buckets, but the request soon backfired. Maeda's colleagues resented the extra work she created for them. They suddenly needed to carry a bucket and additional cleaning supplies. This meant more trips back and forth between the linen closet and the rooms, and more time and energy spent cleaning. "From that point forward my seniors bullied me terribly and gave me a lot of busy work" (*sore kara monosugoku senpaitachi kara ijimerarete. iranai shigoto wo fuyasu natte*).

Despite the bullying, Maeda continued to suggest changes considered common at other ryokan where she had worked. To her they were "incredibly basic" (*konponteki na kihonteki*). The most basic was replacing the *futon* covers every day, instead of once a month or so, as Maeda claimed was common at Yamazakura when she arrived. Her coworkers had believed at the time that since ryokan guests slept in the (clean) *yukata* provided by the inn, and since most of their body would not actually touch the *futon* cover, the *nakai* did not need to change the cover each day. "But the cover's edge will get dirty," Maeda explained emphatically, "and it might smell like cigarette smoke." She couldn't hide her frustration as she recalled explaining something so "basic" to the others, some of whom were still her co-workers at Yamazakura. Eventually Maeda convinced *Okami* that they needed to change the covers every day. The laundry bill might increase, but *Okami* did not want to fall behind her Kurokawa peers. Maeda helped *Okami* keep pace. Unfortunately, the fallout for Maeda continued, as her coworkers complained behind the scenes about the extra work and held her responsible. "We fought all day, every day" (*mainichi mainichi asa kara kenka datta*).

Why did Maeda's colleagues respond with such "incredible friction" (*monosugoi masatsu ga atta*)? Maeda blamed their laziness, which she still saw in shortcuts used around the inn. For instance, she said, "These days when we clean the bathrooms, we are supposed to use a bucket [with cleaning solution] and a rag, right? But even now some people don't do that. They just use a [dirty] bath towel to wipe [the sink and mirror]." I had seen coworkers do this. It was a great way to save time, especially when it seemed guests hadn't even used the sink. But it was unsanitary, and not how Maeda (and by extension, *Okami*) instructed us to clean the bathrooms. I had witnessed some of these shortcuts, but I was sympathetic to my co-workers' resistance to any additional work. It seemed motivated less by laziness and more by their different positions in the company and their different beliefs about the professionalization of hospitality.

### Part-time Power

Maeda and her coworkers stood on different sides of an employment divide that justified both Maeda's self-sacrifice and her coworkers' self-preservation. As the only *nakai* who was a full-time regular employee, Maeda was supposed to put the company first. She earned a monthly salary, a summer and winter bonus, plus benefits like insurance and a pension. Like any full-time regular employee around the country, male or female, she was expected to devote her time and energy to the company and make sacrifices for it, like she did in her first accounting job. The other *nakai* were all part-timers. They earned a daily wage (about $80 a day for ten to twelve hours of work) and no benefits. Most considered the pay fair, but no one wanted to squeeze more work into an already long and exhausting day.

A permanent full-time position might seem appealing for someone lacking the financial support of a spouse, which was the case for all but one of my *nakai* coworkers. However, many told me they preferred to remain part-timers working a full-time schedule. Eguchi, another long-time *nakai* at Yamazakura, explained why. Like Nishihara and Maeda, she had divorced and never remarried. She was married only six years before being left with two children to raise on her own, in a tiny house rented from a neighboring village. Over the years she had worked a variety of part-time jobs to make ends meet, including as a seamstress, which allowed her to work at home while caring for her children. But as her customers gradually bought more clothes in stores and had fewer things made and mended, the work dried up, leaving her in search of more steady work. She heard from friends that Kurokawa's inns were often short-handed, so she tried her hand as a *nakai*. Her children had left home, and there were few other options for a woman in her forties or fifties with a high school education and no real career. Eguchi lacked experience, but that did not matter to the *okami* at Yamazakura. A nice smile and a pleasant personality were enough.

By the time we spoke in 2006 Eguchi had been at Yamazakura for over ten years. In addition to cleaning rooms together, we commuted together each morning in the company van, since Eguchi lacked a driver's license. She could have stayed in the dormitory, but she wanted her privacy and a clear separation between work and home. She had been offered a full-time position, but she preferred to remain a part-timer. When I asked why, she explained matter-of-factly that working part-time gave her complete control over both her time and her commitment to the job. A part-time *nakai* in a busy inn like Yamazakura could work as much or as little as she wanted, up to sixty hours a week, twenty-five days or more a month. Since inns were often short-handed, a *nakai* willing to work so much without expecting full-time status would be doing their *okami* a personal favor. At the same time, a part-timer could request nearly any day off in advance, sometimes even major holidays like New Years, without concern for how her absence might impact those left behind.

If *Okami* begged Eguchi to work an extra day, or to cover for a sick coworker at the last minute, Eguchi had the power to decide. Accept, and *Okami* owed her a favor. Refuse, and *Okami* understood. *Okami* could not expect as much sacrifice and commitment from a part-timer as from a permanent employee like Maeda. Here, Eguchi used the inherent vulnerability of her position (part-time vs. full-time) to her advantage. Maeda, on the other hand, saw this as evidence of Eguchi's laziness and lack of professionalization. Of course, Maeda understood that companies expected different levels of commitment from part-timers and permanent employees, but that didn't prevent Maeda from negatively judging Eguchi.

The different positions of employees on the full-time/part-time divide also extended to daily breaks. Part-timers were more protective of theirs, while Maeda willingly sacrificed hers. This was most obvious around lunch. On a typical day, the rest of us finished cleaning and prepping our rooms at around the same time. Then we sat around a stainless-steel island in the kitchen and ate together, sharing dishes served family style in the middle of the table. Maeda sometimes bustled through, complaining about some small task that she simply *must* complete before she could join us. No one told her to stop and eat, or to not worry about it, as they often did to a part-timer. After all, if Maeda wanted to make such sacrifices, why would anyone question her? As a regular employee, she *should* make sacrifices. She *should* have a fuzzier boundary between work time and rest time. Her dramatic displays of concern for her guests may have been designed to inspire the rest of us to aim for what she considered a higher standard of hospitality, but it only highlighted the structural gulf between the expectations and responsibilities of part-time and full-time employees. We did not consider ourselves lazy. We cared as much for our guests as she did, and we worked just as hard as she during working hours. But as part-timers we knew the limits of what the ryokan should, and could, expect of us. If that meant more work for Maeda, that was her fate as a permanent employee.

Plus, Maeda admitted she wanted to work as much as possible. The alternative was returning to an empty dorm room. Working through the afternoon break made sense for her, but not for Suzuki, who treasured her afternoon nap, or Eguchi, who took a walk most afternoons and rushed home at night to watch Korean television dramas. Takahashi, the rare *nakai* who had married a local and called Kurokawa home, spent most afternoons in her garden. None of these women wanted to work any longer, or any harder, than necessary. When Maeda first arrived at Yamazakura and suggested ways to professionalize their service, they interpreted this as more work for the same pay. The result for Maeda was "incredible friction" from several colleagues that began in 2000 and was still simmering during my most recent visit in 2019.

### Upsetting the Hierarchy

At a more fundamental level, Maeda's suggestions upon her arrival set her on a collision course with two powerful social norms in Japan. First, Maeda failed to respect the company hierarchy. When referring to the *nakai* who were at Yamazakura when she arrived, Maeda called them her "seniors" (*senpaitachi*). This term seemed to acknowledge Maeda's subordinate position in the workplace. Just as a new bride enters a household subordinate to her mother-in-law and gradually learns the family's taste, a new *nakai*, regardless of her age or work experience, is supposed to enter a ryokan subordinate to everyone else and learn the ryokan's flavor from the *senpai*. Maeda upset this hierarchy the moment she asked *Okami* directly to purchase buckets and instructed her *senpai* how to clean the bathrooms. She felt justified doing so because of what she considered her *senpai*'s lack of professionalism. Regardless of the value of her advice, some of her new coworkers resented her for overstepping her boundaries and have held that grudge for years.

Maeda's second transgression of social norms had everything to do with the space in which she undermined this hierarchy. In simplest terms, Maeda presumed to tell a woman how to manage her home. The gendered geography of home in Japan pressures women to accept responsibility for most of its physical and emotional labor. However, home is not simply a trap for women, since they control nearly everything associated with it.[2] They control the budget, which includes paying the bills and purchasing nearly every item inside the home, from groceries to furniture. They control the scheduling and organization of household routines, from meals to baths. And they control when and how to clean the home, from laundry to vacuuming. A wife and mother takes this responsibility so seriously that questioning how a woman manages her home can seem to question her place in the world. Magazines, websites, and television programs abound with cooking, cleaning, and organizing ideas. But no one, with the exception of a mother or mother-in-law, would dare give a woman unsolicited advice on how to run her home.

This is what Maeda did when she told *Okami* to buy buckets and change the *futon* covers every day. And she continued to transgress this norm when she told her new coworkers how to clean and prepare their guestrooms. My coworkers felt responsible for the emotional and physical comfort of their guests, and they did not want anyone to interfere with their process. *Okami* might establish the flavor of hospitality, but the *nakai* were on the front lines translating that flavor into reality. They were telling the joke, asking the questions, pouring the tea, and laying out the *futon*. They wanted full control over that encounter.

More to the point, Maeda sought to professionalize work that many of her coworkers believed was either not work, or at least not *skilled* work. Many *nakai* agreed with those *okami* who believed hospitality is something that comes naturally to women, and therefore cannot—even *should not*—be standardized or professionalized. Their hospitality resembles the everyday unpaid caring work done by a wife and mother in the home; therefore, mobilizing hospitality simply means being a woman. Instead of seeing hospitality training events as opportunities for skill development, such women saw attempts at professionalization as the systematic devaluation of their natural attributes. It signaled a shift in understanding hospitality as something genuine and inseparable from the self, to something anyone could learn through a few sessions with an "expert" like Furukawa or the advice of an upstart like Maeda. When Maeda arrived at Yamazakura, she openly trampled on several Japanese social norms, making it understandable that some of her coworkers pushed back and made her life difficult for years.

### The Puzzle of Perseverance

Why did Maeda stay at Yamazakura? Perhaps she feared gaining a reputation as unreliable or picky, which would damage her future job prospects. Maybe she was exaggerating the difficulties she encountered on arrival at Yamazakura in order to emphasize how much impact she had made. Or maybe she was trying to convince me that some of her coworkers, particularly Eguchi, were lazy; appealing to my fastidious nature in an attempt to turn me against them. Maeda and Eguchi had been rivals for years, both practicing the subtle art of nurturing cliques and exchanging favors behind the scenes, out of view of both guests and *Okami*. Such alliances were useful for trading vacation days or getting help carrying heavy trays of empty dishes back to the kitchen on a busy evening. Maeda may have been trying to solidify my allegiance to her by agreeing to participate in my research and highlighting Eguchi's lax hospitality.

Or perhaps Maeda persevered at Yamazakura because she relished the challenge of professionalizing colleagues like Eguchi. Like the adding machine at her first job, Maeda may have wanted to master the far more complex machinery of the ryokan's social world. Quitting would have meant defeat, something difficult to accept for someone as proud as Maeda. Plus, she had the support of *Okami*, who seemed to have hired her precisely to introduce professional practices she learned in her orientation and monthly training sessions at her previous inn. Maeda could help Yamazakura keep up in the hospitality race. In rare cases, *okami* who want to radically improve the quality of their staff fire everyone and rebuild their team from scratch. But this is an extreme option that obliterates years, or even decades, of social relations between ryokan owners and employees, some of whom were hired by a previous *okami*. At Yamazakura it seemed that *Okami* trusted Maeda to reform her colleagues and professionalize their hospitality. This gave Maeda an unusual amount of power for a new *nakai*, which fostered resentment in some of her colleagues.

Whatever the reason, Maeda stayed, and despite her continued rivalry with Eguchi, she considers her time at Yamazakura a success. She implemented significant changes, helped raise the inn's reputation, and trained many of the newer *nakai*. She has a permanent position and excels at her job. But that does not make her feel any less vulnerable.

Most ryokan are small family businesses that depend on that notoriously unpredictable customer: the tourist. A natural disaster or too many poor reviews might force owners to reduce staff. Under such circumstances, Yamazakura's owners would have little choice but to gradually fire their staff and run the inn themselves, like ryokan owners in nearby Tsuetate (chapter 4). Yamazakura's owners could not endlessly absorb losses, as some Japanese corporations seem to do in order to protect their core of male regular employees. So even Maeda knows her position is precarious. She knows that every day her boss could simply say, "Don't come in tomorrow." Indeed, despite their very different attitudes about the skills associated with their jobs, Maeda and her part-time coworkers shared the same sense of precariousness when it came to the future.

### A Domestic Trap

Many of the *nakai* I worked with at Yamazakura, as well as those I knew at other inns, fell into what I consider a "domestic trap." Like Maeda when she quit her first job, they accepted the notion—widespread in Japan and elsewhere around the world—that a woman's primary place should be in the home. Therefore, they left paid employment as young women and failed to learn the kinds of hard skills that might have helped them secure better jobs after they separated from or divorced their husbands. When these *nakai* were offered the opportunity for professional development through hospitality training, many of them resisted the notion that empathy, politeness, attention to detail, and other keys to their job could be considered skills. They devalued their labor by claiming anyone (any *woman*) could do it. By extension, they acknowledged they were replaceable.

To be certain, leaving home liberated some *nakai* from its limitations, expectations, and dangers. The ryokan offered a safe haven (Kitano called the ryokan a *kakekomidera* in the prologue) when they had "no place to go." The ryokan helped many *nakai* avoid homelessness or the humiliation of imposing on an adult child or a distant relative. However, any sense of emancipation through ryokan work was tempered by her lack of other suitable options. There was nothing glamorous about the position of *nakai*. It was largely devalued in society because it was considered unskilled "women's work," and it had little potential for career advancement. Seniority often does not lead to increased pay or responsibility. Eguchi, the proud part-timer, worked over fifteen years at Yamazakura without a raise. Her employment coincided with Japan's era of economic stagnation from the mid-1990s onward, but if she had been a male full-time regular employee during the same period, she would have enjoyed regular pay increases and bonuses, plus potentially several promotions. Despite the lack of any economic gains or career growth, Eguchi remained loyal to Yamazakura for other reasons: she had the owners' trust and an established position in the employee hierarchy. Moving elsewhere would have meant nearly the same pay and work conditions, plus demotion to the bottom of the pecking order and the stress that comes with being corrected for not knowing the flavor of the ryokan. Under these circumstances, *nakai* become stuck in this "domestic trap," partially by choice, through a desire to remain in one inn, and partially because of the devaluation of their labor in Japanese society as "women's work."

### How Will It End?

There is no retirement age for a *nakai*. She works until she is no longer able, or no longer needed. Even *nakai* with twenty years of experience at a single inn know their loyalty is meaningless if they cannot climb the stairs or if customers stop making reservations. When we last worked together in 2007, Maeda was already in her early sixties and acknowledged that ten to twelve hours a day on her feet was exhausting. I was in my thirties and agreed wholeheartedly. She said that some days her nightly soak in the inn's hot springs was the only thing that kept her moving. She often worried what would happen when she could no longer carry the trays of food, operate the cumbersome vacuum cleaner, and maintain the energy required to serve guests with a smile.

What does a *nakai* do when she is no longer useful? How will this end for Maeda? Where will she go? What will she do? "My daughter is single and wants me to move in with her. She says I work too hard and should retire, but once I quit what will I do all day? If I stop moving, my body and mind might stop working." Indeed, other mature *nakai* constantly worried about how to avoid weak joints, broken bones, and dementia, any of which would threaten their ability to keep working. At the same time, they praised the job for keeping them active. They all had stories of former colleagues and acquaintances who quit working and quickly declined in physical and mental health. These tales served as constant reminders of how fortunate elderly *nakai* in particular were to still earn a living and be valued in a country that economically devalues caring labor overall. "Without work I would go crazy," one said. "Once you stop working, your body and mind will go," said another.

Most *nakai* lived a fine line between job security and insecurity. They knew that as long as the inn remained busy, they were safe, since there were no potential replacements waiting in the lobby. Plus, the *okami* was too busy, or too lazy in the eyes of some employees, to care for guests herself. However, they also knew that once their bodies slowed down too much, they could easily be let go. With rare exceptions, though, most *nakai* did not see professional development as useful to their job security. Instead, they continued to devalue the physical and emotional labor of hospitality by considering it "women's work" that could not, and even *should* not, be profession-alized. In an industry where many business owners believe the flavor of hospitality should be modeled after a particular woman, or believe that all Japanese women are naturally capable of the physical and emotional labor of caring for strangers, no amount of professional development will help a *nakai* feel more secure as the body and face of Japanese hospitality.

## Chapter 9

# Policing Ryokan Space

The period from New Year's to mid-March was cold and lean. It is one of the slowest times of the year at ryokan throughout Japan, with some inns closing for days. Yamazakura never closed during this period due to a lack of guests, but a handful of empty rooms always meant at least one fewer *nakai* on the schedule. This put *Okami* in an awkward position. How do you give everyone enough work to maintain their livelihood, while not wasting money on unnecessary staff? Eguchi, the long-term part-timer, came to the rescue again. Just as she did *Okami* a favor by working extra during busy periods, she worked fewer days during the lean months. She used the opportunity to spend more time with her grandchildren. Komura, the oldest *nakai,* visited her son in Oita. Another *nakai* essentially hibernated in the dormitory, waiting for the front desk to call. I was glad to work less. I used the time to volunteer at other inns, attend training sessions held by the Ryokan Association, and interview employees and *okami* around Kurokawa.

I worked at Yamazakura on weekends, which were still fully booked, and on days when we hosted foreign guests. Because of the slower pace I could devote my undivided attention to a family of four from Switzerland, a group of three couples from Singapore, and others. I had time to explain how to take a bath in Japan (if it was their first time), how to use the remote control for the wall-mounted electric heater, and where to find extra blankets. Of course, the lack of guests also made some days drag. The daily routine could still be unpredictable, but the interruptions came less frequently. The most effective way to make the day pass quickly was to mobilize hospitality—to spend as much time with guests as possible and anticipate their every need—instead of waiting for something to happen.

The winter months also meant working in the cold. We braved the cold winds and icy rain when we carried luggage, food, and clean-

164

ing supplies between buildings. Plus, we still cleaned guestrooms with the windows open, especially to air out the room of a smoker. Colleagues suggested wearing two or three pairs of socks while cleaning, but it was never enough. On particularly slow winter days, the cold seeped into my body early in the morning and clung to my bones until the moment I slid into the bath after 9:00 p.m. The contrast to the summer months was drastic. But which was worse: being understaffed, rushed, and hot, or overstaffed, bored, and cold?

The daylight hours lengthened and the temperatures rose, and by mid-March the national news was full of reports about cherry blossoms. In castle parks, along riversides, and on mountains throughout Japan, the blossoms appeared in a slow wave from Okinawa in the south to the island of Rebun at the northern tip of Hokkaido in May. Each year the blossoms beckon families, work colleagues, schoolchildren, and neighbors from their cozy homes and workplaces into the spring air, where they enjoy sunny afternoons and cool nights sitting on blue tarps sharing meals and drinks under the trees. It is a magical time. It is also when tourists return to Kurokawa in full force.

By the end of March, Yamazakura was back to capacity, bringing with it the stress of too much work and too few employees. I had regularly worked weekends and several days each week to replace a driver or to help prepare and wash dishes for a large lunchtime group. So it was unusual when I took off a Sunday in early April to meet someone in Kurokawa for lunch and an interview. I had been waiting some time for this chance and did not want to miss it. On the way home the night before, I told Sakamoto about my planned day off, and he offered to let me ride in the company van. It would save me the trouble of driving, and I could write at Yamazakura before my meeting.

I arrived with the rest of the commuters around 7:30, then settled into an empty storage shed to write. By 9:45 I needed a break, so I decided to join my colleagues for their morning tea. As I slid open the door to the dining room, I overheard someone complaining about the current staff shortage, the upcoming Golden Week holidays, and the fact that the inn owners did not seem to be actively recruiting.

"Good morning," I said, stepping into the room. Several women replied unenthusiastically, without the vibrancy they used in front of guests. It was a tactic for conserving energy that I understood well. Eguchi and a few more *nakai* sat at the low table. Takahashi handed out sweets she had received as a tip. Three other women lay on the floor with their eyes closed, recharging before cleaning rooms.

I sat in my usual spot at the far end of the table, and Eguchi passed me a cup of tea. "How's the studying?" she asked. We had ridden together in the morning, so she knew my plan for the day. "It's fine," I replied with a tired smile.

Suddenly Komura, our oldest *nakai*, looked up from the day's schedule and breathed a sigh of relief. "Ahh, Chris, I'm glad you're here. You can clean the second floor with me." Then her smile vanished. "Where's your uniform?"

"Actually..." Guilt slowed my reply, "I'm not here to work today. I'm studying."

"What?!" she snapped. "Why are you here if you're not working? If you're not working, I don't want to see you. You shouldn't be here. That's rude!" Then she rose, left the room, and did not return for the rest of the break.

I was speechless. Komura and I had frequently worked together, and she had shared much about her life. She had told me about her husband's unexpected death in his thirties, and the difficulties she faced raising two sons on her own. She had told me about her work history, which included decades as a cleaner at her town hall and positions in hotels and ryokan. She had asked me about my life, and I had revealed all: my complicated family of siblings, step-siblings, and half-siblings, my relationship with my wife and our struggles to have children. She had openly expressed disappointment with Yamazakura's management, and she had complained about coworkers. I thought we had become close colleagues—friends even. Months of trust and camaraderie seemed to disappear in an instant.

What had changed? Years before, when I first stepped into the ryokan and tried to study it by simply watching *nakai*, I only got in their way. I was an obstacle. Komura's reaction reminded me why I put on a uniform in the first place. Only two bodies belong in the ryokan: guests and hosts. If I made a reservation and checked in, Komura could relate to me *as a guest*. If I wore my uniform and worked, she could relate to me *as a fellow host*. On this day I was neither. In Komura's eyes, I was out of place. As a geographer, I took this rebuke personally. I had designed a research project that claimed to take work seriously, a project that aimed to show how much work went into producing this space of relaxation and rejuvenation. And I had spent months doing that exhausting and exhilarating work. In an instant, Komura made it clear that I still did not fully comprehend the complexities of the ryokan.

Komura taught me a valuable lesson about the geographies of ryokan work. Indeed, she policed the boundaries of the ryokan through her anger at my presence and her refusal to share the space with me any longer. Komura reminded me who belonged in this space and who did not. Her designation of me as out of place was not based on age, gender, nationality, marital status, sexuality, religion, education level, or any other attribute that might have marked my marginalization, privilege, or exclusion elsewhere. Instead, it was based on my role.

The ryokan is a space for mobilizing hospitality. Whether evoking an idyllic Japanese village through its landscape or providing intensely personal care associated with the mother, the ryokan is a space in which *hosts* make *guests* feel comfortable. On this day I was neither mobilizing hospitality, nor receiving it. Therefore, I did not belong.

In fact, Komura was not alone in policing different spaces in Kurokawa. Leaders policed the landscape, ensuring that it looked appropriately nostalgic and excluded any elements—including businesses deemed insufficiently local—they considered out of place. Men and women policed spaces and forms of work. Men belonged outside the ryokan, doing work like driving, gardening, making business decisions. Women belonged inside the ryokan, doing work like welcoming guests, serving food, cleaning rooms, and raising a successor. Even many tourists, both Japanese and non-Japanese, policed Kurokawa when expressing surprise at encountering me. On some level, they also thought I did not belong.

Such policing of space hints at the complex geographies running through this book, including the idea at its heart: mobilizing hospitality. Mobilizing hospitality provides a way to conceptualize how landscapes, social norms, Japanese culture, and bodies have been put to work to make strangers feel at home in Kurokawa.

Local business owners and residents have mobilized an idea—the *furusato*—along with its positive cultural associations, to counteract the economic and social devastation of rural depopulation found elsewhere. By populating and shaping the landscape, local business owners have attracted tourists drawn to this idyllic scene. They have even mobilized this national idea to heighten their own local credentials. By upholding landscape principles that perpetuate certain ideas about what a Japanese village should look like, even individuals who have married into local families have *become* local. And this work in turn has led their heirs to return from Japan's cities to take over the family businesses. Indeed, ryokan owners in Kurokawa have mobilized hospitality in a creative and powerful way to revitalize the local economy and population of this isolated hamlet that lies precariously, and contradictorily, at both the periphery and core of the nation.[1]

Within individual business, owners have mobilized powerful social norms located at the intersection of gender and geography. Specifically, Kurokawa's ryokan have mobilized hospitality by entrusting men with the care of ryokan exteriors and landscapes and by ensuring a woman is continually present in this pseudo-domestic space. Just as a Japanese mother and wife is expected to "be there" when her family members return home, ryokan *okami* do the physical and emotional labor that makes guests feel at home. And when the *okami* cannot be there for her guests, she mobilizes hospitality by hiring women to care for guests in her place.

Finally, employees mobilize hospitality by moving their bodies quickly and unobtrusively around the gardens, kitchen, and guestrooms of the ryokan, knowing they may be interrupted at any moment. They mobilize hospitality by making their labor invisible, particularly in their encounters with guests. After all, the finest hospitality requires a visible host who does not appear to be working at all. Ryokan work, and indeed all hospitality, involves giving guests the continuous impression of genuine care for their well-being and enjoyment of the interaction, even when other emotions lie just beneath the surface.[2] At no time was this clearer than when the front desk clerk, Tanaka, flipped an emotional switch, from concern for our founder's health to an enthusiastic welcome for a guest, in the scene that began this book.

At the same time, mobilizing hospitality through a face-to-face encounter with a guest creates one of the most exhilarating and affirming experiences anyone can hope for. Just as actors often praise live theatre over filmmaking, ryokan workers frequently told me that what they enjoy most about their job is the opportunity it gave them to meet and care for strangers. Every day holds the potential for meaningful encounters. Indeed, one of my closest friends in Kurokawa was a young male chef whose greatest complaint was that he never met a guest.[3] Isolated in the ryokan kitchen all day, he felt a kind of sensory deprivation because he could not watch guests as they consumed his cuisine, first with their eyes, then with their noses, and finally with their mouths. He felt that hearing his guests talk about the textures and tastes and watching their faces would make him a better chef. As some *nakai* told me, and as I experienced myself, having the privilege of sharing space with guests and receiving immediate, embodied positive feedback often made us feel as if we were not working at all.

But make no mistake, mobilizing hospitality is hard work. And its internal contradictions remind us again of the complex precarity of Japanese work that has been at the forefront of research on Japan for decades. In the preceding pages I have shown how precariousness is not limited to Japan's underclasses. Certainly, *nakai* in severe financial distress or escaping from an abusive husband fit everyone's image of a precarious worker. However, I have shown that even owners of family businesses with excellent reputations in a successful resort constantly struggle to maintain their status, service their financial debts, please their customers, and plan for the future. By focusing on how hospitality is mobilized across time—whether by the minute or the generation—and space—whether in the public-facing lobby or the darkest corners of the owner's quarters, the employee's dormitories, or the cramped pantries—I have tried to let readers feel the rhythms, constraints, and possibilities of ryokan work.

# Epilogue

**M**uch has changed in Kurokawa since the end of my intensive research in 2007. Some of my Yamaza-kura coworkers are still working, including Maeda and Eguchi; some have retired or moved on, like Suzuki and Sakamoto, the driver; and sadly, some have passed away, including Komura and Kazuko, my fellow dishwasher who once surprised me with a rousing rendition of the "Banana Boat Song" to help us cope with an unprecedented stack of dishes. Some of the young successors who were expected to take over their family businesses have finally done so; others are still waiting, partly because they have not yet married. And there is still a vacant lot where the Kurokawa Onsen Ai Ladies Hotel last stood in 2004.

While this book took longer than expected to complete, time and space away from the ryokan have given me a broader understanding of what constitutes the work necessary to create and maintain Kurokawa. During my intensive research period, I was focused on the daily routine of washing dishes, cleaning rooms, and folding towels. I was consumed by immediate concerns like the pain in my hands, back, and feet, as well as the frustration of abandonment by our bosses, who never seemed concerned about hiring more staff or assisting us on a particularly busy night. Anger and confusion pulsated through my fieldnotes, which captured the repetitive cycle of ryokan work experienced on the ground by me and my coworkers. However, that experience blinded me to the longer-term, generational obligations and planning done by ryokan owners and *okami* in particular. Only with time did I come to understand the risks and concerns they face, which I believe has helped me tell a more complex and comprehensive story about ryokan.

Over the past decade, I have returned to Kurokawa at least once a year, usually with a group of students from Singapore, where I teach. My students experience an overnight stay at a ryokan, and we meet some of the next generation of business leaders, who share their hopes for Kurokawa's future. This next generation of ryokan owners still considers mobilizing hospitality, by maintaining the *furusato* landscape and providing the best service possible, the only way to maintain the economic and social vitality of this tiny hamlet. However, each year the young owners find it more difficult to find employees. One reason is that the number of divorced women seeking work at ryokan in Kurokawa has decreased. Many ryokan have turned to dispatching companies that send workers on short-term contracts. However, the young owners admit that they struggle to attract younger employees to the ryokan industry. The problem is not a lack a qualifications or skills, since most businesses prefer to train staff themselves; it's a lack of willingness to endure the long, irregular hours, the high and low seasons, the demanding and sometimes rude guests, the physical and emotional strain, and the isolation of living in Kurokawa. As one owner told me, "Young people have the language skills and the IT skills, but they don't want to work very hard."

Over the years, an increasing number of ryokan have hired non-Japanese employees to fill the gap. This was rare in Kurokawa before 2010. During my research from 2006 to 2007, there was only one other non-Japanese person working in Kurokawa: a young man from China at the front desk of a small inn. The recent shift toward hiring non-Japanese staff members is due to both a lack of other sources of employees and an increase of non-Japanese guests. As Kurokawa has become known overseas through guidebooks like *Lonely Planet*, travel websites, social networking sites, and other online resources and reviews, the non-Japanese clientele has exploded. One ryokan owner told me that in 2018 nearly seventy percent of his guests were overseas visitors from places like Thailand, Taiwan, Singapore, Malaysia, Hong Kong, and South Korea, as well as places he had never heard of until recently, like Chile, Israel, and Argentina. In response to the large number of recent Chinese-speaking guests, he hired two native Chinese speakers. Such changes indicate that despite the fact that Kurokawa looks like a timeless Japanese rural village, behind the scenes it still provides the hallmark of hospitality: perceiving guests' needs and adjusting accordingly.

In the years and decades to come, Japan will face many challenges, including continued population decline and rural out-migration, a shrinking and aging workforce, and an increased reliance on foreign labor. As the state continues to push for more inbound tourists, both in general and through mega events like the 2019 Rugby World Cup, the (delayed) 2020 Summer Olympics and Paralympics, and the 2025 Osaka Expo, what will happen to Kurokawa and its ryokan? Will Kurokawa continue to be seen as a quintessentially Japanese village, and might this lead to the same overtourism experienced by Barcelona, Venice, and Kyoto in recent years? Will its inns continue to provide a distinctly Japanese form of hospitality, and if so, who will embody that hospitality? How will Kurokawa's business owners and employees continue to mobilize hospitality? I plan to keep returning to find out.

# Notes

**Prologue**

1. Kurokawa Onsen is the real name of the hot springs village where I conducted most of my research. However, I use pseudonyms for all businesses and individuals. I chose the name Yamazakura, which literally means "mountain cherry tree," to identify the ryokan where most of the research took place. In naming the inn, I follow conventional practice of including one or more elements of nature. Unfortunately, in a small resort like Kurokawa, no pseudonym can ensure anonymity among ryokan or ryokan owners. There are only a few dozen ryokan, and therefore, only a few dozen owners. Each ryokan's history is unique, and each ryokan owner's connection to Kurokawa, such as their path into Kurokawa through marriage, is unique. Some owners are public figures who have shared their stories in magazines or personal blogs. Therefore readers may recognize them regardless of pseudonym. However, I only share detailed biographies and direct quotes from owners who explicitly consented to my publishing their stories. I take additional care to protect the identities of ryokan employees, since their lives are often more precarious. I also received explicit written or verbal consent from all ryokan employees whose stories I share, but I changed minor details (like their exact age at the time of an interview or the number of years spent working at a particular inn) to further protect them. There are many more employees than owners in Kurokawa, making it more difficult to identify any individual worker. From the beginning of the project, I worried most about an employee being fired for a comment they made about their employer. Thankfully, enough time has passed and enough of my coworkers have moved on, that such retribution is no longer a concern.

2. Ryokan employees are referred to by a single family name, which appears on a name tag always worn in front of guests. This is usually one's family name, although some female workers may choose a different name, like a stage name. When directly addressing a coworker or talking about

them, we attached the honorific suffix "-san" (the equivalent of Mr. or Mrs.). Therefore, Tanaka was always Tanaka-san. The same was true of titles indicating one's role, such as President (*Shachō-san,* ryokan owner). Exceptions were rare, such as when two employees shared the same family name. The newer colleague's family name appeared on their name tag, but behind the scenes coworkers addressed them by their given name or a nickname. This could offer a constant reminder of their lower status in the workplace hierarchy, or promote a more familiar relationship, depending on the individual. For brevity, I have removed all suffixes throughout the book, except when rendering speech. For more on names in ryokan, see Yoshida, "Joking, Gender, Power, and Professionalism among Japanese Inn Workers."

3. Former Prime Minister Tanaka Kakuei's vision to "remodel" the archipelago and Japan Railways' campaign encouraging the Japanese to "Discover Japan," both dating from the early 1970s, are two examples. On the Tanaka plan, see Sargent, "Remodeling the Japanese Archipelago: The Tanaka Plan"; Tanaka, *Building a New Japan: a Plan for Remodeling the Japanese Archipelago.* On the Japan Railways campaign, see Ivy, *Discourses of the Vanishing: Modernity, Phantasm, Japan.*

4. See Robertson, "*Furusato* Japan: The Culture and Politics of Nostalgia." *Furusato* acquired newfound meaning following the triple disasters (earthquake, tsunami, nuclear accident) of 2011, since some residents may never be able to return home due to the meltdown at the Daiichi Nuclear Power Plant. See Gill, "This Spoiled Soil: Place, People and Community in an Irradiated Village in Fukushima Prefecture."

5. Tokunaga, *Kurokawa: The Story of Sustainable Development.* In an October 2020 email one ryokan owner shared that in 2019 Kurokawa hosted approximately 290,000 overnight guests and roughly three times as many day visitors. 2020 figures will undoubtedly be seriously impacted by Covid-19.

### Chapter 1: Retreat
Portions of this chapter appeared in an earlier form in McMorran, "Mobilities amid the Production of Fixities: Labor in a Japanese Inn."

*Epigraph.* Yado Okyakuya brochure.

1. See Edgington, *Reconstructing Kobe: The Geography of Crisis and Opportunity;* and Murakami, *Underground: The Tokyo Gas Attack and the Japanese Psyche.*

2. See Guichard-Anguis, "Japanese Inns (*Ryokan*) as Producers of Japanese Identity." See also Statler, *Japanese Inn.* For scholarship specifically on ryokan as a workplace, see Yoshida "Joking, Gender, Power, and

Professionalism among Japanese Inn Workers"; and Takahashi, "Omote-nashi to iu rōdō: onsen kankō ryokan no shigoto to jendā."

3. Ministry of Land, Infrastructure, Transport and Tourism, "Kankō ya shukuhaku gyō wo torimaku genjō oyobi kadai nado ni tsuite," 17.

4. Ibid., 17. It is too early to know how the coronavirus pandemic that emerged in 2020 might impact Japan's ryokan industry in the longer term, but the entire tourism industry has been affected by the collapse of inter-national arrivals to Japan, extended lockdowns, and the costs of training staff, securing protective gear, and renovating to ensure the safety of visitors and staff.

5. Japan National Tourism Organization, "Stay at an Upscale Japa-nese Inn: Have the Experience of a Lifetime!"

6. Japan Ryokan & Hotel Association, "What is Ryokan?"

7. Lonely Planet Publications, *Japan: A Travel Survival Kit*, 121.

8. See Clark, *Japan, A View from the Bath*, 66–87.

9. Examples include the ubiquitous Mapple and Walker series of guidebooks, which cover nearly all of Japan. In addition to regularly updated guidebooks on most cities and prefectures, publishers occasionally produce special series, like Mapple's *Shūkan Nihon no meiyu* (Japan's famous hot springs weekly), which ran from September 2003 to May 2004. Each week featured one of 30 hot springs resorts. Issue #2 was on Kurokawa. It devoted half a page to each inn, providing photographs and vivid descriptions of its exteriors, baths, and food, as well as information on the cost, number of rooms, and more. Mappuru, "Kurokawa Onsen."

10. See Japan Ryokan & Hotel Association, "Japan Ryokan and Hotel Association"; and Nihon Hitō wo Mamoru Kai, "Nihon hitō wo mamoru kai ni tsuite."

11. Television dramas include TBS, *Asakusa Fukumaru Ryokan*, and Fuji Terebi, *Watashi wo ryokan ni tsuretette*. The most notable work of fiction is Nobel Prize-winner Kawabata Yasunori's 1957 *Yukiguni* (Snow Country), which mostly occurs in a ryokan in Niigata Prefecture in the dead of winter.

12. The association between bathing and sex stretches back to at least the Edo period, when female bathing attendants (*yuna*) worked in public bath houses. The so-called *onsen* geisha (not to be confused with a profes-sional entertainer who has mastered traditional forms of musical perfor-mance) is a loosely related contemporary iteration of the *yuna*, and can still be found in some *onsen* ryokan. See Clark, *Japan, A View from the Bath*, 31–33, 91–93. For a comprehensive study of Japan's multilayered sex indus-try, see Koch, *Healing Labor: Japanese Sex Work in the Gendered Economy*.

13. I was aware of this perception of ryokan (and *onsen*) as sexualized

spaces prior to my research, but I found no evidence of sex work. In one year spent at Yamazakura, the nearest thing to sex work I witnessed was when a pair of young professional hostesses visited the ryokan from a neighboring village to serve drinks to a group of five male guests during dinner. Like *onsen* geisha of old, they facilitated communication between guests, but were dressed in skirts and blazers, and they promptly departed after their two-hour shift. As for the employees, the *nakai* I knew were too busy to engage in any sex work. Plus, ryokan had strict policies against *nakai* drinking with guests, including after work.

14. In her classic study of emotional work, Arlie Hochschild acknowledged that just as a factory worker becomes alienated from their labor when making an object, a service worker may become alienated from their emotions when they are the product being consumed. Hochschild highlighted this growing occupational hazard in the early 1980s, which has only expanded in the decades since. Hochschild, *The Managed Heart: Commercialization of Human Feeling*.

15. See Allison, *Nightwork: Sexuality, Pleasure, and Corporate Masculinity in a Tokyo Hostess Club*; Broadbent, *Women's Employment in Japan: the Experience of Part-Time Workers*; Cole, *Japanese Blue Collar: The Changing Tradition*; Dalby, *Geisha*; Hankins, *Working Skin: Making Leather, Making a Multicultural Japan*; Kondo, *Crafting Selves: Power, Gender, and Discourses of Identity in a Japanese Workplace*; lewallen, *The Fabric of Indigeneity: Ainu Identity, Gender, and Settler Colonialism in Japan*; McVeigh, *Life in a Japanese Women's College: Learning to Be Ladylike*; Ogasawara, *Office Ladies and Salaried Men: Power, Gender, and Work in Japanese Companies*; Roberts, *Staying on the Line: Blue-Collar Women in Contemporary Japan*; Rohlen, *For Harmony and Strength: Japanese White-Collar Organization in Anthropological Perspective*; Stevens, *On the Margins of Japanese Society: Volunteers and the Welfare of the Urban Underclass*; Tsuda, *Strangers in the Ethnic Homeland: Japan Brazilian Return Migration in Transnational Perspective*; Whitelaw, "Learning from Small Change: Clerkship and the Labors of Convenience."

16. For critical studies of these figures, see Dasgupta, *Re-reading the Salaryman in Japan: Crafting Masculinities*; Hendry, "The Role of the Professional Housewife"; Borovoy, *The Too-Good Wife: Alcohol, Codependency, and the Politics of Nurturance in Postwar Japan*.

17. See especially Kondo, *Crafting Selves*. For more on small family firms, see Bestor, *Tsukiji: The Fish Market at the Center of the World*.

18. See especially Roberts, *Staying on the Line*.

19. On dispatched work, see also Fu, *An Emerging Non-Regular*

*Labour Force in Japan: The Dignity of Dispatched Workers*. On service work, particularly in peripheralized sectors of the economy like sex work and sex work-adjacent jobs, see Koch, *Healing Labor*, and Takeda, *Staged Seduction: Selling Dreams in a Tokyo Host Club*.

20. On the stagnation of the lifetime employment system since the early 1980s, see Gordon, "New and Enduring Dual Structures of Employment in Japan: The Rise of Non-Regular Labor, 1980s–2010s." On shifts in female participation in the labor force, see Allison, *Nightwork*; Broadbent, *Women's Employment in Japan*; Ogasawara, *Office Ladies and Salaried Men*; Roberts, *Staying on the Line*.

21. Indeed, precariousness and precarity have recently become widely used to explain contemporary Japan. See especially Allison, *Precarious Japan*. However, even during the high economic growth of the 1970s and 80s, social scientists revealed the underlying precariousness of life in Japan, particularly for those not protected by the security of the lifetime employment system.

22. See Cook, *Reconstructing Adult Masculinities: Part-time Work in Contemporary Japan*; Fu, *An Emerging Non-Regular Labour Force in Japan*; Gill, *Men of Uncertainty: The Social Organization of Day Laborers in Contemporary Japan*; Slater, "The 'New Working Class' of Urban Japan: Socialization and Contradiction from Middle School to the Labor Market."

23. See Yoshida, "Joking, Gender, Power, and Professionalism among Japanese Inn Workers."

24. Japanese rooms are often measured in number of *tatami* mats. Mat sizes vary slightly by region but are approximately 90cm x 180cm. A 10-mat room is around 15 square meters.

25. See Wright, "Severing the Karmic Ties that Bind: The "Divorce Temple" Mantokuji."

26. Scheper-Hughes, *Death without Weeping: The Violence of Everyday Life in Brazil*, 29.

27. Gordon, "New and Enduring Dual Structures of Employment in Japan."

28. Yoshio Sugimoto notes the casualization of labor as one factor in widening economic divides in Japan. However, he characterizes the emergence of a *kakusa shakai* not as a reflection of a drastic drop in job security and growth of an underclass (*karyū shakai*), but rather as a sudden focus on preexisting variations, made more obvious by a looming sense of precariousness due to two decades of very little economic growth. As he points out (p. 12), one important consequence is that it is becoming more commonly recognized that "Japanese society is not as classless and egalitarian

as the conventional theory suggests." See Sugimoto, *An Introduction to Japanese Society*, especially chapter 2.

29. Glenda Roberts makes this point when dispelling myths about the homogeneity of class values in contemporary Japan. As she shows, some families do not share the widely held goal of a child successfully advancing to a top university and a coveted position in the private or public sector. Instead, they would prefer a child return home to take over the family business, marry, and raise a family nearby, or even under the same roof. Roberts, "Shifting Contours of Class and Status." See also Kondo, *Crafting Selves*, especially 132–137.

### Chapter 2: Landscaping the Countryside

Portions of this chapter appeared in an earlier form in McMorran, "Understanding the 'Heritage' in Heritage Tourism: Ideological Tool or Economic Tool for a Japanese Hot Springs Resort?," and McMorran, "A Landscape of 'Undesigned Design' in Rural Japan."

1. Lonely Planet, "Kurokawa Onsen."

2. Gotō, *Kurokawa Onsen no don: Gotō Tetsuya no "saisei" no hōsoku*, 6. Gotō was a minor celebrity in Japan, frequently interviewed by the press and sought out for advice by business owners and tourism officials around the country. He authored several books about Kurokawa. Importantly, Gotō wrote in dialect, which was a significant marker of his "local" identity and bolstered the authenticity of his advice on matters like the importance of protecting local businesses and recognizing the uniqueness of one's region.

3. For discussion of these state initiatives, see McCormack, *The Emptiness of Japanese Affluence*; Johnson, *MITI and the Japanese Miracle: The Growth of Industrial Policy, 1925–1975*.

4. Scott Schnell argues that rice-growing villages in particular have been held up as exemplars of Japanese culture. Schnell, "The Rural Imaginary: Landscape, Village, Tradition."

5. Numerous authors have shown why these links are problematic. Gluck, *Japan's Modern Myths: Ideology in the Late Meiji Period*; Gordon, "The Invention of Japanese-Style Labor Management"; Ryang, *Japan and National Anthropology: A Critique*.

6. Marilyn Ivy in particular notes that a "vanishing" countryside triggered anxiety in the 1970s and 80s. Ivy, *Discourses of the Vanishing: Modernity, Phantasm, Japan*. See also Graburn, "The Past in the Present in Japan: Nostalgia and Neo-traditionalism in Contemporary Japanese Domestic Tourism."

7. Gotō, *Kurokawa Onsen no don: Gotō Tetsuya no "saisei" no hōsoku*, 6.

Gotō's use of *inaka*, which ranges in meaning from "rural" to "backwards" or even "the sticks," indicates a position for Kurokawa as clearly *not* urban. In fact, Kurokawa's *inaka* atmosphere is not just *not* urban. Sometimes it is depicted as "a rural atmosphere surrounded by mountains" (*yaman'naka no inaka no fun'iki*). This portrays Kurokawa as literally cut off from the rest of the country by the mountains that encircle it. This further distances Kurokawa from the country's urban centers and their landscapes, values, and ways of life, thus bolstering its *furusato* credibility.

8. Robertson, "It Takes a Village: Internationalization and Nostalgia in Postwar Japan," 117.

9. Robertson, "*Furusato* Japan: The Culture and Politics of Nostalgia," 495–496.

10. Ibid., 494.

11. Hiramatsu, *Isson ippin no susume.*

12. See Knight, "Rural Revitalization in Japan: Spirit of the Village and Taste of the Country" and Thompson, "Depopulation in Rural Japan: 'Population Politics' in Towa-Cho."

13. Ivy, *Discourses of the Vanishing: Modernity, Phantasm, Japan.*

14. Roy, *Poverty Capital: Microfinance and the Making of Development.*

15. Sōmushō (Ministry of Internal Affairs and Communications), "Heisei no gappei ni tsuite no kōhyō."

16. Suganama, *Mura ga kieta: heisei gappei to wa nan datta no ka*; Fujii, *Kieru mura ikinokoru mura: shichōson gappei ni yureru sanson.*

17. See Furusato Choisu, "Furusato nōzei to wa."

18. An NHK special in early 2015 noted that many donors choose their recipient based on the products they will receive as thanks, thus creating more of an economic relationship (as opposed to an emotional one) than some municipalities prefer, and creating intense competition among municipalities to produce the most desirable gifts for donors. NHK, *Kurōsu appu gendai* #3605.

19. A website that helps potential donors both understand the tax break and search for desirable "thank you" gifts, assures visitors that they can select two or more places to receive their *furusato* tax donation. Furusato Choisu, "Furusato nōzei to wa."

20. See, for instance, Williams, *The Country and the City,* or more recently Thompson, *Unsettling Absences: Urbanism in Rural Malaysia.*

21. Minami-Oguni Town, "Machi no jinkō."

22. Mitchell, *The Lie of the Land: Migrant Workers and the California Landscape*; Duncan, J. S. and N. Duncan, *Landscapes of Privilege: Aesthetics and Affluence in an American Suburb*; Trudeau, "Politics of Belonging in

the Construction of Landscapes: Place-Making, Boundary-Drawing and Exclusion."

23. Price, *Dry Place: Landscapes of Belonging and Exclusion*.

24. Kurokawa Onsen Kankō Ryokan Kyōdō Kumiai, "Rekishi no yado: Okyakuya."

25. For more on ryokan in this early postwar era, see Guichard-Anguis, "Japanese Inns (*Ryokan*) as Producers of Japanese Identity."

26. Tokunaga, *Kurokawa: The Story of Sustainable Development*, 58.

27. Kumamoto Nichinichi Shinbun, *Kurokawa Onsen 'kyūseichō' wo yomu*.

28. Gotō, *Kurokawa Onsen no don: Gotō Tetsuya no "saisei" no hōsoku*, 6.

29. Kumamoto Nichinichi Shinbun-sha, *Kurokawa Onsen 'kyūseichō' wo yomu*; Matsuda, "Kurokawa Onsen 24 no yu yado"; Niwa, "Kurokawa Onsen no niwa"; Gotō, *Kurokawa Onsen no don: Gotō Tetsuya no 'saisei' no hōsoku*; Terebi Tokyo, "Kurokawa Onsen saisei no ketsudan"; Tokunaga, *Kurokawa: The Story of Sustainable Development*.

30. Gotō also built a cave bath (*dōkutsu burō*) in the hillside next to his inn. These baths, particularly the cave bath, have become like pilgrimage sites for tourists hoping to understand the origins of today's Kurokawa. On busy days, guests must sometimes wait an hour or more to enter the baths.

31. Officially known as the Kurokawa Onsen Kankō Ryokan Kyōdō Kumiai, or literally the Tourist Inn Cooperative. Hereafter, I call it the Ryokan Association.

32. Gotō, *Kurokawa Onsen no don: Gotō Tetsuya no "saisei" no hōsoku*, 6–8.

33. These plantation forests provide a constant reminder of high domestic lumber prices in the 1960s, before the market opened to less expensive imports. Totman, *The Green Archipelago: Forestry in Preindustrial Japan*.

34. Niwa, "Kurokawa Onsen sono niwa no miryoku."

35. The bath pass was also reminiscent of travel behaviors already found in Japan. For instance, the stamp inked on the pass at each ryokan resembles the unique stamps found at railway stations, shrines, temples, and other destinations around Japan, which are avidly collected by some travelers.

36. Kumamoto Nichinichi Shimbun-sha, *Kurokawa Onsen 'kyūseichō' wo yomu*.

37. Kurokawa sold its first million passes by 2001 and its second million passes only six years later. Kurokawa Onsen Kankō Ryokan Kyōdō

Kumiai, *Shisatsu shiryō*. Currently, the *nyūtō tegata* generates more than twenty million yen each year for the *kumiai*.

38. Niwa, "Kurokawa Onsen sono niwa no miryoku," 7. Another iteration of this is found in Mori, "Nihonichi genki na Kurokawa Onsen no himitsu," 32: "The entire *onsen* is one complete inn" (*onsenchi zentai ga, sanagara hitotsu no ryokan*). Elsewhere Gotō Tetsuya stresses the importance of maintaining what he calls Kurokawa's "complete image" (*zentaizō*). See Gotō, *Kurokawa Onsen no don: Gotō Tetsuya no "saisei" no hōsoku*, 118.

39. ST Kankyō Sekkei Kenkyūjo. *Kurokawa furusato no shizen, kurashi, motenashi no fūkeizukuri: kurokawa chiku machizukuri kyōtei*.

40. ST Kankyō Sekkei Kenkyūjo, *Kurokawa Onsen no fūkeizukuri*, 34.

41. Tokunaga, *Kurokawa: The Story of Sustainable Development*. Examples often appear in the *Yu no hata shinbun*, published monthly by Minami-Oguni Town, in association with the internationally linked nonprofit organization Nihon no mottomo utsukushii mura (The Most Beautiful Villages in Japan). The emphasis again is on the role of locals in continuing to make the village beautiful. This contrasts with geographical scholarship on landscape in the North America context, which tends to emphasize landscape's role in naturalizing unequal power relations, in part due to its impression as a completed scene. As is the case in Kurokawa, a particular landscape becomes a powerful tool to reinforce not only the aesthetic choice it represents, but also the social relations involved in reproducing it. However, the labor that produces the landscape is often made invisible in the North American context. The prevalence of visible landscaping efforts in Kurokawa shows that landscape labor is not always hidden, but may in fact be considered an essential factor of belonging. See especially Mitchell, *The Lie of the Land: Migrant Workers and the California Landscape*; and Duncan and Duncan, *Landscapes of Privilege: Aesthetics and Affluence in an American Suburb*.

### Chapter 3: Pariah in Paradise

Portions of this chapter appeared in an earlier form in McMorran, "Understanding the 'Heritage' in Heritage Tourism: Ideological Tool or Economic Tool for a Japanese Hot Springs Resort?" and McMorran, "A Landscape of 'Undesigned Design' in Rural Japan."

1. Lonely Planet, "Kurokawa Onsen." The lot remains vacant as of November 2020.

2. Niwa, "Kurokawa Onsen rotenburo gaido," 95.

3. Mappuru, "Kurokawa Onsen."

4. The disease is named for G. H. Armauer Hansen, who discovered

the bacterium responsible for the disease in 1873. See Burns, "From 'Leper Villages' to Leprosaria: Public Health, Nationalism and the Culture of Exclusion in Japan"; Burns, "Making Illness Identity: Writing 'Leprosy Literature' in Modern Japan."

5. The World Leprosy Conference in Berlin in 1897 stated that "every leper is a danger to his surroundings," and "isolation is the best means of preventing the spread of the disease." Lower House member Saito Hisao stated in 1902, "The government pays no attention to the regulation of leprosy. This behavior causes extreme loss of face for our nation even as we are trying to maintain equal relationships with other civilized nations." Kitano, "The End of Isolation: Hansen's Disease in Japan," 40.

6. Ibid., 40.

7. Even after the law was repealed, most residents decided to remain in these facilities, where they had built communities based on a common struggle against prejudice.

8. BBC, "Japan Lepers Reject Spa Apology"; Japan Times, " 'Onsen' Hotel Named for Discriminatory Behavior."

9. The Japan Times, " 'Onsen' Hotel Named for Discriminatory Behavior."

10. According to former hotel employees some people also called and faxed to support its decision. More troubling is the fact that over the next few months Kikuchi Keifuen also received hundreds of inflammatory phone calls and faxes criticizing its role in the incident. Comments ranged from anger at patients' reliance on taxpayer money to support both their livelihoods and their overnight stay at a famous hot spring, to remarks that showed Japanese society's continued fear and misunderstanding of hansenbyō (e.g., "I don't want to take a bath with you!" [issho ni ofuro iyada]). Pearson, "Bigotry Hounds Former Hansen's Patients"; Japan Law Foundation, "Hansenbyō mondai ni kansuru kenshō kaigi: saishū hōkokusho."

11. Japan Times, "Apology Fails to Placate Angry Hansen's Patients."

12. BBC, "Japan Lepers Reject Spa Apology."

13. Kondo later called these Kurokawa's "town-making principles" (machizukuri no rinen), which include conforming to its design guidelines and participating in its landscaping efforts. These principles are outlined in the 2003 Town-Making Pact (ST Kankyō Sekkei Kenkyūjo, Kurokawa furusato no shizen, kurashi, motenashi no fūkeizukuri: Kurokawa chiku machizukuri kyōtei).

14. Kurotani, Home Away from Home: Japanese Corporate Wives in the United States.

15. Gotō, Kurokawa Onsen no don: Gotō Tetsuya no "saisei" no hōsoku.

16. See Kumamoto Nichinichi Shinbun, "Kyōgi 7-nen yureru yu no machi."

17. Eighty percent of Kurokawa's inns and hotels have twenty rooms or fewer.

18. Over the years I received a handful of the internal documents related to these negotiations, including the "confidential" letter from the Association to KM, dated May 20, 2013, and a draft of a letter dated February 2015, from the Association to the Minami-Oguni mayor. The latter letter summarizes the Association's consultations with KM, noting, for instance, that the parties met nine times between June 2011 and June 2014, with no discernible progress. The Association concludes by expressing its disappointment with KM and requests the mayor's assistance in convincing the company to build elsewhere. Finally, I received a copy of the Kurokawa Onsen Furusato Charter, which was ratified in mid-2015 in order to establish a set of "principles of, from, and for the area" (*chiiki no, chiiki ni yoru, chiiki no tame no gensoku*) that goes beyond the mere aesthetic rules set out in the 2003 Town-Making Pact.

19. Geographer Cindi Katz crystallizes Gotō's concern with her concept of "vagabond capitalism," which identifies capitalism as "that unsettled, dissolute, irresponsible stalker of the world." Katz, "Vagabond Capitalism and the Necessity of Social Reproduction," 709.

20. "*Nihonjū doko e den itte mo onaji fūkei-bakari ni natte shimattorun desu na.*" Gotō, *Kurokawa Onsen no don: Gotō Tetsuya no "saisei" no hōsoku*, 18.

## Chapter 4: Inside Job

1. Geographers Blunt and Dowling (2006) have pointed out the problems with what they call "dualistic thinking" about home vs. work, thus highlighting the fuzzy boundaries between them. See Blunt and Dowling, *Home*.

2. Sand, *House and Home in Modern Japan: Architecture, Domestic Space, and Bourgeois Culture, 1880–1930*; Neitzel, *The Life We Longed For: Danchi Housing and the Middle Class Dream in Postwar Japan*.

3. Anne Allison discusses the heavy burden Japanese mothers accept for their children's educational successes or failures, which is encapsulated in the term commonly used to describe such women: *kyōiku mama*, or "education mother." See chapter 5 in Allison, *Permitted and Prohibited Desires: Mothers, Comics, and Censorship in Japan*.

4. Roberts, "Shifting Contours of Class and Status," (see chap. 1, n. 29). Roberts makes this point when dispelling myths about the homogeneity of class values in contemporary Japan. As she shows, some families do

not share the widely held goal of a child successfully advancing to a top university and a coveted position in the private or public sector. Instead, some families would prefer a child return home to take over the family business, marry, and raise a family nearby, or even under the same roof. See also Kondo, *Crafting Selves: Power, Gender, and Discourses of Identity in a Japanese Workplace*, especially 132–137.

5. The so-called American *okami* Jeanie Fuji preferred the term "proprietress." Born and raised in the United States, the tall, blond, blue-eyed woman moved to Yamagata Prefecture to teach English as a second language on the JET Program in the late 1980s. There she met her future husband, the successor of Fujiya ryokan, located in Ginzan Onsen, Yamagata, which had been in the family for fourteen generations. Her future in-laws initially rejected her as unsuitable. However, she was eventually accepted not only by her family, but also by the nation, precisely because she insisted on being *more* Japanese than the Japanese. For a time in the late 2000s she was a minor celebrity, often appearing on television in kimono and speaking about the beauty and uniqueness of Japanese hospitality. She authored books on the subject and even served on an ill-fated government committee tasked with certifying the authenticity of Japanese restaurants abroad (dubbed the "sushi police" in the English-speaking press). Her case actually strengthens the argument that an *okami* should be Japanese, since she was only accepted because of her attempts to authentically embody the finest elements of Japanese hospitality. In December 2006 she shared with me her eight-year struggle to please her mother-in-law and take over as *okami* as we walked around her newly rebuilt ryokan, designed by internationally renowned architect Kengo Kuma. She commissioned the rebuild as her first and defining act as *okami* as soon as she was officially promoted to take over from her mother-in-law. Incidentally, she eventually stepped down as *okami* after separating from her husband and returning to the US. Fuji, *Nipponjin wa, Nihon ga tarinai*; Fuji, *Amerikajin okami ga mananda Nihon no omotenashi kokoroechō*.

6. For a lucid discussion of the importance of a Japanese woman "being there" in domestic space, see Kurotani, *Home Away from Home: Japanese Corporate Wives in the United States*.

Kurotani examines Japanese women whose husbands have been temporarily (two to five years) transferred to the US by their Japanese corporations. The women are expected to "be there" when their husbands and children return home each day, thus making them anchors of Japanese femininity and identity who serve the interests of Japanese corporations whose employees (the husbands) must eventually re-integrate into their workplaces in Japan. As well, the children must re-integrate into Japanese schools, in order to minimize any disruption to the employee's life. The presence of the wife/mother at home is believed to be essential to maintaining the well-being (and Japaneseness) of the rest of the family.

7. Nakano, *Makiko's Diary: A Merchant Wife in 1910 Kyoto*, 2.

### Chapter 5: How to Succeed in Business

1. The eldest son is the preferred heir, even if he has one or more older sisters. This preference echoes the practices of Japan's Imperial household. According to the Imperial House Act of 1889, succession can only pass through male heirs. Thus, the only child of Emperor Naruhito and Empress Masako, a daughter named Aiko, cannot succeed her father. Instead, her uncle, Crown Prince Fumihito, is currently second in line, followed by his son (and Aiko's younger cousin), Prince Hisahito. Until Prince Hisahito was born in 2006, there was great speculation about whether or not the Constitution should be changed to enable a female successor. At the time, the pressure to bear a male heir was hinted at as the cause of various physical and mental ailments suffered by then-Princess Masako. As I show in this chapter, the preference for a male heir creates stress for ryokan families, too, in particular for the would-be mother, who often feels personally responsible for bearing a son. Indeed, she often blames herself if she fails to do so.

2. See Ueno, "Genesis of the Urban Housewife" for a vivid depiction of the regional diversity of non-samurai households during the Tokugawa period. See also Ueno, "The Position of Japanese Women Reconsidered."

3. Being the second or third son can be liberating for some men, while for others it can feel unfair, since they grow up knowing they must leave behind the comforts of home and find success on their own. The practice of *norenwake* (lit. splitting the shop curtain) is still found among some family business owners. This involves setting up a second or third son with a branch of the main business, as can be found in the restaurant business. However, *norenwake* is uncommon among ryokan owners, largely because ryokan are particularly geographically fixed businesses. Family reputations are built in specific communities, making it difficult to open a "branch" ryokan somewhere else. On *norenwake*, see Bestor, *Tsukiji: The Fish Market at the Center of the World*.

4. A growing exception is widowed or frail elderly parents moving in with their middle-aged children and grandchildren. This arrangement tends to impact women more than men, since they are expected to care for both child and parent. See Rosenberger, *Dilemmas of Adulthood: Japanese Women and the Nuances of Long-Term Resistance*.

5. Although difficult to generalize, some signs show that aversion to life in the countryside by Japanese young people may be dissipating, especially among environmentally conscious individuals who wish to pursue organic farming or raise children close to nature. See Reiher, "Embracing the periphery: urbanites' motivations for relocating to rural Japan."

The availability of high-speed internet also means new rural inhabitants may feel less socially isolated. In 2018 I stayed at a small pension along the Kumano Kodō pilgrimage route run by a couple in their early thirties who had recently moved from Tokyo. They had no connections to the tiny mountain village in Wakayama Prefecture, but after learning about the availability of abandoned properties and deciding they were tired of their jobs in advertising, they decided to move to the countryside. When we met, they seemed to have settled into their new life and joked that their primary nuisance was protecting their garden from wild boars and monkeys.

6. For a comprehensive analysis of matchmaking agencies, see Ishikawa, "Role of Matchmaking Agencies for International Marriage in Contemporary Japan."

### Chapter 6: A Day in the Life
1. Scott, *Weapons of the Weak: Everyday Forms of Peasant Resistance.*

### Chapter 7: Women without Homes
Portions of this chapter appeared in an earlier form in McMorran, "Practicing Workplace Geographies: Embodied Labour as Method in Human Geography," McMorran, "Mobilities amid the Production of Fixities: Labor in a Japanese Inn," and McMorran, "Liberating Work in the Tourist Industry."

1. Lebra, *Japanese Women: Constraint and Fulfillment.*

2. Goldstein-Gidoni, *Housewives of Japan: An Ethnography of Real Lives and Consumerized Domesticity.*

3. Borovoy, *The Too-Good Wife: Alcohol, Codependency, and the Politics of Nurturance in Postwar Japan;* Kurotani, *Home Away from Home: Japanese Corporate Wives in the United States;* Goldstein-Gidoni, *Housewives of Japan.*

4. See Borovoy, *The Too-Good Wife.*

5. The M-curve has become less extreme in recent years, particularly with more women delaying marriage, delaying the birth of their first child, continuing to work past marriage and childbirth, or not marrying at all.

6. Goldstein-Gidoni, *Housewives of Japan,* 110.

7. Borovoy, *The Too-Good Wife*, 161.

8. Doi, *Yoku wakaru hoteru gyōkai*, 95.

## Chapter 8: Professional Care?

1. Hochschild, *The Managed Heart: Commercialization of Human Feeling*.

2. See Borovoy, *The Too-Good Wife*; and Kurotani, *Home Away from Home*.

## Chapter 9: Policing Ryokan Space

Portions of this chapter appeared in an earlier form in McMorran, "Practicing Workplace Geographies: Embodied Labour as Method in Human Geography."

1. For other approaches by peripheral communities to their precarious position, see Manzenreiter, Lützeler, and Polak-Rottmann, *Japan's New Ruralities: Coping with Decline in the Periphery*, and Traphagan, *Cosmopolitan Rurality, Depopulation, and Entrepreneurial Ecosystems in 21st-Century Japan*.

2. This intersection of visible and invisible work can be problematic. As Arlie Hochschild (*The Managed Heart*) showed, employees who are expected to display emotions like concern and excitement to their customers can suffer an emotional toll in their private lives. Outside the workplace, they can struggle to separate their genuine emotions from "fake" emotions, since so much emotional labor is needed on the job. This can be a hazard of ryokan work, too, since there is constant pressure to embody the "flavor" of okami's hospitality and make all guests feel at home.

3. I feature this chef's story in depth in McMorran, "Mobilities amid the Production of Fixities: Labor in a Japanese Inn."

# Bibliography

Allison, Anne. *Nightwork: Sexuality, Pleasure, and Corporate Masculinity in a Tokyo Hostess Club.* Chicago: University of Chicago Press, 1994.

———. *Permitted and Prohibited Desires: Mothers, Comics, and Censorship in Japan.* Boulder; Oxford: Westview Press, 1996.

———. *Precarious Japan.* Durham, NC: Duke University Press, 2013.

BBC. "Japan Lepers Reject Spa Apology." November 21, 2003. Accessed December 10, 2020. http://news.bbc.co.uk/2/hi/asia-pacific/3228200.stm.

Bestor, Theodore C. *Tsukiji: The Fish Market at the Center of the World.* California Studies in Food and Culture. Berkeley: University of California Press, 2004.

Blunt, Alison, and Robyn M. Dowling. *Home.* New York: Routledge, 2006

Borovoy, Amy Beth. *The Too-Good Wife: Alcohol, Codependency, and the Politics of Nurturance in Postwar Japan.* Ethnographic Studies in Subjectivity. Berkeley: University of California Press, 2005.

Broadbent, Kaye. *Women's Employment in Japan: The Experience of Part-Time Workers.* London; New York: RoutledgeCurzon, 2003.

Burns, Susan. "From 'Leper Villages' to Leprosaria: Public Health, Nationalism and the Culture of Exclusion in Japan." In *Isolation: Places and Practices of Exclusion,* edited by Carolyn Strange and Alison Bashford, 104–118. London; New York: Routledge, 2003.

———. "Making Illness Identity: Writing 'Leprosy Literature' in Modern Japan." *Japan Review* 16 (2004): 191–211.

Clark, Scott F. *Japan, A View from the Bath.* Honolulu: University of Hawai'i Press, 1994.

Cole, Robert E. *Japanese Blue Collar: The Changing Tradition.* Berkeley: University of California Press, 1971.

Cook, Emma E. *Reconstructing Adult Masculinities: Part-Time Work in Contemporary Japan.* London: Routledge, 2015.

Dalby, Liza Crichfield. *Geisha.* Berkeley: University of California Press, 1983.

Dasgupta, Romit. *Re-reading the Salaryman in Japan: Crafting Masculinities.* London: Routledge, 2012.

Doi, Kyūtaro. *Yoku wakaru hoteru gyōkai* [All about the hotel industry]. Tokyo: Nihonjitsugyō Shuppansha, 2009.

Duncan, James S., and Nancy Duncan. *Landscapes of Privilege: Aesthetics and Affluence in an American Suburb.* New York: Routledge, 2004.

Edgington, David W. *Reconstructing Kobe: The Geography of Crisis and Opportunity.* Vancouver: UBC Press, 2010.

Fu, Huiyan. *An Emerging Non-Regular Labour Force in Japan: The Dignity of Dispatched Workers.* The Nissan Institute/Routledge Japanese Studies Series. New York: Routledge, 2011.

Fuji, Jeanie. *Amerikajin okami ga mananda Nihon no omotenashi kokoroechō* [Everything an American okami learned about Japanese hospitality]. Tokyo: Gentosha, 2004.

———. *Nipponjin wa, Nihon ga tarinai* [The Japanese lack enough Japan]. Tokyo: Nihon Bungeisha, 2003.

Fujii Mitsuru. *Kieru mura ikinokoru mura: shichōson gappei ni yureru sanson* [Vanishing village, surviving village: mountain villages buffeted by city/town/village amalgamation]. Tokyo: Atto Wākusu, 2006.

Fuji Terebi. *Watashi wo ryokan ni tsuretette.* Japan, 2001. Television.

Furusato Choisu. "Furusato nōzei to wa" [What is the furusato tax?]. Accessed December 7, 2020. http://www.furusato-tax.jp/about.html.

Gill, Tom. *Men of Uncertainty: The Social Organization of Day Laborers in Contemporary Japan.* Albany: State University of New York Press, 2001.

———. "This Spoiled Soil: Place, People and Community in an Irradiated Village in Fukushima Prefecture." In *Japan Copes with Calamity: Ethnographies of the Earthquake, Tsunami and Nuclear Disasters of March 2011,* edited by Tom Gill, Brigitte Steger, and David H. Slater, 201–233. Bern: Peter Lang, 2013.

Gluck, Carol. *Japan's Modern Myths: Ideology in the Late Meiji Period.* Princeton, NJ: Princeton University Press, 1985.

Goldstein-Gidoni, Ofra. *Housewives of Japan: An Ethnography of Real Lives and Consumerized Domesticity.* New York: Palgrave Macmillan, 2012.

Gordon, Andrew. "The Invention of Japanese-Style Labor Management." In *Mirror of Modernity: Invented Traditions of Modern Japan,* edited by Stephen Vlastos, 19–36. Berkeley: University of California Press, 1998.

———. "New and Enduring Dual Structures of Employment in Japan: The Rise of Non-Regular Labor, 1980s–2010s." *Social Science Japan Journal* 20, no.1 (2017): 9–36.

Gotō Tetsuya. *Kurokawa Onsen no don: Gotō Tetsuya no "saisei" no hōsoku* [Kurokawa Onsen's don: Gotō Tetsuya's revitalization rules]. Tokyo: Asahi Shinbunsha, 2005.

Graburn, Nelson H. H. "The Past in the Present in Japan: Nostalgia and Neo-Traditionalism in Contemporary Japanese Domestic Tourism." In *Change in Tourism: People, Places, Processes*, edited by Richard Butler and Douglas Pearce, 47–70. London: Routledge, 1995.

Guichard-Anguis, Sylvie. "Japanese Inns (*Ryokan*) as Producers of Japanese Identity." In *Japanese Tourism and Travel Culture*, edited by Sylvie Guichard-Anguis and Okpyo Moon, 76–101. London and New York: Routledge, 2008.

Hankins, Joseph D. *Working Skin: Making Leather, Making a Multicultural Japan*. Asia Pacific Modern. Oakland, CA: University of California Press, 2014.

Hendry, Joy. "The Role of the Professional Housewife." In *Japanese Women Working*, edited by Janet Hunter, 223–241. London; New York: Routledge, 1993.

Hiramatsu Morihiko. *Isson ippin no susume* [Suggesting one village, one product]. Tokyo: Gyōsei, 1982.

Hochschild, Arlie Russell. *The Managed Heart: Commercialization of Human Feeling*. Berkeley: University of California Press, 1983.

Ishikawa, Yoshitaka. "Role of Matchmaking Agencies for International Marriage in Contemporary Japan." Geographical Review of Japan Series B, 83, no. 1 (2010): 1–14.

Ivy, Marilyn. *Discourses of the Vanishing: Modernity, Phantasm, Japan*. Chicago: University of Chicago Press, 1995.

Japan Law Foundation. "Hansenbyō mondai ni kansuru kenshō kaigi: saishū hōkokusho" [Final report on the meeting considering problems related to leprosy]. https://www.mhlw.go.jp/topics/bukyoku/kenkou /hansen/kanren/4a.html.

Japan National Tourism Organization. "Stay at an Upscale Japanese Inn: Have the Experience of a Lifetime!" Accessed March 12, 2014. http:// www.jnto.go.jp/webmaga/en/nov/trends.html.

Japan Ryokan & Hotel Association. "Japan Ryokan and Hotel Association." Accessed March 12, 2014. http://www.ryokan.or.jp/english/.

———. "What is Ryokan?" Accessed March 12, 2014. http://www.ryokan .or.jp/past/english/what/index.html.

Japan Times. "Apology Fails to Placate Angry Hansen's Patients." November 21, 2003.

———. " 'Onsen' Hotel Named for Discriminatory Behavior." November 19, 2003.

Johnson, Chalmers. *MITI and the Japanese Miracle: The Growth of Industrial Policy, 1925–1975*. Stanford: Stanford University Press, 1982.

Katz, Cindi. "Vagabond Capitalism and the Necessity of Social Reproduction." *Antipode* 33, no. 4 (September 2001): 709–728.

Kawabata Yasunari. *Yukiguni* [Snow Country]. Japan: Shinchō Bunko, 2006.

Kitano, Ryūichi. "The End of Isolation: Hansen's Disease in Japan." *Harvard Asia Quarterly* 6, no. 3 (2002): 39–44.

Knight, John. "Rural Revitalization in Japan: Spirit of the Village and Taste of the Country." *Asian Survey* 34, no. 7 (July 1994): 634–646.

Koch, Gabriele. *Healing Labor: Japanese Sex Work in the Gendered Economy*. Stanford: Stanford University Press, 2020.

Kondo, Dorinne K. *Crafting Selves: Power, Gender, and Discourses of Identity in a Japanese Workplace*. Chicago: University of Chicago Press, 1990.

Kumamoto Nichinichi Shinbun. "Kyōgi 7-nen yureru yu no machi" [Seven years of consultations stir up hot springs town]. September 30, 2015, 37.

Kumamoto Nichinichi Shinbun-sha. *Kurokawa Onsen 'kyūseichō' wo yomu* [Reading into the 'rapid growth' of Kurokawa Onsen]. Kumamoto: Kumamoto Nichinichi Shinbun Jōhō Bunka Sentā, 2000.

Kurokawa Onsen Kankō Ryokan Kyōdō Kumiai. "Rekishi no yado: Okyakuya" [Historical inn: Okyakuya]. Accessed September 28, 2015. http://www.kurokawaonsen.or.jp/oyado/syosai.php?intYKey=3.

———. *Shisatsu shiryō* [Annual report]. 2012.

Kurotani, Sawa. *Home Away from Home: Japanese Corporate Wives in the United States*. Durham, NC: Duke University Press, 2005.

Lebra, Takie Sugiyama. *Japanese Women: Constraint and Fulfillment*. Honolulu: University of Hawai'i Press, 1984.

lewallen, ann-elise. *The Fabric of Indigeneity: Ainu Identity, Gender, and Settler Colonialism in Japan*. Santa Fe: University of New Mexico Press, 2016.

Lonely Planet. "Kurokawa Onsen." Accessed September 15, 2013. http://www.lonelyplanet.com/japan/kyushu/kurokawa-onsen.

Lonely Planet Publications. *Japan: A Travel Survival Kit*. Berkeley: Lonely Planet Publications, 1997.

Mappuru (Mapple). "Kurokawa Onsen." *Shūkan Nihon no meiyu* [Japan's famous hot springs weekly], 2003.

Matsuda Tadanori. "Kurokawa Onsen 24 no yu yado." [Kurokawa Onsen: 24 hot springs inns]. *Onsen shugi* (Hot springs principles), September 1, 2001, 16–40.

McCormack, Gavan. *The Emptiness of Japanese Affluence.* Japan in the Modern World. Rev. ed. Armonk, NY: M. E. Sharpe, 2001.

McMorran, Chris. "Understanding the 'Heritage' in Heritage Tourism: Ideological Tool or Economic Tool for a Japanese Hot Springs Resort?" *Tourism Geographies* 10, no. 3 (2008): 334–354.

———. "Practicing Workplace Geographies: Embodied Labour as Method in Human Geography." *Area* 44, no. 4 (2012): 489–495.

———. "A Landscape of 'Undesigned Design' in Rural Japan." *Landscape Journal* 33, no. 1 (2014): 1–15.

———. "Mobilities amid the Production of Fixities: Labor in a Japanese Inn." *Mobilities* 10, no. 1 (2015): 83–99.

———. "Liberating Work in the Tourist Industry," in *Rethinking Japanese Feminisms*, Bullock, Kano, and Welker, eds., Honolulu: University of Hawai'i Press (2018): 119–130.

McVeigh, Brian J. *Life in a Japanese Women's College: Learning to Be Ladylike.* London and New York: Routledge, 1997.

Minami-Oguni Town. "Machi no jinkō" [Town population]. Accessed November 2, 2020. http://www.town.minamioguni.kumamoto.jp/profile/town/000007.php.

Ministry of Land, Infrastructure, Transport and Tourism. "Kankō ya shukuhaku gyō wo torimaku genjō oyobi kadai nado ni tsuite" [About the current situation and problems surrounding the tourism and hotel industry]. January 28, 2019. Accessed November 27, 2020. https://www.mlit.go.jp/common/001271444.pdf.

Mitchell, Don. *The Lie of the Land: Migrant Workers and the California Landscape.* Minneapolis: University of Minnesota Press, 1996.

Mori Mayumi. "Nihonichi genki na Kurokawa Onsen no himitsu" [Secrets from Kurokawa Onsen, Japan's most energetic]. *Tabi* [Travel], January 2001, 29–35.

Murakami, Haruki. *Underground: The Tokyo Gas Attack and the Japanese Psyche.* Translated by Alfred Birmbaum and Philip Gabriel. London: Harvill, 2000.

Nakano, Makiko. *Makiko's Diary: A Merchant Wife in 1910 Kyoto.* Translated by Kazuko Smith. Stanford: Stanford University Press, 1995.

Neitzel, Laura Lynn. *The Life We Longed For: Danchi Housing and the Middle Class Dream in Postwar Japan.* Portland, ME: MerwinAsia, 2015.

NHK. *Kurōsu appu gendai* [Close-up today] #3605. "Furusato nōzei: būmu ga tou mono wa" [The hometown tax: what the boom means]. Aired January 26, 2015.

Niwa. "Kurokawa Onsen no niwa" [The gardens of Kurokawa Hot Spring Resort]. *Niwa* [The Garden], 2002.

―――. "Kurokawa Onsen rotenburo gaido" [Guide to Kurokawa's outdoor baths]. *Niwa* (The Garden), 2002, 94–99.

―――. "Kurokawa Onsen sono niwa no miryoku" [Fascinating gardens of the hot spring resort, Kurokawa]. *Niwa* (The Garden), 2002, 5–7.

Nihon Hitō wo Mamoru Kai. "Nihon hitō wo mamoru kai ni tsuite" [About the Japan Association of Secluded Hot Spring Inns]. Accessed March 1, 2014. https://www.hitou.or.jp/static/about_us.

Ogasawara, Yuko. *Office Ladies and Salaried Men: Power, Gender, and Work in Japanese Companies.* Berkeley: University of California Press, 1998.

Okyakuya. "Yado Okyakuya." Kumamoto: Kurokawa Onsen, 2004.

Pearson, Natalie Obiko. "Bigotry Hounds Former Hansen's Patients." *The Japan Times,* August 27, 2004.

Price, Patricia L. *Dry Place: Landscapes of Belonging and Exclusion.* Minneapolis: University of Minnesota Press, 2004.

Reiher, Cornelia. "Embracing the Periphery: Urbanites' Motivations for Relocating to Rural Japan." In *Japan's New Ruralities: Coping with Decline in the Periphery,* edited by Wolfram Manzenreiter, Ralph Lützeler, and Sebastian Polak-Rottmann, 230–244. London: Routledge, 2020.

Roberts, Glenda S. "Shifting Contours of Class and Status." In *A Companion to the Anthropology of Japan,* edited by Jennifer Ellen Robertson, 104–124. Malden, MA: Blackwell Publishing Ltd., 2008.

Roberts, Glenda S. *Staying on the Line: Blue-Collar Women in Contemporary Japan.* Honolulu: University of Hawai'i Press, 1994.

Robertson, Jennifer. "*Furusato* Japan: The Culture and Politics of Nostalgia." *Politics, Culture, and Society* 1, no. 4 (1988): 494–518.

―――. "It Takes a Village: Internationalization and Nostalgia in Postwar Japan." In *Mirror of Modernity: Invented Traditions of Modern Japan,* edited by Stephen Vlastos, 110–129. Berkeley: University of California Press, 1998.

Rohlen, Thomas P. *For Harmony and Strength: Japanese White-Collar Organization in Anthropological Perspective.* Berkeley: University of California Press, 1974.

Rosenberger, Nancy. *Dilemmas of Adulthood: Japanese Women and the Nuances of Long-Term Resistance.* Honolulu: University of Hawai'i Press, 2013.

Roy, Ananya. *Poverty Capital: Microfinance and the Making of Development.* New York: Routledge, 2010.

Ryang, Sonia. *Japan and National Anthropology: A Critique*. New York: Routledge, 2004.

ST Kankyō Sekkei Kenkyūjo. *Kurokawa furusato no shizen, kurashi, motenashi no fūkeizukuri: kurokawa chiku machizukuri kyōtei* [Creating Kurokawa's furusato landscape of nature, life, and hospitality: Kurokawa area town-making agreement]. Minami-Oguni Town: Minami-Oguni Town, 2003.

———. *Kurokawa Onsen no fūkeizukuri* [Total landscape design of Kurokawa Onsen]. Fukuoka: ST Kankyō Sekkei Kenkyūjo, 2008

Sand, Jordan. *House and Home in Modern Japan: Architecture, Domestic Space, and Bourgeois Culture, 1880–1930*. Cambridge, MA: Harvard University Asia Center, 2003.

Sargent, John. "Remodeling the Japanese Archipelago: The Tanaka Plan." *Geographical Journal* 139, no. 3 (1973): 426–435.

Scheper-Hughes, Nancy. *Death without Weeping: The Violence of Everyday Life in Brazil*. Berkeley: University of California Press, 1992.

Schnell, Scott. "The Rural Imaginary: Landscape, Village, Tradition." In *A Companion to the Anthropology of Japan*, edited by Jennifer Ellen Robertson, 201–217. Malden, MA: Blackwell Publishing Ltd., 2008.

Scott, James C. *Weapons of the Weak: Everyday Forms of Peasant Resistance*. New Haven, CT: Yale University Press, 1985.

Slater, David H. "The 'New Working Class' of Urban Japan: Socialization and Contradiction from Middle School to the Labor Market." In *Social Class in Contemporary Japan: Structures, Sorting and Strategies*, edited by Hiroshi Ishida and David H. Slater, 137–169. London; New York: Routledge, 2010.

Sōmushō (Ministry of Internal Affairs and Communications). "Heisei no gappei ni tsuite no kōhyō" [Announcement on the Heisei-era amalgamations]. Tokyo: Ministry of Internal Affairs and Communications, 2010.

Statler, Oliver. *Japanese Inn*. Honolulu: University of Hawai'i Press, 1983.

Stevens, Carolyn S. *On the Margins of Japanese Society: Volunteers and the Welfare of the Urban Underclass*. London and New York: Routledge, 1997.

Suganama Eiichiro. *Mura ga kieta: Heisei gappei to wa nan datta no ka* [Vanished village: what was the great Heisei amalgamation?]. Tokyo: Shōdensha, 2005.

Sugimoto, Yoshio. *An Introduction to Japanese Society*. 3rd ed. Cambridge, UK: Cambridge University Press, 2010.

Takahashi Satsuki. "Omotenashi to iu rōdō: onsen kankō ryokan no shigoto to jendā" [What Is 'Omotenashi'? Hospitality and Gender in Hot Spring Town, Hakone]. *Annals of Ochanomizu Geographical Society* 49 (2009): 49–65.

Takeyama, Akiko. *Staged Seduction: Selling Dreams in a Tokyo Host Club.* Stanford: Stanford University Press, 2016.

Tanaka, Kakuei. *Building a New Japan: A Plan for Remodeling the Japanese Archipelago.* Tokyo: Simul Press, 1973.

TBS. *Asakusa Fukumaru Ryokan.* Japan, 2007. Television.

Terebi Tokyo. *Rubikon no Ketsudan.* "Kurokawa Onsen saisei no ketsudan" (Kurokawa's regeneration decision). Aired May 7, 2009, on TV Tokyo, Japan. 60 min.

Thompson, Christopher S. "Depopulation in Rural Japan: 'Population Politics' in Towa-Cho." In *Demographic Change and the Family in Japan's Aging Society,* edited by John W. Traphagan and John Knight, 89–106. Albany: State University of New York Press, 2003.

Thompson, Eric C. *Unsettling Absences: Urbanism in Rural Malaysia.* Singapore: NUS Press, 2007.

Tokunaga Satoshi. *Kurokawa: The Story of Sustainable Development* (Kurokawa Onsen kankō ryokan kyōdō kumiai setsuritsu 50-shūnen kinensatsu). Minami-Oguni Town: Kurokawa Onsen Kankō Ryokan Kyōdō Kumiai, 2012.

Totman, Conrad D. *The Green Archipelago: Forestry in Preindustrial Japan.* Athens: Ohio University Press, 1989.

Traphagan, John W. *Cosmopolitan Rurality, Depopulation, and Entrepreneurial Ecosystems in 21st-Century Japan.* New York: Cambria Press, 2020.

Trudeau, D. "Politics of Belonging in the Construction of Landscapes: Place-Making, Boundary-Drawing and Exclusion." *Cultural Geographies* 13, no. 3 (July 2006): 421–443.

Tsuda Takeyuki. *Strangers in the Ethnic Homeland: Japanese Brazilian Return Migration in Transnational Perspective.* New York: Columbia University Press, 2003.

Ueno, Chizuko. "Genesis of the Urban Housewife." *Japan Quarterly* 34, no. 2 (April-June 1987): 130–142.

———. "The Position of Japanese Women Reconsidered." *Current Anthropology* 28, no. 4 (August-October 1987): S75-S84.

Whitelaw, Gavin H. "Learning from Small Change: Clerkship and the Labors of Convenience," *Anthropology of Work Review,* 29 (2008): 62–69.

Williams, Raymond. *The Country and the City.* New York: Oxford University Press, 1973.

Wolfram Manzenreiter, Ralph Lützeler, and Sebastian Polak-Rottmann, eds. *Japan's New Ruralities: Coping with Decline in the Periphery.* London: Routledge, 2020.

Wright, Diana E. "Severing the Karmic Ties That Bind: The 'Divorce Temple' Mantokuji." *Monumenta Nipponica* 52, no. 3 (Fall 1997): 357–380.

Yoshida, Mitsuhiro. "Joking, Gender, Power, and Professionalism among Japanese Inn Workers." *Ethnology* 40, No. 4 (Autumn 2001): 361–369.

# Index

Note: Page locators in **bold** denote photographs or maps.

accommodation, Western and Japanese style, 8
accommodation denial incident (*shukuhaku kyohi jiken*), 47–48, 49
adoption of males as successors, 86–87
agricultural history and associated values and beliefs, 27–28
Ai Ladies Hotel (*Ai Redīzu Kyūden Hoteru*), 170; closure of, 48; consequences of cancelling Kikuchi Keifuen reservations, 46–47; demolition of, 44, 50; sale of site, 51. *See also* Aistar Co., Ltd.; Kyōritsu Mentenansu (KM)
Aistar Co., Ltd., 47, 48–49, 51
Allison, Anne, 183n3
*Asakusa Fukumaru Ryokan* (television series), 175n11

bath crawl (*onsen meguri*), 39
bathing: privatization, 9–10; wooden bath pass (*nyūto tegata*), 39, 180n35, 180–181n37. *See also dōkutsu burō* (cave baths); *onsen* (hot spring resorts); *rotenburo* (outdoor baths)
Beppu Onsen (Oita Prefecture), 35
biological reproduction, 58; *okami's* interior work, 23, 60; succession in family business, 72
Borovoy, Amy, 131
business culture, 52–53

caregiving as women's work, 66–67, 145, 163
carework, 63, 67, 95
cave baths (*dōkutsu burō*), 180n30
childcare provided by employer, 135–136
*chōjo* (eldest daughter), 83
*chōnan* (eldest son), 82–83, 185n1; measures taken to hide familial obligations, 93; media portrayal of issues affecting, 92; responsibility in family business succession, 78–79, 86–87
Clark, Scott, 9–10
class values, myths about, 178n29, 183–184n4
collective identity, landscape as, 34, 35
company hierarchy, 159–160
contract-based dispatch work (*haken*), 14
Coronavirus pandemic and impact on tourism industry, 175n4
countryside: difficulty attracting workers to, 171; ideological power of, 22, 55; nostalgic appeal, 32; rice growing, 28, 92, 178n4; trend of young people moving to, 185–186n5
culture: business, 52–53; use as disruptor in urban–rural power relations, 53–54

Daiichi Nuclear Power Plant disaster, 174n3
dekasegi (seasonal domestic migrant workers), 14
dezain shinai dezain (undesigned design), 41–42, 54–55
Discover Japan campaign, 30, 174
disparity society, 20, 177–178n28. See also gap society
divorced women: decrease in numbers working in ryokan, 171; vulnerability to exploitation in workforce, 134–135; work as nakai, 129, 131–134
Doi Kyūtarō, 136
dōkutsu burō (cave baths), 180n30

eldest daughter (chōjo), 83
eldest son. See chōnan (eldest son)
employees: duties, 96–97; flexibility required by those living onsite, 105–106; job satisfaction as, 168–169; kitchen duties, 98–100; micro geographies, 95; morning tea break, 103–106; occupational hazards, 176n14, 187n2; onsite living conditions, 16–17; reaction to formal hospitality training (kenshū), 144, 151; sources of internal friction, 155–158; spirit of perseverance and suffering, 113–115; staff meals as bonding exercise, 112; staff who commute, 97–98, 105; upsetting social norms, 159; ways to demonstrate dissatisfaction with working conditions, 108–109, 121; work schedule/roster, 11–12
Endō Keigo, 36

farming mechanisation, 32
feminized workforce. See nakai (maids/cleaners); okami (female co-owners)
fixity in ryokan, 81, 185n3
food, 57, 104; gendered division of labor, 69–70, 99; kaiseki meal,

69–70, 99; as reflection of owner's distinct taste of hospitality, 69, 70; as women's work, 65–66
Fuji, Jeanie, 184n5
Fujiya ryokan (Yamagata Prefecture), 184n5
furusato (hometown), 22; as collective identity, 34; creating, 28–29, 179n7; foundation for local and national identities, 59; state-sponsored campaigns to revive, 30–31, 174, 179n18; steps in creating elements of, 36–43; ways Kurokawa residents embody, 54–55; ways of mobilizing hospitality, 167–168
Furusato Creation Plan, 30
Furusato Parcel Post, 30, 31
Furusato Return Project, 45–46
Furusato Tax (furusato nōzei), 31, 179n18

gap society, 20, 177–178n28
gender bias, 59–60, 163; succession, 86–87, 185n1
gendered division of labor: association with family home, 28; blurring boundaries, 65; food preparation in ryokan, 69–70, 99; in ryokan, 15–16, 148; ways boundaries are policed, 64–66, 167
Ginzan Onsen (Yamagata Prefecture), 184n5
"Good Design Award," 41
Gotō Tetsuya: celebrity status, 178n2; cultivating furusato, 26, 28, 37, 42–43; commentary on Kurokawa's anonymous period, 35–36; concerns about other towns not harnessing furusato values, 55; concerns about "outside capital" (gaibun shihon), 50, 53. See also Shinmeikan ryokan
guests: as number one priority, 4, 116, 121; preparations for VIPs, 147–150, 152–154

Hansen's disease, 22, 181–182n4; accommodation denial incident

(*shukuhaku kyohi jiken*), 47–48; marginalization of sufferers, 47, 182n5, 182n10; national controversy (2003), 5; state-run sanitorium, 46. *See also* Kikuchi Keifuen
Hochschild, Arlie, 176n14, 187n2
hometown. *See furusato* (hometown)
hospitality (*omotenashi*): *aji* (flavor) of, 23, 60, 68, 95, 124–125, 126; balancing intimacy and, 59; characteristics of Japanese, 67–68; physical and emotional labor associated with, 150–151. *See also* hospitality training, formal (*kenshū*); professionalization of hospitality
hospitality, mobilizing, 116, 120–121, 160; how *okami* utilize, 5, 167–169; how rural communities utilize, 167–168, 171
hospitality training, formal (*kenshū*), 143–144, 147–150, 152–154; *nakai*'s reaction to, 151; standardizing greetings, 149–150
hotels, difference from ryokan, 8

ideological power, countryside as source of, 22, 55
Imperial family succession and heirs, 185n1
Imperial House Act 1889, 185n1
*isson ippin* (One Village, One Product) movement, 29

Japan Institute of Design Promotion, 41
Japan National Tourism Organization, 9
Japan Post, 30
Japan Railways (JR), 30, 174
Japan Ryokan & Hotel Association, 9
Japan Travel Bureau, 46–47

Kagaya ryokan, 136–137
*kaiseki* meal: gendered division of labor, 69–70, 99; as important part of experience in ryokan, 117–119; preparation and service, **118**

Kawabata Yasunori, 175n11
*kenshū See* hospitality training, formal (*kenshū*)
Kikuchi Keifuen, 46, 182n10
Kumamoto City, 6
Kumamoto Prefecture, 32
"Kurokawa Area Town-Making Pact," 41, 49, 50, 51, 182n13
Kurokawa Onsen: aerial view, **38**; anonymous period, 35–36; challenges of over tourism, 172; factors for success and appeal, 3, 22, 179n7; geographic location, **33**; history as *onsen* area, 35; incompatibility of local and non-local values, 49; in mid-1990s, 6–7; overnight and day guests in 2019, 174n5; permanent resident population, 32, 60–61; recreating *furusato* as collective identity, 34–35, 36–37; regional branding, 52–53; as regular travel destination, 45; shaping landscape to conjure time-slip, 7, 26–27; size of typical ryokan in, 51; winning "Good Design Award," 41–42
Kurokawa Onsen Furusato Charter, 183n18
Kurokawa Onsen Ryokan Association (*Kurokawa Onsen Kankō Kyōdō Kumiai*), 35, 37, 47–48, 61; codifying and standardising aesthetic, 41, **42**; cooperative network, 54–55; fears about "outside capital" influence on landscape, 50–51; opposition to KM's redevelopment of Ai Ladies site, 51–52, 183n18; professional development sessions, 146–147; removal of Ai Ladies Hotel from membership, 47–48; wooden bath pass (*nyūto tegata*), 39
Kurokawa Onsen Tourist Association (*Kurokawa Onsen Kankō Kumiai*), 61
Kusastu Onsen (Gunma Prefecture), 45

*kyōiku mama* (education mother), 183n3

Kyōritsu Mentenansu (KM), 183n18; demolition site, 45; locals' objection to redevelopment of Ai Ladies site, 51–54

landscape: in North American context, 181n41; power over who belongs, 54, 167, 181n41; work in creating undesigned design, 41–42. *See also* rural landscape

language: dialect as marker for local identity, 149, 178n2; standardising greetings, 149–150

leprosy. *See* Hansen's disease

Leprosy Prevention Law, 46

lifetime employment system, 13, 14, 128, 177n20

local identity, 52; dialect as marker for, 149, 178n2; *furusato* as foundation, 59; intersection with national identity, 26–27

*Lonely Planet*, 9, 26, 171

Mapple and Walker guidebooks, 175n9

marriage, 23; women's expectations, 131

media: depiction of Kurokawa's rise to prominence, 36; gender bias in coverage of ryokan, 59–60; Kurokawa as regular travel feature in, 45; portrayal of issues affecting *chōnan* in rural families, 92; role in promoting ryokan as Japanese retreat, 10

Meiji Civil Code, 82

men's work (*otoko no shigoto*), 64; role and responsibilities, 25; ryokan duties, 97–98, 116–117

*michi no ryokka* (street greening), 37–39

Minami-Oguni: mayor's correspondence with Kurokawa Onsen Ryokan Association, 51, 183n18; population, 32

Minami-Oguni Town Chamber of Commerce and Industry Youth Branch, 61

Ministry of Justice, 46–47

Ministry of Tourism 2019 report, 8

mothers. *See* education mother (*kyōiku mama*); divorced women; single mothers

mothers-in-law: role in training daughters-in-law, 71, 72–74, 76, 89; as traumatic element of succession work, 88

*nakai* (maids/cleaners), 5, 24; burden of ryokan work, 121–122; cleaning guestrooms, 106–109; devaluing own labor, 147, 160; food preparation and service, 99, 100–101, 119, 120; full-time employment and obligations, 156–157; full-time employment and precarity of situation, 161; full-time versus part-time employees, 157–158; internal rivalries, 121, 140–141, 160–161; job insecurity, 125–126; job satisfaction, 130–131; *kaiseki* meal service, 117–119; married women working as, 137–139; morning tea break meeting, **104**; part-time roles and flexibility, 164; physical and emotional labor, 124–126, 150–151; policies against drinking with guests, 176n13; pre-check-in duties, 123–124; professionalization of, 126–127; reaction to external influence in running ryokan, 153–154; reaction to formal hospitality training, 144, 151; reasons for choosing part-time employment, 156–158; reasons for internal friction, 155–156; roles and duties in ryokan, 7, 15–16; single mothers working as, 135–137; skill at adapting to needs of guests, 124; source of tension between *okami*

and, 24, 144–145; turnover rate, 126; ways of demonstrating dissatisfaction with working conditions, 108–109; ways of mobilizing hospitality, 109. *See also senpai* (experienced *nakai*)
national identity: *furusato* as foundation, 59; intersection with local identity, 26–27; rural landscape as source of, 22
*Niwa* (magazine), 44–**45**, 181n38
*norenwake* (business branches), 185n3
nostalgia. *See* time-slip
Nozawa Daizō, 47
*nyūto tegata* (wooden bath pass), 39, **40**, 180n35, 180–181n37

*okami* (female co-owners), 5, 60, 64; American, 184n5; different women's paths to becoming, 73–75; emotional and physical labor of bearing successor, 81–82, 83; as face of the inn, 71; juggling business and family tasks, 60; lack of media coverage of, 59–60; managing ryokan's taste of hospitality, 70, 124; outsourcing hospitality training to experts, 130, 143–144, 148; outsourcing training of replacement, 75–77; preference for hiring divorced women, 135; preparation for New Year, 112–113; pressure to produce male heirs, 185n1; role and responsibilities, 23; roles reflecting gendered division of labor, 64–66; source of tension between *nakai* and, 24, 144–145; Tsuetate Onsen (Kumamoto Prefecture), 56–57; ways of mobilizing hospitality, 168; ways to define, 67. *See also* biological reproduction
Okyakuya ryokan, 35
*omotenashi*. *See* hospitality (*omotenashi*)
One Village, One Product (*isson ippin*) movement, 29

*onsen* (hot spring resorts), 9–10; associated perceptions with sex industry, 10, 175–176n13; Kurokawa Onsen as regular travel feature, 45
*onsen meguri* (bath crawl), 39
*Otoko wa tsurai yo* (It's Tough Being a Man), 58
outdoor bath (*rotenburo*), 37, 39, **40**
outside capital (*gaibu shihon*), 50–51, 52, 53, 54–55

perseverance, 114–115
post-World War II: importance of housewives to economy, 128; resurgence of Japanese economy, 2, 6, 27; social mobility, 63–64
power hierarchies, 159–160
Price, Patricia, 34
professional development, 146–147; *nakai* appreciation for, 154–155
professional housewife (*sengyō shufu*), 13, 128
professionalization of hospitality: as areas of tension between *nakai* and *okami*, 24; consequences of implementing, 155–156, 160; *nakai*'s reaction to, 151; outsourcing training, 130, 143–144, 147–150, 152–154; standardizing greetings, 149–150

regional branding, 52–53
residents' association (*jichikai*), 51, 54
Roberts, Glenda, 178n29
Robertson, Jennifer, 29
*rotenburo* (outdoor bath), 37, 39, **40**
rural communities: amalgamation process, 31; challenges successors face in, 91–94; depopulation, 2, 27–28; match-making schemes, 92–93; multi-generation cohabitation, 91; programs to reinvigorate, 2–3, 30–31; ways of mobilizing hospitality, 167–168
rural landscape: ideological power of,

22, 181n41; time-slip, 7. *See also* countryside

ryokan: childcare for single mothers, 136–137; cleaning baths, 109–112; cleaning guestrooms, 106–109; closing time, 120–122; company trip to boost morale, 121; creating distinctive taste of hospitality, 68–69; daughters as successors of, 79–80; declining associations with sex industry, 10; difference from hotels, 8; driving duties as break from predictable working day, 116–117; duties before guests' arrival, 1; employee and nonemployee space, 12; factors determining succession, 90; formal hospitality training (*kenshū*), 143–144, 148–150; gendered division of labor, 15–16; guests as highest priority, 4, 116, 121; importance of baths in, 9–10; increase in non-Japanese clientele and staff, 171–172; isolation felt by chefs, 168–169; kitchen duties, 98–100; laundry room duties, 112–116; morning tea break, 103–106; outsourcing training of *okami* replacement, 75; pantry duties, 100–101; perceived associations with sex industry, 175–176n13; physical and emotional labor, 187n2; as place of safety and exploitation, 19–21, 24, 161–162; popularity, 59; pre-check-in process, 123–124; predictable duties, 115; preparing for VIP guests, 147–150, 152–154; rarity of full-time regular *nakai*, 126; reliance on outside help, 59; role and duties of *nakai*, 15–16; role of media in promoting, 10; as safe workplace option for women, 18, 19–20; seasonal work cycle, 164–165; size of rooms, 177n24; sources of unpredictability, 97, 107, 120; staff turnover, 126; staff work ethic, 3–4, 63; television series featuring, 10, 175n11; using remote location to advantage, 3; washing dishes, 101–103; ways boundaries are policed, 166–167; ways *nakai* show dissatisfaction with working conditions, 108–109; ways to achieve high levels of hospitality, 121; ways to ensure fixity, 81; Westerners' first experience, 7–8

ryokan (family-run): balancing hospitality and intimacy, 59; blurred home and work boundaries, 61–63; difficulty establishing *norenwake* (business branches), 185n3; formal hospitality training (*kenshū*), 143–144, 147–148, 148–150, 152–154; pressure to produce male heirs, 83; reasons for permanent closure, 64; reliance on outside help, 11–14; ways families lure children back to business, 87–88

ryokan owners: lifestyle and work ethic, 2–4; long-term generational work responsibilities, 95–96, 170; next generation, 171; onsite living conditions, 2; return of eldest sons to run business, 37

Ryūichi Kitano, 46

*shachō*, 64, 67; preparation for New Year, 112–113

Saitō Yuki, 114

*sararīman* (salaryman), 13

Scheper-Hughes, Nancy, 19

Schnell, Scott, 178n4

Scott, James, 108

seasonal domestic migrant worker (*dekasegi*), 14

*Seinenbu*, (Young Adult's Association), 54, 90–91

*sengyō shufu* (professional housewife), 13

*senpai* (experienced *nakai*), 154

sex industry and associations with ryokan, 10, 175–176n13

Shinmeikan ryokan, 37
Shūkan Nihon no Meiyu, 175n9
shukuhaku kyohi jiken (accommodation denial incident), 47–48
single mothers, 135–137; lack of
   childcare provision, 135–136
social mobility, 63–64
social norms, 159, 168
staff in ryokan See employees; nakai
   (maids/cleaners); okami (female
   co-owners); shachō
street greening (michi no ryokka), 37–39
succession: adoption of males as
   successors, 86–87; burden on
   women, 77, 88–89; challenges
   successors face, 91–94; daughters
   as successors, 79–80; families with
   multiple daughters, 84–85;
   families with no children, 86–87;
   families with only daughters,
   85–86; gender bias, 86–87;
   mothers' reluctance to use harsh
   training on daughters, 71, 75–77,
   90; preparation and challenges of
   succession work, 87–91; responsibility and burden, 80–81; responsibility of being chōnan (eldest
   son), 78–79, 86–87; signs of
   successors' maturity, 90, 91; ways
   families choose successor, 81–82
sugi (Japanese cedar), 37
Sugimoto Yoshio, 177–178n28

Takigawa, Christel, 67–68
Tanaka Kakuei, 174
television series featuring ryokan, 10,
   175n11
time-slip, shaping landscape to
   conjure, 7, 26–27
tourism: impact of Coronavirus
   pandemic, 175n4; Minami-Oguni's reliance on, 32; onsen and
   furusato boom, 39
tourism association (kankō kyōkai), 54
training. See hospitality training,
   formal (kenshū); professional
   development

transportation, improved rail and road
   networks 1960s, 35
travel boom, 35
travel guidebooks, 9, 26, 171; hot
   springs special series, 175n9
tree planting, 37–39
Tsuetate Onsen (Kumamoto Prefecture), 35, 56; difficulties with
   succession, 64; slow decline, 57

undesigned design (dezain shinai
   dezain), 41–42, 54–55
urban–rural power relations, using
   regional culture to disrupt, 53–54

Vanished Village: What Was the Great
   Heisei Amalgamation? 31
Vanishing Village, Surviving Village:
   Mountain Villages Buffeted by City/
   Town/Village Amalgamation, 31

Watashi wo ryokan ni tsuretette
   (television series), 175n11
women: burden of children's educational success or failure, 183n3;
   importance of presence at home,
   184–185n6; importance to ryokan
   work, 5; juggling paid employment
   and home life, 13–14, 128–129,
   138–139; marginalization in
   society, 139–141; pressure to
   produce male heirs, 185n1. See
   also divorced women; kyōiku mama
   (education mother); single mothers
women and work: M-curve trend, 128,
   186n5; precariousness of work in
   ryokan, 20–21, 161–163; workforce participation, 14. See also
   nakai (maids/cleaners); okami
   (female co-owners); yuna (female
   bathing attendants)
women escaped from domestic
   violence: ryokan as place of safety
   and exploitation, 19–21, 24;
   ryokan as safe workplace, 18
women's work (onna no shigoto), 64;
   caregiving as, 66–67, 145, 163,

185n4; devaluing, 161–162, 163; food service, 65–66; as non-work, 66–67; *yuna* (female bathing attendants), 175n12
wooden bath pass (*nyūto tegata*), 39, **40**, 180n35, 180–181n37
workplace: insecure working conditions, 20–21, 169; myths surrounding, 13; trend since 1980s, 14, 177n21
World Leprosy Conference (1897), 182n5

World War II (post). *See* post-World War II

Yamanami Highway, 35
Young Adults' Association (*Seinenbu*), 54, 90–91
Yufuin Onsen (Oita Prefecture), 35
*Yukiguni* (Kawabata), 175n11
*yuna* (female bathing attendants), 175n12
Yusai ryokan, 51

# About the Author

Chris McMorran is associate professor of Japanese studies at the National University of Singapore. He is a cultural geographer of contemporary Japan who researches the geographies of home across scale, from the body to the nation. He has also published research on tourism, disasters, gendered labor, area studies, and field-based learning. He is co-editor of *Teaching Japanese Popular Culture* and co-producer of *Home on the Dot*, a podcast that explores home in Singapore through the lives of NUS students.